Who was Mrs Willett?

Landscapes and Dynamics of Mind

Chris Nunn

imprint-academic.com

Copyright © Chris Nunn, 2011

The moral rights of the author have been asserted.
No part of this publication may be reproduced in any form
without permission, except for the quotation of brief passages
in criticism and discussion.

Published in the UK by
Imprint Academic, PO Box 200, Exeter EX5 5YX, UK

Published in the USA by
Imprint Academic, Philosophy Documentation Center
PO Box 7147, Charlottesville, VA 22906-7147, USA

ISBN: 978184540 219 8

A CIP catalogue record for this book is available from the
British Library and US Library of Congress

Contents

Acknowledgements		v
Introduction		1
1	Of Spooks and the Gentry	5
2	What Size Tells Us	19
3	Picturing Mentality	33
4	The Boundaries of Mind	51
5	Turning on the Lights	79
6	The Shape of Consciousness?	115
7	Of Matter, Laws and Time	133
8	The Wilder Shores of Experience	161
9	Making Sense of 'Mrs Willett'	201
10	The End of Time?	217
Bibliography		227
Index		234

Acknowledgements

As the thesis of this book implies, I really ought to thank everyone whom I have ever known, corresponded with, or whose books I have read, for all must have contributed to it however indirectly. But special thanks to contributors to the *Journal of Consciousness Studies*—one of the first journals in its field (issue no. 1 appeared in 1994) and still perhaps the benchmark one. I have read over 1500 papers, published and unpublished, describing their ideas, arguments, interests and findings. Nearly all have influenced me in one way or another, although I've given only a few specific references to their work. Fay Dunbar probably still holds the record for the greatest number of references (over 5000) quoted by a single author. Her monumental survey of the psychosomatic literature was written in a more leisurely age, the late 1940s. Any attempt to follow her example would have turned this into a very different sort of book and I have followed the opposite strategy to hers. Apologies, however, to any authors who feel that their names have been unfairly omitted from what follows.

Another reason for keeping references to a minimum is that some of the papers that impressed me most have never seen the light of publication, such is the lottery of academia in general and peer review in particular. It's perhaps invidious to single out particular authors in this category, but nevertheless I am especially grateful to Erhard Bieberich for conveying his enthusiasm for fractals, Peter Henningsen for his wonderful insights into brain attractor dynamics and Vadim Vasilyev for getting me to think about symmetries and consciousness—all of them, of course, have successfully published papers elsewhere on other topics.

Many thanks, too, to Mike Beaton, Bill Faw, Penelope Rowlatt and Max Velmans for extremely helpful comments on drafts of various chapters and to Alfredo Pereira Jr. for keeping me up to date on a range of topics, especially ones to do with astrocytes and their activities. I'm also grateful to participants in a 'Nature-groups' invited workshop, who spent a week discussing and refining some of the ideas described in this book. Professor Max Velmans has kindly allowed me to quote (in chapter 2) remarks that he sent in a private email, while Christian MacLean of Floris publishers permitted reproduction here (in chapter 3) of a table first printed in a previous book of mine. Other quotations given in this book adhere to the 'fair dealing' convention and are fully attributed to their authors: should there be any queries about them, please contact me.

Apart from these intellectual debts, I owe a huge amount to my wife, Ruth, for her love, patience and forbearance. Incidentally, other than having both suffered in the cause of consciousness studies, she has no connection with the 'Ruth' whose story is told in chapter 8.

Introduction

This book is a report from the front line of 'consciousness studies', woven around an attempt answer questions raised by the story of 'Mrs. Willett', an early 20th century medium. It's basically a broad brush account of where the subject has got to nowadays, plus a search for evidence that may prove especially helpful to its future development. Although neuroscience plays a large part in the picture that I'll be describing, like most people I see the study of consciousness as necessarily covering a much wider field, ranging from philosophy and physics, through psychology and anthropology, to things like arts and history. And my account is of course to some extent an idiosyncratic one. People who prefer to reduce everything to its simplest components — as do some neuroscientists and artificial intelligence experts for instance — might say that the main campaigns are elsewhere and I'm describing side issues only. A few remaining diehards (e.g. so-called 'Eliminative Materialists' and their co-travellers) could well mutter something about a picture of the battle between Centaurs and Lapiths being as realistic as the one I offer here. But, the way things have been going in this new century, they themselves are likely soon to join the Centaurs and fade into mythology — as did the Behaviourists before them. In any case, like any reporter, I can only tell it as *I* see it, so here goes.

First, I need to introduce some words. I use 'consciousness' to refer to the sort of thing you or I experience when we see someone's face, or feel an emotion, or know that we are thinking a thought. But, as we shall see later (in chapter 5), it's not nearly as simple as this suggests. Scientists and philosophers attach many different meanings to the word, some of which are mutually incompatible though most overlap. Nevertheless, there is a sense in which consciousness is us. When we are deeply asleep or anaesthetized, for example, the lights have gone out and there is no longer any 'us' from our own personal points of view, even though others can still point to our bodies and say 'that's him or her'.

'Mentality' or 'mind' is a broader concept than consciousness, if only because it always refers to our unconscious minds in addition to our conscious ones. Ideas about 'extended mind' are attracting ever more interest nowadays from psychologists and others. They think it useful to regard 'mind' as also occupying aspects of our bodies, environments, tools and societies, not just our brains alone. I'm with them in this. Some philosophers (Idealists, Panpsychists and Property Dualists), and even a few physicists, go further still, supposing that mind may be co-extensive with the universe. Arguments offered for their views are better than you might think. But, whatever its boundaries may be, mind is nevertheless to do with information and meaning, and is dynamic—it flows and changes and does things.

In my last book (*From Neurons to Notions*), I developed a picture of mentality aimed at showing that it can usefully be viewed in terms of 'state spaces' containing 'attractors', which in turn could be pictured as forming 'landscapes'. Don't worry about what these terms mean if they seem unfamiliar; all will be revealed in due course. It was a good picture in that it could be used to explain a whole lot of puzzles, ranging from why we need to sleep to why bureaucracies are often so awful. And, crucially for a wannabe scientific view, it predicted things that we may (or may not) discover in the future; it was refutable in other words. However, the book ended with a sort of cliff-hanger and contained a feature that I'm not at all happy about.

The cliff-hanger had to do with the size of the 'state space' relevant to some particular aspect of mentality. This may sound dry and boring, but in fact raises all sorts of fascinating questions. If you go to a football match, for example, is what you regard as your own mind confined within your own skull, or does it belong, in a very fundamental sense, to the whole crowd of which you are part? Common experience shows that sometimes you will feel you are an autonomous self and other times you will feel 'part of the crowd' in a way that can seem a lot more than just metaphorical. What is responsible for the difference, how does it arise and what does it mean? I want to try to get to the bottom of questions like these in this new book.

The bit I wasn't happy with concerned the status of consciousness. The picture of mind offered in my earlier book implied that 'consciousness' is simply our word for whatever the small part of the content of mentality may be that one can tell oneself about at any given moment. It is defined, in other words, by being 'introspectible' or 'reportable' (if only to oneself), and should probably be regarded as basically something that comes for free as a consequence of certain types of memory. Mentality is where the interest and action mostly is, while consciousness is a sort of decorative add-on, according to this view. Well, there's something basically right about some of this, as we shall see later on. Many people probably would say it's the whole story. But I think there is more to consciousness than that alone. I want both to describe reasons for thinking there's more to the story than reductionists often suppose, and to outline some ideas about what the extra parts of the story could be like.

The telling will involve asking deep questions about causation, the status of physical law, the origins of things like electro-magnetism, the nature of selves and other matters. Some of the concepts we'll need are primarily mathematical, but there won't be many equations (only two) you may be relieved to hear — if only because I lack the technical competence to deal with them!

So that's what this book is mainly about. It offers a view of what we currently understand about mind, consciousness and aspects of personhood, then explores some ideas about possible future understandings. After providing a 'taster' to indicate the scope of the problems (the 'Mrs Willett' history described in chapter 1), I'll be taking a look at the boundaries and basis of mentality, especially conscious mentality, in chapters 2 to 4; then I'll go on to explore how consciousness itself might possibly arise in chapters 5 to 7. Chapter 8 deals with some of the experiential evidence that's relevant to ideas described earlier, while chapter 9 circles back to try to make sense of Mrs Willett's somewhat bizarre story in the light of everything discussed in the interim.

We shall be seeing that consciousness and some forms of memory are certainly linked, while there are all sorts of hints that time and temporality have essential parts to play in the unfolding story, albeit ones that are hard to pin down because our understanding of time is so poor. The final chapter 10, therefore, is to do with seeing whether we can find any good questions to ask about the nature of time—following the principle that, if you don't understand something, the first step towards gaining understanding is often to find the right questions to ask.

People have probably always pondered over questions to do with their minds, conscious experience and temporality. A particularly talented group was doing so around a hundred years ago, using approaches very unlike modern neuroscientific ones although they were admirably rigorous and logical in their own way. As a warm-up exercise, therefore, I start off by describing this remarkable piece of history because it nicely shows that there's a lot more needing explanation than is apparent to most of us as we go about our everyday routines; more, indeed, than is apparent to most contemporary psychologists and neuroscientists as they follow their professional interests.

Chapter 1

Of Spooks and the Gentry

Mrs Winifred Coombe-Tennant (1874–1956) was an Edwardian *grande dame*. Imaginative, rather plump and somewhat shy as a child, she had grown to become a formidable support of society and empire. The imperious Lady Bracknell, from Oscar Wilde's play *The Importance of Being Ernest*, could by all accounts have been regarded as more portrait than caricature of Winifred's public *persona*. With an estate in Wales and a townhouse in London, she was chairperson of the War Pensions Commission, briefly UK delegate to the League of Nations, hard-working local magistrate and a general promoter of good works. In addition, she was the doting mother of four children. But, in another and more secret life, she was also the remarkable 'Mrs Willett'.

The story I shall outline is no 'Batman' fantasy, where the reclusive millionaire turns into the masked crusader. The facts about both Coombe-Tennant and Willett have been documented in meticulous detail (see bibliography) and I shall try simply to summarise them in this chapter. Whatever one's opinions about the validity of beliefs held by the lady herself and other characters in the story (beliefs that I shall delay examining critically until chapter 9), it is nevertheless a fascinating tale that raises all sort of relevant issues — especially questions to do with the stability and boundaries of the conscious selves of some of the people involved, and the nature of temporality.

A League of Extraordinary Ladies and Gentlemen

The society in which Winifred had grown up was astonishing, but tragic. All the Victorian achievements in science, technology and humanitarianism had failed to deliver freedom from death and pain. Children were nearly as likely to die as to survive; brothers, sisters, fiancés and spouses regularly proved only too mortal. The comforts of the church appeared increasingly threadbare to many. Private anguish and loss lurked behind public triumphalism. These were strong incentives to explore mysteries of the human spirit; to search for meaning and hope in the face of an apparently cruel, or at best indifferent, universe. One possible way forward had been suggested by the craze for Mesmerism that had swept the country (and indeed much of the world) in the first half of the 19th century. Many amazing things had been associated with it, but also a great deal of distinctly less wonderful hype, showmanship, trickery and fraud. A more 'scientific' approach was needed; one in accord with the spirit of the age. Among the many would-be explorers of the psyche who came forward, a group based at Cambridge university were pre-eminent.

Two principal stars of the group were Edmund Gurney and Frederic Myers, both with established reputations for 'brilliance' in their fields (classics, music and literature). They were said to have been sensitive, compassionate people who had been scarred by bereavements earlier in their lives. Having done exploratory studies and developed some expertise in psychology, hypnosis, interviewing techniques and the like, they worked to establish a 'Society for Psychical Research' (The SPR, founded in 1882). A highly respected Professor of Moral Philosophy at Cambridge, Henry Sidgwick,[1] was pressured into becoming first president and became enthusiastically involved along with his wife Eleanor; herself a respected mathematician and a principal of Newnham, Cambridge's first women's college.

---

[1] Sidgwick had been something of a mentor for Myers since the latter's undergraduate days. He was intellectually more cautious and critical than Myers but had had an interest in spiritualism and related matters for a good many years prior to the foundation of the SPR.

Quite soon, a surprising number of the great and the good had joined in, including six of the country's leading physicists and a future Prime Minister — Arthur Balfour who was Eleanor Sidgwick's brother. William James, that greatest of American philosopher/psychologists and a good friend, first of Gurney and later of Myers, was also an active participant.

These people and others, having powers of mind and morality unequalled, perhaps, by any comparable group in human history, were lured on by curiosity but also by hopes of immortality. Naturally, therefore, 'spiritualism' was a chief focus of interest for them. Indeed a majority of the original SPR council members were avowed spiritualists, though Gurney and Myers were not. They were particularly interested in 'telepathy' (a word coined by Myers) and saw themselves as investigators of this along with spiritualist claims. Some of the spiritualists were later to complain of what they regarded as the excessive rigour of the methods and standards of proof demanded. But both rigour and standards were nevertheless maintained.

Spiritualism was a movement with very ancient origins, invigorated in the 19th century by aspects of mesmerism, reports of poltergeists and the like. The 18th century writings of Count Swedenborg had already given a boost to the whole field. These works had proved popular in some intellectual circles, though not always with churchmen. Charles Wesley the founder of Methodism, for example, thought they were hokum though his objections were based mainly on theological grounds. Swedenborg, the son of a bishop, was a Swedish philosopher and mining expert who published several books describing his 'visits' to the afterlife and his frequent encounters with 'angels', by which he meant the souls of the dead. His reports were especially attractive, no doubt, to people tired of the threats of judgement and damnation that issued from so many pulpits across the land. He wrote that you would go to hell only if you in some sense 'chose' to do so, and the sort of hell you found would in any case very likely be one that catered to your (depraved) tastes. And his credibility was bolstered by a famous anecdote, widely believed to be true if now impossible to verify. While at a high society dinner party in Gothenburg, he was said to have gone into a trance and described in accurate detail the progress of a major fire occurring in Stockholm at the same time, hundreds of miles away.

Myers and his colleagues were fascinated by questions about the origins of evidence, from 'channelling' and so forth, that spiritualists assumed pointed to survival after death. Fraud and trickery could account for only some of it, they felt, and it isn't easy to disagree with them if one looks at the measures they took to exclude such things. One of the physicists, for example, changed his entire household staff while an American medium (Mrs Piper) was staying with him, so that she wouldn't be able to gather information from that source for use in her séances. And of course an apparently complete range of more obvious precautions had already been taken, including having her tailed by a detective to make sure *she* hadn't hired detectives to ask about stuff that she could later attribute to the spirits. Moreover the investigators were fully aware of the propensity of mediums to use 'cold reading'. Usually, though not always, they took what *seem* to have been adequate precautions against it.

Questions asked by the investigators included: could the evidence be down to telepathy or clairvoyance in this life? Might sensitives be accessing some sort of universal memory field? Were they actually in contact somehow with discarnate spirits and, if so, how? Time passed and firm answers remained elusive. Then people started to die. Gurney went first (1888), followed by Henry Sidgwick (1900) and Myers himself (1901). The core group of the SPR shifted. Eleanor Sidgwick remained somewhere near the centre. Several physicists (especially Sir Oliver Lodge, he of the household staff change) played an increasingly active part and so, independently, did Arthur Balfour's and Eleanor Sidgwick's (she was born a Balfour, you will recall) brother Gerald, who was also a politician and President of the Board of Trade for quite a while. Gerald had a protégé,

John Piddington, who did a lot of the detailed work involved. I've tried to keep the names to a minimum; lots of other people were also involved but there's no point listing them here. Gerald Balfour, however, is particularly important as he later became central to the 'Mrs Willett' story, to which we shall soon return. In the meantime, a little more background information is needed.

Shortly after Myers' death, Margaret Verrall, a friend of his and a colleague of Eleanor's, offered to take up automatic writing in order to give Myers the opportunity to communicate with the living if he was in a position to do so. Her efforts apparently met with some success but many of the records were later destroyed at the insistence of his widow. As things turned out, this did not matter too much as other communicators with the dead soon appeared on the scene.

One was Margaret Verrall's daughter Helen; another Mrs Leonora Piper, a Boston housewife and medium who had already been extensively investigated by the SPR and by William James; yet another, a 'Mrs Holland', lived in India and later turned out to be Rudyard Kipling's sister. Quite soon, all these people were writing words 'dictated' by, or reporting 'conversations' with, Edmund Gurney, Frederic Myers and Henry Sidgwick, plus occasional interlopers. Then, a couple of years later, 'Mrs Willett' entered the arena.

'Mrs Willett'

That lady of the manor, Mrs Winifred Coombe-Tennant, came from a naval family. There seems to have been nothing very unusual about her early life, and she married slightly up-market at age 22, to a landowner in his forties. But they apparently got on all-right and soon had a son (born 1897). The birth, however, had not been easy and they did not have another child until 10 years later. This was a daughter, Daphne, who survived for only 17 months. Winifred was grief stricken at the death, shut herself away from society for quite a while, took up automatic writing, joined the SPR and got in touch with Margaret Verrall.

Some of Margaret and Helen Verrall's writings provided what Winifred took to be good evidence of Daphne's continued existence—and Winifred's association with the automatists and channellers escalated from there. Quite soon, she became the star turn, at least as far as 'Gurney', 'Myers' and 'Sidgwick' were concerned. And it was necessary to keep quiet about her talent in this direction. To be known as a communer with spirits of the dead isn't good for the reputation of ladies of the manor—or that of future League of Nations delegates—hence 'Mrs Willett' was born. And the secret was kept until after her death.

The story that unfolded had three principal threads. First, the trio of spirits were anxious to prove that they had indeed survived death with personalities intact. As all were excellent classical scholars, 'they' decided that the best method of proof was to make obscure classical references in their communications with channellers, which could later be shown to form a pattern—to 'cross-correspond' as the SPR researchers said. The idea was that, if Mrs Willett in England, for example, got a message from 'Myers' referring to a little-known inscription on some Italian tomb, and around the same time Mrs Holland in India got a different reference to the same tomb, while Mrs Piper in America reported a third, this couldn't be put down to the subconscious minds of the channellers being in telepathic communication, since none of them were that well educated. Equally it was hard to see how they could themselves have accessed relevant information in some hypothetical universal memory field because, to access information, you have to know what to look for. And fraud or collusion among them was ruled out, not only by the presumed integrity of the participants, but also by the distances involved (no emails in those days; letters took too long and telegrams would have been detected). Hence communication from the dead was left as the only reasonable explanation, said the 'spirits', though actually they were wrong here since their (alleged) argument depended on assumptions about temporality that could be questioned.

Gerald Balfour and his sidekick Piddington were especially active in tracing and collating these cross-correspondences, which kept on coming over a period of nearly 30 years (1901–30). They often sat with Winifred in particular for long periods while she was communicating. One suspects that this may have at first appealed to her especially because she was something of a social climber and the Balfours were *very* aristocratic. Other motives surfaced later.

Another thread was far more romantic and concerned reunions in the afterlife with significant others who had been lost in this life. There were claims that Myers had re-met a girl with whom he had been in love before his marriage. She came from a family with a history of mental disorder and had drowned herself in lake Ullswater while depressed. News of this re-union was apparently what inspired Myers' widow (who was, incidentally, Winifred's sister-in-law; they were a close-knit group in all sorts of ways) to try to have records of it suppressed or destroyed. Then the spirits were sometimes aided by a 'dark young man' who turned out to be the Balfour's youngest brother, killed in a climbing accident. But the most romantic story of all had to do with Arthur Balfour and a girl who had been in love with him but had died young of some fever, allegedly typhus. Her love had been undimmed by death, it seemed.

The final thread was utterly bizarre. Winifred had had another son, presumably by her husband, in 1909. But in 1913 a third son, Henry, arrived; an arrival that had been planned by the spirits, who also promised to guide his development. The spiritual father was Edmund Gurney, so it was believed, while the putative physical one was Gerald Balfour. The aim of the spirits was to provide a Messiah who would bring peace to the world. As it turned out, they were too late. Wars multiplied and Henry, after a moderately distinguished career as a soldier in World War II, became a type of spook himself—a military intelligence officer of some sort. He never married, however, and ended his life as a Benedictine monk.

Winifred died in 1956 but her story continued, which may come as no surprise to anyone who has followed the gist of her tale thus far. An Irish medium, Geraldine Cummins, began to receive messages from a spirit who turned out to be 'Winifred', communicating from beyond the grave—a somewhat autocratic Winifred indeed, liable to refer to Geraldine as a 'secretary' and to admonish her to 'pay attention'; as much lady of the manor as 'Mrs Willett', it seemed. And she reminisced about her experiences in both guises while still alive, but went on to recount stories about what had happened next. One particularly poignant claim was that she had met her daughter Daphne, whose death in infancy had so distressed her and which had set her on the road to becoming 'Mrs Willett'. Daphne, meanwhile, had 'grown up' and showed no great interest in her mother; a rejection that devastated poor Winifred all over again.

What Was it Like for Winifred?

There's a popular myth that all communications purporting to be from 'spirits' are banal, rambling, fatuous and evasive. Many of those reported are indeed like that to some degree, but the ones involving Winifred were mostly in a very different category. They were often cogent, thoughtful and reasoned. Moreover they conveyed personality traits: Gurney's sardonic humour for instance, or Myers' impetuous enthusiasm, or Sidgwick's measured wisdom. Even the 'grow-your-own Messiah' thread was consistent with well-intentioned, high-minded Victorian hubris at its most ambitious. Winifred 'herself' (via Geraldine Cummins) recalled:

> You must understand that the experience of these sittings was exciting for me. One might describe it as a heightened life. The emotional memory of the experience remained with me, but so often the details, the words, vanished from my memory—were not with me when I passed out of a dazed condition after sittings. But not all were so. On occasions I was not drowsy (Toksvig (ed.), 1971, p. 101).

If this was no more than a projection of Cummins' personal experience of mediumship, it probably still describes something of what Winifred felt during her own sittings.

Again via Cummins, 'Winifred' offered accounts of what it felt like to try get messages across to a medium from the spirit world. For example:

> When we [i.e. spirits] converse through a medium or with a medium and automatist we become, as it were, dependent on her thoughts, words and images, and we go wrong, we stray in that tide (*Ibid.*, p. 25).

Much earlier, 'Frederic Myers' had commented (via 'Mrs Holland'):

> The nearest simile I can find to express the difficulties of sending a message—is that I appear to be standing behind a sheet of frosted glass—which blurs sight and deadens sound—dictating feebly—to a reluctant and very obtuse secretary (Roy, 2008, p. 178).

However, things were not always quite as difficult, reminisced the deceased 'Winifred':

> The Group Cross-Correspondence Case might be likened to an orchestra's perfect performance. The several communicators were scholars, whose intellects were married to imaginations that cherished an ideal image of scholarly perfection. The investigators and the mediums had sufficient imagination to envisage the ideal image, the objective of perfection. Thus deep called to deep in a unified desire … That is how the high standard of evidence was maintained over a period of thirty years … (Toksvig (ed.), 1971, p. 58).

So there was excitement, frustration, striving, romance, wonder, a sense of dedication and no doubt many other emotions too, especially surrounding the origins of Henry. Winifred was a sexy lady under her starchy exterior, it appears, but she also liked and admired Gerald Balfour's wife; guilt can't have been altogether absent. This all says something about what it was like *for* Winifred. But there's a much larger question lurking in the background. One that will provide a central theme for the remainder of this book; namely, who *was* Winifred?

Who Was Winifred?

If asked 'who are you?' many of us nowadays would point vaguely to our heads and say something like 'I'm what's in there.' We can't be referring to the material of our brains—proteins, microtubules and the like—because almost all of that gets recycled every month or two. But we probably mean something to do with our brains; some characteristic pattern, perhaps, or set of memories. Mrs Coombe-Tennant was a fairly standard issue person of that sort. She had phases—childhood, adolescence, young motherhood, old age, and so forth—which were superficially very different from one another, but possessed some sort of continuity. She had *personae* adapted to roles—the young, blushing bride no doubt differed greatly, to all appearances, from the respected Justice of the Peace. But we're all like that; a sort of mish-mash of phases and stages and role-playings. And we don't have problems, usually, with pointing to any one of them and saying 'that's me'. Just occasionally, we catch ourselves doing or saying something surprising and we think 'surely that wasn't really me?'

Mrs Willett, on the other hand, was rather different, both less and more than the usual type of person. She was less in that she sometimes seemed to become little other than a sort of radio receiver for the spirits. Indeed 'they' quite often referred to her and the other mediums as 'machines'. But she could also seem to be more, or larger in some sense, than what we ordinarily take to be an individual, in that her identity appeared often to encompass the whole group of which she was part. The home-grown Messiah episode for example, which resulted in her having Henry and subsequently bringing him up as a very 'special' son, was central to her life as both Willett and Coombe-Tennant for many years. It can probably be regarded as a rationalisation of, or justification for, her fling with Gerald Balfour; there's no need to put it down to spirits of the dead! Even leaving them out of the equation, however, it was still the construct of a quite large group of people, including Gerald, his wife, Piddington and others, along with Winifred herself. Most remarkable of all, an atemporal or extra-temporal aspect of herself could, to all appearances, turn up in someone else after her death; namely in the Irish medium Geraldine Cummins.

The 'less' aspect is in some respects reminiscent of multiple personality (now somewhat confusingly re-named 'dissociative identity disorder', rather as cooks for example have turned into 'food preparation operatives' or whatever). People with the disorder typically have several distinct 'personalities', who may or may not be aware of one another, taking turns to *be* the person, rather as if they were queuing up behind the scenes awaiting their chance to appear centre stage.

The 'more' aspect, as we shall see later, can be seen as an exaggeration of what is true of all of us. It looks stranger than it is mainly because the interests and activities of the group(s) in question were so way-out. Even Winifred's *post-mortem* appearances in Geraldine's mind, have their less dramatic parallels in all of us, perhaps, when we remember the dead, especially those to whom we were close. The mental boundaries between individuals and their associates are always fuzzy at best, and can be indiscernible.

'But surely', someone might object, 'people are real, even Mrs Willett was real most of the time. Alleged discarnate spirits are not real. Who, then, was Mrs. Willett when she was occupied by "Myers" and the gang? Was she Mrs Willett simply play-acting at being Myers? Was "he" some sort of *alter ego* of the normal Mrs Willett? Similarly, who or what was the "Winifred" that surfaced in Geraldine Cummin's mind? What was going on?' Good questions, but it's going to take us quite a while before we can even begin to say what sort of answers they might have. In the meantime, we need to decide what 'real' means.

What is 'Real'

'Real' is one of those words like 'time' that we all know the meaning of — until we think about it, that is. My dictionary gives a range of definitions, the most relevant being: 'existing or occurring in the physical world; not imaginary, fictitious or theoretical.' Let's see how that works. Most people now would regard atoms as real (although, in Myers' time, there was still dispute about this) and acceptance of them as such came about on theoretical grounds long before scanning tunnelling electron microscopes were invented and some types could actually be seen. Neutrinos provide an even better example, for the bulk of them can never be detected—not even in principle, let alone in practice. We accept that they are part of physical reality because we know from experiments involving atoms and other particles that 'spin conservation' would be broken if neutrinos did not exist and because extremely rare events in huge detectors can plausibly be attributed to them. Clearly, therefore, the exclusion of 'theoretical' by the dictionary definition doesn't work. But we still need a criterion of some sort for distinguishing 'real' from 'unreal'.

The one I like to use is to say that anything is 'real' that has effects, regardless of whether we know about the effects from established theory or from direct observation, In any case, so-called 'direct observation' is never so theory-free as is sometimes believed, if only because our perceptual apparatus operates largely on Bayesian, predictive principles (see e.g. Frith, 2007). Thus, neutrinos are 'real' because both well-founded theory and indirect observations show that they do have consequences for aspects of the physical world, even though individual neutrinos are nearly always completely 'invisible'. A unicorn, on the other hand, is not real because it has no existence of any sort that does or could produce any effects whatsoever. But it's important to note that this does not apply to my *idea* of a unicorn, which *is* real because it has caused me to type these words. The reality of the idea, we would generally assume nowadays, is down to its physical embodiment in some memory structure or pattern of activity in my brain.

It's a particularly nice criterion, I think, because it relates what is 'real' to 'information'; in fact it suggests that 'reality' and 'information' can be regarded as synonymous terms for some purposes, although they are commonly used in different contexts. Anthropologist and polymath Gregory

Bateson famously proposed that the most general definition of information is to say that an item of it is 'a difference that makes a difference'. Thus, information has to be 'real' and what is 'real' has to contain information since it either is making a difference of some description to other 'real' things with which it is in contact, or at least has the potential to make a difference when conditions are right. The close relationship of information to reality is a truth that has surfaced in various guises over the years. In the 1930s, for instance, the astronomer Sir James Jeans wrote that the universe is 'more like a great thought than like a great machine'. One of the most influential 20th century physicists, John Wheeler, coined the phrase 'its from bits', by which he meant that information (i.e. bits) is fundamental and should be considered to somehow generate the 'its' that comprise our material world. However, it's also worth noting that, on this definition, 'reality' extends beyond matter as such to include natural law, since that too has effects and consequences.[2]

On this criterion at least, which is arguably the best available, all aspects of Winifred Coombe-Tennant can clearly be regarded as having been 'real' in some way. However, this does not mean that the 'spirits' were in fact the discarnate entities that 'they' claimed to be. There are all sorts of other possibilities, many of them more consistent than the notion of 'spirits-as-discarnate-souls' with current mainstream thinking about such matters. We need to gather ideas about the sorts of 'reality' likely to have been involved. But, to get anywhere near the ideas needed, we shall first have to take a look at a whole lot of other concepts, with plenty of digressions and diversions along the way. The next chapter makes a fairly gentle start in this direction by describing some anecdotes and theories which strongly suggest that 'mind' is both a broader and more fluid concept than is often supposed, while aspects of it that we often like to consider

---

[2] Another way of putting this would be to say that 'reality' refers to Aristotle's 'material', 'efficient' and 'formal' causes, the status of his 'final' causes being left open.

fixed, especially those relating to 'personality', can be quite malleable.

Chapter 2

What Size Tells Us

Popular science writers like to congratulate us on the size of our brains. After all, there's not much else to pick on in our biology that distinguishes us from the apes. And the fact that some dolphins match us, while elephants and whales outclass us in the size department, can always be put down to them having bigger bodies and the claim that it's *relative* size (of brain to body) that matters[1]. However our predecessors in Europe, both the Neanderthals and the Cro-Magnons, seem to have had slightly larger brains on average than us. The figure often given for the Neanderthals is around 10% bigger and the Cro-Magnons may have been about the same, though estimates in their case are based on fewer available skulls. Their (average) body size, however, appears to have been similar to that of a well-fed modern population, except possibly in youth—it's been suggested that the Neanderthals at least may have grown up faster than us.

Big brains cost. They cause increased maternal and infant mortality because they need a lot of rather special nutrients to grow, and they have a hard time getting out into the world. Even if they are delivered safely, they require a lot of maintenance afterwards. Weight for weight, brains need around ten times as many calories as the rest of our bodies. So there are (or were until very recently) strong evolutionary pressures to reduce brain size, countering whatever led

---

[1] Relative to body size, the brains of humans, bottlenose dolphins and apes are in the ratios of 7.0 to 4.14 to 3.21 (Marino, 2004). There are also a range of anatomical differences between animal brains and ours, quite big differences in the case of cetaceans, the consequences of which are unknown.

to big ones in the first place[2]. Even so, it's a puzzle as to why we've been able to dispense with a little of what the Cro-Magnons had. Surely we need even bigger brains than them to cope with all the complexities of civilisation, don't we?

All sorts of explanations can and have been offered, but one stands out as by far the most plausible (though it does not exclude other possible explanations from playing a part as well). It is that our cultures supply a whole lot of things that individual Cro-Magnons had to supply for themselves. We don't need quite so much brain as them because our societies have taken over some of the functions that were originally the province of nerve cells; society can be regarded, in other words, as quite literally having mental aspects. The picture is that Cro-Magnons, as relatively recent arrivals in a harsh environment, had to work out for themselves everything needed to keep them alive. As civilisation developed, a lot of what was necessary became a matter of custom and routine. After all, it *is* easier to strike a match than to use a fire drill, and a lot easier to shop in the supermarket than kill a mammoth for food — and even in Neolithic times there were many similar short-cuts enabling people to avoid having to do it *all* themselves. Although our social environments are more complex in some ways than those that would have been experienced by Cro-Magnons, these also encompass savings on cognitive requirements, such as the physical conveniences already mentioned, defined social positions, clear-cut roles, predictable career trajectories and so forth.

Incidentally, this is not to claim that hunter-gatherer lifestyles always demand more neural capacity than so-called 'civilised' ones. Customary use of a natural environment can be equivalent to having constructed an artificial one as far as requirements for neural processing are concerned. Thus we would not necessarily expect Australian aborigi-

---

[2] There are a large number of suggestions about what did lead to the huge increase in brain size through the primate lineage, culminating in our immediate predecessors. Many of the ideas centre on its having had something to do with coping with the increasing complexity of social interactions in groups of increasing size.

nes, for instance, to have bigger brains than us. They have had 30,000 years or more to develop customs allowing them to fit in with their environment(s), whereas we in Europe have had only around half that time to make environments that fit us. It could be said that they have put part of their mentality into the wild nature around them, while we have mostly put it into artefacts and our domesticated natural surroundings. Indeed, the aborigines themselves appear to be saying something like that when they talk of their relationship with animals or landscapes — their totems, their 'dreamlines' and so forth.

Navigators

Edwin Hutchins (1996) has described a specific example of how mental functions can be displaced into cultural artefacts. He is an American anthropologist, interested in both cognitive psychology (i.e. the sort of academic psychology that has been 'mainstream' for the last 30 or more years) and small boat navigation. Combining his interests, he made a detailed study of how US Navy navigators go about their business.

As he pointed out, the horizons of cognitive psychology have generally been confined to looking at what goes on in individual brains. But the actual cognitive system used in navigation depends on teams of people equipped with conceptual and physical tools that have been developed over long periods of time within some particular cultural tradition. Methods used by the Navy, for instance, are very different from those used by Polynesian navigators — although both were about equally effective until the advent of GPS and the like.

The cognitive essence of navigation, Hutchins showed, is not in the individual navigator so much as in the team of which he is a part, his charts and his ancestors. It's reasonable to infer that the same applies to most cognitive systems. A lot of the computation needed to make these systems work is undertaken, not in the brains of individuals, but in their tools and traditions. So individuals don't have to do nearly as much neural information processing as would be needed if they didn't have the tools and the pre-existent knowledge. I guess it's a fairly obvious point really. It would have taken me a lifetime of deep thought and effort to build my own boat, for instance, if I had had to start from scratch. As it was, I bought the drawings and instructions and went to the appropriate suppliers of materials, and the whole thing was done in a couple of years with not much personal brainpower needed. We can all supply similar examples from our own lives. Nevertheless, the implications have been lost on most cognitive psychologists until quite recently.

Incidentally, a fascinating consequence of Hutchins' new outlook on cognition is that it helped him programme a computer model of the effects of increasing the level of communication between individuals in a team on their ability to reach consensus decisions; in this case decisions about how to interpret a given set of data. As communication increased from an initially very low level, the speed at which individuals decided on one or other of two possible interpretations of the data also increased. Then came a stage at which everyone adopted the same interpretation, tending to stick to it even if the weight of evidence was against it—a phenomenon that manifested in the history of academic psychology, for example, with its long-lasting adherence to Behaviourism. As a body, psychologists stuck with it for over 30 years despite its many and, to us in the light of hindsight, obvious failings. Similar examples have cropped up in most fields. At higher communication levels still, people sometimes simply milled about and never arrived at any coherent interpretation whatsoever; best not to worry, perhaps, about the implications for our democratic decision-making, given the ever more frenetic pace and coverage of modern communications!

Cultures and People

It's not just technical skills like navigation or boat-building that blur the boundaries between the minds of individual people and their environments, especially their cultural environments, and it's worth giving a few more examples.

Wilhelm Wundt (1832–1920), often acclaimed as the 'father' of modern psychology and famous for setting up (in Leipzig) one of the first psychology laboratories, actually advocated two entirely different lines of study. The first was to be a search for general laws, analogous to Newton's laws of motion, that may govern mentality; the second was to be a sort of cultural/historical account of mind that might be more like one of the humanities (e.g. art studies or whatever) than like our present concept of a social or psychological science. Of course nearly every academic over the last one hundred years has aimed for the first type of psychology and has ignored the second; the main exceptions being some Russian psychologists of the Stalinist era, scattered anthropologists and a few others including Michael Cole (1997), who tells us that he was originally a 'first psychology' psychologist (i.e. a would-be searcher for general laws of mentality) and is based at the University of California, San Diego.

Perhaps the most obvious characteristic of present-day psychology (except for the sub-discipline of neuropsychology, including cognitive neuroscience), Cole averred, is its relative failure to measure up to the standards of the hard sciences. Any universal laws of mentality, human behaviour or the like have proved elusive and the discipline as a whole has sometimes become fixated on unsatisfactory paradigms, of which Behaviourism was the most egregious example. Cole argued that this may be largely because Wundt's 'second psychology' has been so neglected. His change of heart resulted partly from the influence of Russians (such as Luria and Vygotsky), and partly from personal experience in cross-cultural work that he undertook early in his career.

An example of the type of difficulty he met is provided by IQ tests, which were first developed to measure and predict the performance of French schoolchildren. When Cole gave conceptually similar tests to Liberian tribesmen, they appeared fairly 'dumb', he found; but their behaviour in other respects showed that they were actually smart. Even when he tried his best to make the tests fit the tribesmen's culture, there were still discrepancies. He then concluded firstly that tests of this sort are useful only in relation to some particular cultural milieu, and secondly that psychologists don't know how to make measurements that might provide a basis for a worthwhile 'first psychology'—remember these conclusions were the ones he came to *early* in his career.

We can certainly accept the first conclusion. There's lots of subsequent evidence that IQ measurements, which are supposed to be relatively culture-independent, are nothing of the sort. But your IQ is a basic aspect of your personality, so it is usually assumed. And, if the sort of IQ you have depends on the culture you live in, this means that an important part of *you* is culture dependent.

Coles' second conclusion, that psychologists don't know how to make adequate measurements, is a lot more 'iffy', since it appears to imply that a successful 'first psychology', focussing on individuals tested in laboratory-like settings, should be achievable in principle. But that seems to clash with the first conclusion, which suggests that *any* successful psychology will have to take culture into account, along with individuals. He himself soon came to accept this and a lot of his later career has centred on trying to construct 'sub-cultures' that will optimize children's learning and development—hopes which are now shared by some participants in the new field of 'social neuroscience' (Frank, 2009), although they tend to focus more on possible benefits of specific, neuro-cognitive interventions than on general 'culture'.

Still more thought provoking is Daniel Everett's story, told in a recent book (*Don't Sleep There Are Snakes*), about his work in Amazonia. He first went there, along with wife and two children, as a Baptist missionary assigned to a tribe called the *Piraha*. He managed to learn their language, probably the first outsider to do so properly, which turned out to have all sorts of unusual characteristics. For instance, there's an almost complete absence of words for abstract concepts, not even numerals; sentences are probably never 'recursive', meaning that you *can* say 'The man came into the house. He was tall' in their language, but you *can't* say 'The man who was tall came into the house.'

Another characteristic, especially relevant for a would-be missionary, is that the tribe have special forms of language for different types of report. If you see something yourself, you use different verb endings than if you're telling about something that your brother told you he had seen.[3] And if there are no direct eye-witnesses involved, the *Piraha* aren't interested. Hence, as soon as Everett told them that there were no living eye-witnesses to his stories about Jesus, they politely suggested they didn't want to hear any more on the topic.

Nevertheless they're a happy people, who are constantly chattering to one another; indeed, they chatter most of the night, it appears, because they view sleep as potentially dangerous. Everett was warned not to snore: 'Jaguars will think a pig is nearby and come to eat you', he reports being told — though actually the *Piraha* would probably have used two sentences to say this. They have hardly any material possessions, other than a few clothes, disposable baskets that they weave, and bows and arrows. If they do acquire metal tools from traders, they tend to neglect them. Skilled use of jungle and river is what keeps them alive but they don't appear to plan ahead much and, in general, show remarkably little concern for the future. After all, there are no eye-witnesses to it, so it is outside their sphere of interest.

One might suppose that, with their aversion to abstractions, they would be entirely tied to the material here and now. But it turns out that they treat dream experiences as

[3] There's also a third set of verb endings for use if you're telling about something you've deduced from what you have seen personally — maybe all experimentalists should learn Piraha. Except for the aversion to abstractions, it sounds ideally suited to their purposes! The Tibetan language allegedly has a similar, but more sophisticated, system of using special words in relation to particular sources of evidence and inference. It's been found that, presumably as a consequence of this, Tibetan children are better at drawing inferences than comparable American children (de Villiers and Garfield, 2009).

being on a par with waking ones and they are also prone to seeing jungle 'spirits' even when awake, whose reality they accept apparently without question. Everett's book opens with an account of how he was woken one morning by a group of *Piraha* excitedly chatting about a spirit that they could all plainly see on the beach by the river in front of them, though he couldn't.

It's a remarkable culture, beautifully described, but one of the most interesting things about the book is the sub-text, which shows how the tribe converted the would-be missionary. Everett studied them for thirty years, spending long periods living in their villages. He was fascinated by their language and the counter-examples it provided to Noam Chomsky's theories about 'innate grammar', gaining a PhD in linguistics in the process and becoming 'visiting scholar' at the prestigious Massachusetts Institute of Technology for a while. And his former faith? Well, his ending to the 'Prologue' of the book says it all:-

> The Pirahas showed me that there is dignity and deep satisfaction in facing life and death without the comfort of heaven or the fear of hell and in sailing towards the great abyss with a smile. I have learned these things from the Pirahas, and I will be grateful to them as long as I live.

He didn't 'go native' to the same extent as some officials in remote outposts of empire were prone to do in days gone by. Indeed, he seems to have managed to integrate two cultures in himself admirably well. All the same, exposure to the *Piraha* culture clearly resulted in a major conceptual, and probably personality, re-organisation. He did show that, like all of us, he had what one might call leaky boundaries.

Embodied Mind

The fact that our minds are 'embodied' became a bit of a buzzword in the 1990s. The idea was promoted by groups of psychologists and philosophers as a corrective to the tendency, which was mainly a hangover from the previous decade, to view minds as being like computers—information processors able to do their thing more or less independently of their environments. One of the movement's leading lights was Francisco Varela (1946–2001), a Chilean biologist who became a Tibetan Buddhist and subsequently took up neuropsychology. The last 15 years of his life were spent in Paris where he held a number of prestigious appointments, latterly heading a neuroscience research group.

The notion of 'embodiment' that Varela and others adopted often referred to the views of French philosopher Maurice Merleau-Ponty,[4] who had been heavily influenced by the earlier ideas of Husserl and Heidegger. Luckily, many of us find Ponty's prose a little easier to understand than his predecessors' writings![5]

> For Merleau-Ponty, as for us, *embodiment* has this double sense: it encompasses both the body as a lived, experiential structure and the body as the context or milieu of cognitive mechanisms (Varela *et al.*, 1993, p. xvi).

Basically, the idea was that you can't do cognitive psychology properly unless you take into account a person's body as well as their brain, along with their history and environment. And the functional role of mind is always played out in relation to a body and its environment. In some ways it was[6] much the same message as Michael Cole's plea for taking cultural/historical factors into account, but with differences too. One difference was that many of the 'embodiment' group were heavily influenced by post-modernism and deconstructionism; an influence which seems to have resonated with Varela's Buddhist views. They were fond of quoting David Hume's (the 18th century Scottish

---

[4] Merleau-Ponty was an existentialist and a contemporary of Jean-Paul Sartre, though he rejected the latter's Marxist views.

[5] Personally, I find Heidegger in particular to be almost incomprehensible. Merleau-Ponty's apparent lucidity may, however, have had a lot to do with the relative clarity of French as compared to German. The thoughts behind the words are perhaps equally difficult in both cases.

[6] And still is; for the whole approach, once seen as highly innovative, has now become almost mainstream. Even many Artificial Intelligence experts, whose approaches used to be entirely 'computational', have adopted it and are giving robots senses, motor functions and training in their use, on the basis that these are all integral components of 'intelligence'.

philosopher) musings about how, when he looked inside himself, he was unable to find anything that he could confidently call a 'self'. Buddhist psychologists have long claimed, of course, that our experience of 'self', along with our experience of the world, is illusory. To quote Varela again:

> We began with our common-sense as cognitive psychologists and found that our cognition emerges from the background of a world that extends beyond us but that cannot be found apart from our embodiment. When we shifted our attention away from this fundamental circularity to follow the movement of cognition alone, we found that we could discern no subjective ground, no permanent and abiding ego-self (*ibid.*, p. 217).

Our minds not only emerge from, and spill over into, our bodies and environments according to this view, but lack any abiding core. As we have begun to see from what's been said in this book so far, the first part of this claim appears to fit the facts; there are no clear boundaries between our minds, our bodies and their physical and social *milieus*. The second part of the claim (nothing exists that can be properly be called an enduring 'self') is not so clear-cut. Varela appears to imply that we *might* find an 'enduring ego-self' if we were to take the 'fundamental circularity' (i.e. the reciprocal involvement of 'cognition' with body and 'world') into account. I suspect he may have been ambivalent about this possibility, for his Buddhist leanings probably suggested to him that *any* notion of 'self' is illusory. Nevertheless, this is a question that we'll need to keep in mind. Could a lasting 'self' emerge from the dynamic that he describes?

How Big is Experience?

The question above probably comes across as one of those nonsense ones that children like to ask. But it's a problem nonetheless. If scientifically minded, we tend to think of experience as being inside our brains in some way. And brains are quite little, only a few inches across. But what we actually experience is different. If we have a pain in a toe at the same time as an itch in a finger, the combined experience of both apparently extends across several feet. Listen to a concert and the sound seems to fill the entire hall. Look at a distant scene and it is miles big. So how does it all fit inside one's head?

'You might as well ask how a photo of St Paul's cathedral fits inside the camera', some people would say, 'It's a silly question'. However, there's a big difference between a photo and a conscious experience in that the photo is simply another object—a representation of something that can be picked up and moved around. But an experience of something either is, or at least seems as though it is, the thing itself. A pain in the toe is felt in the toe, not in the brain. The sun at sunset is sitting on the horizon, not at the back of your head where your visual cortex is sited—and it's the visual cortex that's equivalent to the photo since that is where the scene is registered. The actual experience is something, and apparently somewhere, else.

Psychologist Max Velmans first raised issues like these in a paper published in 1990 in a journal titled *Philosophical Psychology*, and the debate has rumbled on ever since. His most recent account of them is in a 2009 book—see the Bibliography. Possibly the commonest reaction to his arguments that people have is to try to brush the problem under the carpet and say something like: 'Oh well, the fact that a pain in your toe is in your toe, not in your head, is simply what experience of pain is like'. 'So what's the difficulty?' they add. Others hypothesize that we construct 'virtual realities' in our heads and then 'project' the results out into the environment, apparently ignoring the fact that a virtual reality machine doesn't itself do anything of the sort; it's only us who can do any 'projecting' when we use the machine.

As Velmans' thinking has developed over the last 20 years, he has come to advocate a view that he names 'reflexive monism'. It says that (conscious) perceptual experience results from preconscious reflexive interactions of goings-on in the brain with goings-on in the environment—and the products of these interactions just *are* the experienced environment. So the answer to the 'how big is experience?' question, according to him, would presumably be 'the same size as whatever it is that you are experiencing'. This does not mean that, if you were looking at the sun for example, your experience should be regarded as being the same size as the actual sun, far bigger than the whole earth, only that it would have to be regarded as the same size as the perceived sun — that bright disc in the sky.

All this seems to be telling us something important about experience, and there's something basically right about it. But there are questions to ask. For instance how is it that, if you view a stereoscopic image of the Grand Canyon, it can look as huge and as real as the actual Grand Canyon, even though the stereo apparatus is far smaller than the real thing? Well, according to 'reflexive monism', the causal interactions between brain and environment are prior to the experience itself. Thus, if they (i.e. the causal interactions) are similar in the two cases, similar experiences will result — and evidently the stereo picture does mimic causal interactions produced by the real canyon well enough for that to happen and for us to therefore perceive the image as if it were the same size as the reality.

A more fundamental question is to ask how there can be any 'monism', which implies an indivisible unity, between for example the scene outside my window and the happenings in my visual cortex which are responding to the scene? Common sense tells us these are two entirely different things, only tenuously and indirectly linked by one-way chains of causes — photons reaching the eye, nerve impulses and so forth.

Velmans has of course tackled this issue. The quotation below summarizes the views he has arrived at:

> Reflexive Monism argues that 'the basic stuff of which the universe is composed has the potential to manifest both physically and as conscious experience (a dual-aspect theory in the tradition of Spinoza). In its evolution from some primal undifferentiated state, the universe differentiates into distinguishable physical entities, at least some of which have the potential for conscious experience, such as human beings. While remaining embedded within and dependent on the surrounding universe and composed of the same fundamental stuff, each human, equipped with

perceptual and cognitive systems has an individual perspective on or view of both the rest of the universe and him or her self. In this sense, each human participates in a process whereby the universe differentiates into parts and becomes conscious in manifold ways of itself, making the entire process reflexive.' So, I would argue for a primal unity — but of course fully accept that the world we live in has differentiated into many parts that have causal interactions with each other (Max Velmans, 2009, personal communication).

His answer involves ideas about both an original universal holism and a form of what is called 'dual aspect theory' (he refers to his picture as a 'dual aspect monism'). We'll be taking a look at the issues involved in subsequent chapters and will come up with a variety of holism that probably differs from Velmans' version or, even if similar in some ultimate sense, at least rests on rather different concepts and arguments. I shall also, in Chapter 4, describe my own doubts about the usefulness and validity of the type of 'dual aspect theory' that is most widely discussed these days. Although Velmans uses a more traditional version of the theory (the one advocated by the philosopher Spinoza (1632–77)), I shall be suggesting that it may not actually be needed because its function in his theory, as the theory now stands, is to introduce *consciousness* into perception. But consciousness, I'll be arguing, may have origins that are better described in more specific terms.

Conclusions

We've seen, in chapter 1 and in the first part of this one, how mentality and even personality seem often to be rather fluid. Individual minds and their characteristics can apparently swap or share identities to some extent, and also spill over into their environments. An impoverished social environment, as evidenced by actual or perceived loneliness, can have major effects on people's cognitive function as well as manifesting in increased mortality and physical illness (Cacciopo and Patrick, 2008). Even something as familiar as everyday perception of our bodies and the world around us is, according to Max Velmans, an holistic happening not confined to brains alone.

The trouble is that our habitual ways of thinking about brains and cognition, in terms of nerve impulses or synaptic weightings or computational metaphors for instance, are of no direct help when it comes to trying to understand the things we've been looking at; indeed that sort of thinking can often get in the way of understanding. And commonsense isn't much better. I'll describe the outlines of what may be a more useful description of mentality in the next chapter; a picture which has its origins in a whole range of strands of thinking that have been developing over the last 20 or more years, most clearly articulated, perhaps, in the work of Walter Freeman (1999). As we shall see later on it provides, among a good many other things, what seems to me a natural basis for the 'monism' in 'reflexive monism'. It'll be one that differs somewhat from Velmans' own suggestions, but leads to similar conclusions about an underlying unity of brain and environment when it comes to perception — along, probably, with a unity involving some other manifestations of mind that I'll be discussing. However, my argument about 'unity' will relate to mentality in general, rather than to conscious experience in particular; we have a lot of groundwork to lay first, and won't begin to tackle specific 'consciousness' issues until we get to chapter 5.

Chapter 3

Picturing Mentality

'Mentality' or 'mind' are words of a sort that automatically make you think of things (so I assume; they certainly make me do it!); objects out there that you could maybe pick up and weigh if you had a mind to do so. But of course they're not things, they are processes. The closest thing-like analogies for them would be candle flames or swirly patterns in a waterfall. Try to pick up either of those and they are liable to vanish or change form, which tells us quite a bit about the difficulties faced by psychology in general; neuropsychology in contrast, which *can* pick things up and 'weigh' them, has on the whole been making faster progress lately. Mentality is thus all about dynamics, and the first question to tackle is: the dynamics of what? A scheme that I think especially useful is set out in the table below:

Atemporal Entanglement 'Dynamics' (based on particle entanglements)
Social Dynamics (based on memes)
Level 2 Dynamics in Brains (mostly conscious: based on interactions between level 1 attractors)
Level 1 Dynamics in Brains (mostly unconscious: based on interactions between neurons in neural nets)
Brain Genetic Dynamics (based on development processes guided by genes)

- There are linkages running both up and down the hierarchy.
- Links proceed up the hierarchy step by step, except for the top stage (entanglement dynamics) which may be directly affected by all lower stages.
- All ascending links are mediated by ordinary, straightforward physical causation.
- Descending links do not necessarily go step by step — e.g. 'social dynamics' may directly affect the bottom level ('genetic dynamics') as well as the two levels immediately below it.
- Descending links often appear to be mediated by law-like influences, which act in conjunction with ordinary physical causation as far as the four lower levels of the hierarchy are concerned (Nunn, 2007, pp. 163–64).

I'm not going to say anything about the top category ('entanglement dynamics') just now as it depends on quantum theoretical possibilities that don't have any immediate relationship to most day-to-day concerns. That's why there's a dotted line under it. We'll get to topics of that sort later in the book. The remaining categories, however, all contribute directly to making our minds and I had better explain what they are about, starting from the bottom and working up.

Brain Genetic Dynamics

This is about the 'hardware' of our minds. Genes provide information which guides the enormously complex processes that result in the growth and development of brains. As they develop, different genes are called into play, switching on and off under the influence of feedback from the nerve cells they occupy, in an elaborate dance.

Processes occur on all sorts of time scales. There's the underlying Darwinian one that works over the millennia while genes jostle for 'fitness' as evinced by the brains that they have helped to form. Then there is the activation and de-activation (mostly down to the chemical changes called de-methylation and methylation it is thought) associated with the formation of different types of nerve cell and their growth or destruction. This happens over days, weeks or months. On shorter scales still there are events like the consolidation of short term memories into long term format, which require protein synthesis and thus gene activation, while de-activation due to 'small interfering RNA' production also occurs. Times of the order of a few minutes are involved here.

Processes working on longer time scales, interacting with environments that we encountered as we were growing up, are responsible for the 'hereditary' aspects of our minds; characteristics like how readily things frighten us, how extroverted we are, etc., which are known to be partly down to our genetic inheritance. Even some specific fears, such as that of snakes, are thought to be of genetic origin; and specific likings, too, such as the instinctive tenderness we all feel for little creatures with large heads and big eyes. The shorter time-scale processes, however, generally seem to be responsive to dynamics further up the hierarchy, though even here there may be feedback from other genes — perhaps, for instance, influencing things like degree or type of response to what's going on further up.

Level 1 Brain Dynamics

This refers to basic neural processes, such as the ones responsible for detecting the outline, colour or motion of an object that you see. As lots of work on visual perception over the last 50 or more years has shown, these three different characteristics are analysed separately to start off with and are only later combined into meaningful wholes, such as 'that's a car coming towards me, I'd better get out of the way!' A good deal of neural processing, perhaps all of it, is similar in that it involves information being dealt with in smallish, separate chunks at first that are then put together into the sorts of assembly that mean something to us as conscious individuals.

Processing of this sort is done in smallish networks, perhaps containing a few hundred or a few thousand nerve cells each. The dynamics of *artificial* neural networks has been a hot research topic for quite a while, but it is worth noting that the model 'nerve cells' used in this research are invariably extremely simple compared to real neurons and usually lack components of types thought to be crucial in natural networks, such as 'memristors' (Pershin and Di Ventra, 2009). Moreover few of the artificial networks contain nearly as many 'cells' as these smallest of natural ones.

Level 2 Brain Dynamics

The idea here is that the level 1 neural networks can be regarded as able to organise themselves functionally into units (the term 'attractor' in the table will be explained later), which will then interact with one another rather like the individual neurons in a 'level 1' network. Activity in these networks of networks (i.e. 'level 2' networks) underpins what we usually regard as our mentality, especially conscious mentality.

There are intimate inter-relationships between levels 1 and 2. Level 2 activity is a product of what goes on at level 1 but also feeds back to affect level 1. For instance, reading this page is, overall, a level 2 activity; but it depends on level 1 analyses of the shapes of individual letters, etc. and would cease if this information were not available. Equally, if level 2 reading switched off, if you lost interest for instance, most of the relevant level 1 analyses would very likely switch off too.

Social Dynamics

This depends on people interacting in groups of varying sizes ranging from family units, through workplaces, schools, clubs, towns and and so forth, up to nations and beyond. A lot of the interactions, however, depend on 'memes', used as a shorthand term for memorable concepts that people have in their minds or which are manifest in their environments. Going back to the navigation example, the idea of making charts would be a 'meme', shared by most navigators the world over, while an actual chart would be an instance of that meme—you might call it a 'memic representation'.

Discovery of the mirror neuron systems, which translate meaning as well as information between people, shows that social dynamics have far greater immediacy than we used to suppose. They directly link (aspects of) the brain dynamics of interacting individuals:

> ... we've got a system of brain cells [i.e. the mirror neuron system(s)] that process my actions and your actions in a holistic way in one and the same procedure. They simulate and re-create not only others' actions but also their intentions and feelings ... Our nervous systems are directly connected (Marco Iacoboni, quoted in Frank, 2009, pp. 163-4).

Memes are sometimes regarded as too abstract or vague in conception to be thought useful in the context of social dynamics. However, as I argued in the earlier book, they always involve emotions of one sort or another, sometimes the most intense passions; their interactions are responsible, not only for the positive aspects of culture, but also for phenomena like the 'dancing manias' of the middle ages, or the craze for Mesmerism that swept Europe two hundred years ago, or the recent epidemic of 'alien abduction'; moreover their concrete embodiments in 'memic representations' provide most of the fabric of our everyday surroundings.

Although each meme no doubt had its origin, often lost in the mists of time, in some individual person, once they get out there into society and are propagated in lore, education, the media and so forth, they frequently appear to take on a life of their own, which feeds back to mould the minds (i.e. mainly the level 2 dynamics) and lives of individual people. In aggregate, memes *are* culture, and our minds would be unimaginably impoverished if our cultures somehow disappeared. Nevertheless, their roles can often be of ambiguous benefit from our points of view. Consider the meme 'patriotism', for example, which came to the fore along with the development of nation-states. Admirable though it is in some respects, it's also partly responsible for the huge slaughter of modern warfare.

It is worth noting, too, the increasing recognition nowadays that culture can affect evolution, via both traditional Darwinian and so called 'epigenetic' mechanisms, as well as via behavioural ones. In other words, social dynamics influences genetic dynamics through a range of long chains of causation. The situation isn't nearly so straightforward as used to be pictured at one time, where the only influences were upwards; so that our inherited sexual preferences, say, determined aspects of culture. The processes are actually two-way, with our brain dynamics sandwiched in the middle.

State Spaces and Attractors

Perhaps the most obvious feature of the scheme outlined above is its almost unimaginable complexity; hugely complicated dynamics on each of four levels which also reciprocally affect one another, giving an overall dynamic across the levels. Is there any way of taming this complexity to let us build a more intuitive picture of mentality? Well, a first step in this direction involves a standard way of representing dynamical systems of any sort; namely in terms of 'state spaces'.

These are basically just a development of graphs. In a graph, you have two dimensions — the 'x' axis and the 'y' axis. Any point on the graph situated between the two axes represents some value of whatever both 'x' and 'y' mean. In other words, with one point, you can represent two variables. Now suppose you want to represent the momentary state of a dynamic system with just one point — simple! You merely have to assign one dimension to each variable that the system possesses. Think of a ball thrown through the air for instance; each moment it will have some defined position in space and also some defined speed and direction of travel. So, to represent the dynamic state of the ball (at any given instant of time) with a single point, you need a *six* dimensional space — one dimension for each position in our ordinary 3-D space, and one for speed in each possible 3-D direction. As time passes the ball will trace a line through the state space that represents a complete description of its dynamics from start to finish.

The bad news is that the number of independent dimensions you need depends not only on the number of variables required to describe a single entity like a ball, but also on the number of relevant entities. If you wanted to describe the dynamics of 100 aircraft approaching Heathrow airport, for instance, a six hundred dimensional state space would be required, six dimensions for each aircraft. And this was supposed to be a step towards simplification!

The saving grace is that these high dimensional state space descriptions will often include features called 'attractors'. In the case of the aircraft, the single line representing the evolution of the dynamics of all of them over time will show two types of feature. It will converge on positions in the space corresponding with the air traffic control stacking areas and the speeds and directions allowed while in them, and will oscillate round those positions for a time. Then it will head off for the position and landing speeds of Heathrow itself, finally coming to a stop there. The oscillatory areas are called 'periodic' attractors and the Heathrow position is a 'point' attractor.

Remember, the dynamic description we're talking of 'knows' nothing about aerodynamics, or air traffic control, or passengers' requirements, or fuel limitations, or anything like that. All it can 'see' is that the line describing the state is first drawn towards small areas of the space, where it wanders to and fro for a bit, and is then drawn to another area where it stops. And, with really complicated systems, that's often all we ourselves can see, for we know little or nothing about the chains of causation leading to some particular bit of dynamic behaviour, and we may frequently be ignorant of the relevant 'laws' (corresponding to air traffic control and its rules) that constrain the behaviour. Indeed 'attractors' can themselves appear to be like laws, putting constraints on what dynamical systems are able to do. As we shall see later, this appearance of being law-like is not so misleading as you may think at first hearing.

You might suppose that, if a system is chaotic or verging on the edge of chaos — which is what many systems such as the weather, brain activity, the stock market, or indeed the banking system so it now appears, are in fact like (see for example Kitzbichler *et al.*, 2009, for an up-to-date discussion of 'self-organized criticality' in the brain) — their state space descriptions would simply be a blur of random points scattered throughout the relevant, very high dimensional space. However, this is not the case, for they usually harbour what have been dubbed 'strange attractors' — regions of the state space, often with a very complicated shape, towards which the evolution of the system appears to be drawn, or within which it is confined.[1]

But what are these 'attractors'? What do they correspond with in the systems that we've been discussing? They are, or more correctly they *manifest*, simply as the things we've already been discussing. In genetic dynamics, they show up as neural structures like cells or axons or synapses. In brain dynamics, the most extensive ones manifest as things like personality traits and emotional states, while smaller ones are mostly memories of all the longer-term types. In social dynamics, they are organisations like political parties on large scales and, on smaller scales, memes in all their guises, both in abstract form (e.g. ideas in books) and concrete form (artefacts of all sorts that embody concepts). You may well be thinking at this stage that we've gone round in a big circle to get nowhere useful. All we've done, it could be said, is to take familiar, manageable concepts and translate them into a concept which, for its proper description, requires us to imagine 'spaces' with trillions upon trillions of dimensions. How on earth is that supposed to help?

Actually it does help, and this comes about in two principal ways. The first is that the attractor concept takes all the apparently disparate elements that contribute to mentality and gives them a common descriptive grounding as features of dynamical state spaces. We'll be exploring some of the implications of that in subsequent chapters.

The second way it helps is that it immediately suggests what seems to me a very intuitive description of the overall

---

[1] It's well worth googling 'strange attractor' if you're not familiar with their wonderful variety and beauty — a range of excellent websites picture them.

appearance of mentality, which is down to the fact that attractors can be fitted into what can be regarded as 'landscapes'. And this is more than just a pretty picture, for it directly implies possible answers to two of the biggest questions in science and one of the bigger questions in sociology. Or, to be more precise, it shows how and why answers to these apparently separate questions are simply the *same* answer manifesting in three different contexts. First, what are these 'landscapes'?

Attractor Landscapes

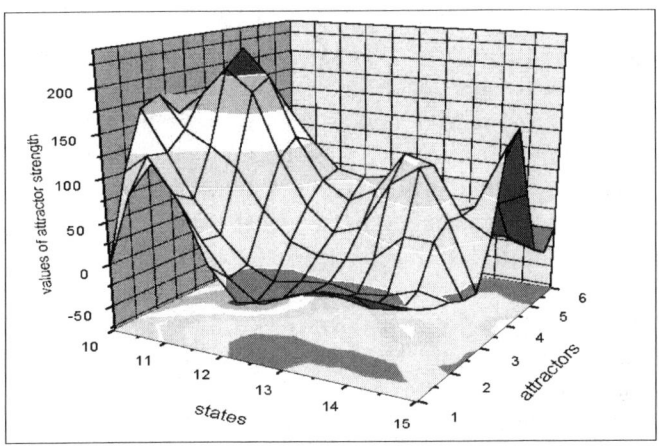

A simple attractor Landscape
(from J. A. Jensen and O. E. Rasmussen, *Mental Landscapes*, Proceedings of ECCON annual meeting, 2004)

The idea is to take each attractor that exists in some relevant state space — and there will be very large numbers of attractors in the systems we've been discussing; many millions in the case of brain dynamics — and map them into an 'attractor space', showing their relative positions, shapes and volumes. Of course it's impractical to actually *do* any such mapping at present, except for very simple systems like that pictured above (which describes influences on problem solving by a model 'agent'), as we simply don't know enough about the relevant dynamics. All the same, it is still useful to *imagine* that the mapping can be done because such maps have various interesting general properties.

Although 'attractor space' will generally inherit the multidimensionality of the state space to which it refers, it can be pictured, for many practical purposes, in familiar 3-D, so that its contents can be viewed (in imagination, of course) as just like an ordinary landscape. Each attractor can be envisaged as sitting at the bottom of a valley, or depression, or minor dent in the landscape, so that any process which reaches a downward slope will end up in whichever state the attractor describes.[2] Some attractors, of course are much larger than others (i.e. they have deeper and more extensive 'basins' of attraction), so they will form bigger features of the landscape, probably with lots of lesser attractors dotted around within them, which in turn may house even smaller ones, and so forth. The whole scene is likely to be 'fractal', therefore, just as real landscapes are often fractal.

It's an idea first popularised in biology over fifty years ago by Conrad Waddington (though he didn't know about fractals, of course—they were described later), who was mainly interested in how embryos grow. He imagined that genes work together to form what he called 'epigenetic landscapes', consisting of inter-connecting valleys down which the ball of development can roll until adult form is finally reached. Stuart Kauffman (1995) of the Santa Fe 'complexity' institute is an enthusiast for a related notion: that of genetic 'fitness landscapes' where evolution drives genomes to achieve hard-to-attain peaks of fitness. Another closely related idea—that of 'conformal spaces'—is now often used by biologists in connection with things like protein folding.

The landscapes of mentality are vast and mountainous; and behave as if viewed on a geological timescale, con-

---

[2] The picture at the start of this section actually shows the attractors as 'mountain peaks', but it's easier to understand how the sorts of landscape envisaged here work if you think of the attractors as occupying valley bottoms—if you turn the picture upside down, in other words.

stantly heaving, changing shape, obliterating some features and forming new ones. At least that's how they need to behave when they are working properly. Minds are nothing if they're not flexible and fluid when necessary. However, there's a problem here because it is a general feature of such landscapes that the more some particular route through them is taken, the more readily it will be taken in the future. It's as if use grinds wheel ruts into the landscape which are hard to get out of. Now this is fine for Waddington's developmental biology, for it is usually a good idea if development *does* follow well established paths. But it is not such a good idea in relation to many aspects of mentality because the environment in which the mentality is trying to survive doesn't stand still. Although well-worn routes are sometimes useful, they are often not the best possible ones and can be positively dangerous. Moreover, if some routes were to become too well-worn, it might be hard to switch from them even to other familiar tracks when the need arose. Behaviour could end up as completely stereotyped, with all adaptability lost. Which is why we're in a position to explain the puzzles described below. The answer to all of them depends on a need to keep attractor landscapes fairly rut-free in order to survive.

Sex, Sleep and Elections

Why do we have sexual reproduction? The basic problem here is that it seems incredibly inefficient from an evolutionary point of view because it results in half the number of off-spring that could have been obtained via non-sexual reproduction (because you need two individuals to make a baby instead of one[3]). All sorts of plausible-sounding explanations have been proposed. One group of proposals centres on the role of sex in creating and spreading potentially useful variations that could, for example, help us as a species to keep up in the evolutionary arms race with parasites.

---

[3] Except in the cases of those hermaphrodites able to fertilize themselves. The relative rarity of this lifestyle also suggests that 'normal' sex must usually have big evolutionary advantages.

Another group of explanations has to do with the possible roles of sex in minimising harm from DNA and chromosome abnormalities; some arguing that, if two sub-optimal genomes get together, they may function as well as one optimal genome; others in contrast have proposed that, if two not-so-goodies get together, the result is likely to be fatal, thus eliminating relative baddies from the species' gene pool which is good for the species. However, when examined in detail, each of these specific explanations has turned out to be less than convincing, whichever group they belong to; so the debate rumbles on.

The picture of genetic dynamics that we've built up suggests, however, that all such explanations are right but they have to be considered as a group, not separately, because they are not mutually exclusive. What can stop the wrong sorts of rut from developing in the relevant landscapes? Genetic mutations are going to help since they can remodel whole areas of landscape, which will be rut-free at least to start off with. Trouble is they are more likely than not to remove desirable features along with any ruts. But combining genomes via sex may allow retention of what's wanted in an existing landscape along with either filling in unwanted ruts or at least engendering a possibility that they will be filled in one day as further mutations occur.

However, mutations work on rather long timescales so that's unlikely to be the whole story. Of at least equal importance, probably, is the likelihood that simply shuffling genomes, which is what sexual reproduction does, will (on average) prevent ruts deepening over succeeding generations, and this benefit can more than outweigh the disadvantage implicit in the fact that a parent is a proven successful reproducer, whereas the child (the outcome of the reshuffle) is slightly less likely to turn out successful than would a child produced asexually (i.e. without any genetic reshuffle), provided the environment hadn't changed in the meantime. Thus sex can not only ameliorate the downside of mutations, while retaining and even enhancing the occasional long-term benefits, but is also likely to ameliorate any trend towards excessive rigidity as each generation succeeds the last.[4]

Sleep presents the same sort of puzzle for evolutionists, in that simple evolutionary arguments suggest that it ought often to be more disadvantageous than whatever it's worth. But all higher animals sleep, even though it's very dangerous for some of them. When particularly dangerous, they don't give up sleep, they simply evolve strategies to mitigate the dangers — as dolphins sleep only one brain hemisphere at a time, or herd animals on the African plains sleep in short snatches while some companions remain awake. Yet, apart from showing that it has what appears to be a relatively minor role in enhancing learning and memory, nobody knows what sleep actually does, nor why it is evidently so important to survival.

There is a big hint available, though. Sleep deprivation does result in behaviour becoming more stereotyped and less adaptable; a finding which has been in most of the textbooks for forty years or more, but which is not generally given much prominence. Daily routines wear grooves in the attractor landscapes of the brain, and it looks very much as though one function of sleep, perhaps the most important function, is to remove them. The high amplitude, rather simple, slow waves that sweep over the head during deep sleep seem well adapted for this purpose.

While 'rut removal' from brain landscapes is likely to have been the original reason for sleep evolving, it may also have acquired the secondary, related function of so to speak 'tuning' recently acquired landscape features (i.e. attractors) to fit in as well as possible with pre-existing features.

---

[4] This explanation can be regarded as a generalisation of the proposal made by some geneticists that cloning is worse than sex in the medium to long term because it allows minor harmful mutations to accumulate over the generations and has no means of getting rid of them. They go on accumulating until a tipping point is reached and a species that relies on cloning goes extinct. However, there are a few species that reproduce by cloning only which have been around for a very long time, while the DNA in our mitochondria is always cloned but seems to be as good now as it was 2 million years ago. Other factors, present somewhere in the generalisation but lacking in this specific instance of it, must also be important.

It's tempting to use this suggestion to account for why we have two different sorts of sleep (slow wave and rapid eye movement or REM). Maybe slow wave sleep deals mainly with 'rut removal', while REM is responsible for 'tuning'. It has long been supposed, on the basis of suggestive but not conclusive evidence, that REM sleep may have something to do with 'rehearsing' and/or 'consolidating' learning and other memories — processes which could mimic tuning. However, there is recent evidence that neural patterns reflecting previously acquired information are replayed during *slow wave* sleep (Peyrache *et al.*, 2009); if so there would appear to be functional overlap between the two types of sleep. It has also been suggested that slow wave sleep helps to coordinate

> the re-activation and redistribution of hippocampus-dependent memories to neocortical sites, whereas during REM sleep, local increases in plasticity-related immediate-early gene activity ... might favour the subsequent synaptic consolidation of memories in the cortex (Diekelmann and Born, 2010).

The suggestion made by these authors about slow wave sleep would seem to fit in with a 'rut' removal or redistribution role, and the more tentative one to do with REM is not inconsistent with a 'tuning' role for that type of sleep.

So I guess it's now pretty obvious now why elective democracy has turned out to be the least unsatisfactory form of government of any. Superficially, it seems kind of crazy to change governments so frequently. Those involved tend to get kicked out just when they have finally learned their jobs, it seems, in favour of a new lot who inevitably make all sorts of 'teething' mistakes. But the old guard equally inevitably get stuck in ruts in the landscapes of social dynamics — indeed there's a sense in which they *are* the ruts — and the advantages of getting rid of them apparently outweigh the disadvantages.

Multidimensionality May Matter

Although thinking of attractors as forming 3-D landscapes is fine from some points of view, and certainly helps with getting an imaginative handle on them, it may not be so alright from others. In very complex systems, the landscapes are going to be a lot more than *three* dimensional and there is evidence from another sort of high dimensional space that this can result in counter-intuitive properties. The space in question (a 'sequence' space) is one that relates the sequence of components in RNA molecules to how the molecule will fold — i.e. it relates the sequence of nucleotides within the RNA molecule to the molecule's final shape. And of course there are a whole range of different frequently occurring final shapes, but these are a lot fewer than the number of possible different sequences since many of the various possible sequences fold into *same* shape. The space is closely analogous to an attractor one in many ways; in fact the final shapes of the molecules can be thought of as *being* attractors.

The final shape of an RNA molecule can actually be calculated nowadays from knowledge of its component (i.e. nucleotide) sequence. Evolutionary biologists have wanted to know how many different sequences can produce any particular example of the frequently seen final shapes, how these sequences relate to one another and how they relate to the sequences that generate other frequently seen shapes. The number of random changes in sequence needed to get from one frequently seen shape to another is of special interest to them, because it is directly relevant to how easily evolutionary changes can occur. If you were thinking in 3-D terms, you'd probably say that you would have to 'explore' at least half the volume of the sequence space to be fairly sure of finding close links between any one (frequently seen) shape and any other — and even then you might miss a few. But, in fact, you can be certain of finding sequences capable of producing *every* commonly seen shape within a much smaller volume, so calculations show.

To put some figures on this, for RNAs containing 100 nucleotides, the radius of the higher dimensional 'sphere' in sequence space that is certain to contain representatives of *all* frequently seen shapes is *not* 50, as you'd expect by analogy with an ordinary 3-D sphere. It is actually only 15

(Wagner, 2005, p. 46). And this has consequences for the real world, not just for the imaginations of mathematically inclined biologists. For it means that random substitutions of individual nucleotides (due to random genetic mutations) can get you from one shape to any other in far fewer steps than might be expected, which is something that really does occur in nature. It's a remarkable result, and almost certainly carries implications for our attractor landscapes. What could they be?

One is that links between attractors are going to behave a bit like the 'small world' networks that have been the focus of so much interest lately. Far fewer steps will be needed, in other words, to get from one attractor to another than intuition suggests. But a better analogy would be to go back to the mountain and valley 3-D picture and imagine the valley bottoms (the attractors) connected, not only by roads along ravines and across passes and down other valleys, but also by a network of invisible air links and underground tunnels that can often directly connect landscape features which would look remote from one another from an ordinary 3-D perspective.

This could be especially relevant to the dynamics of memory. If one thinks of memory in Information Technology terms, with addressable contents that need to be dealt with in orderly sequences, it is extremely hard to understand how our own memories function as they do; recognizing faces in an instant, for example, or recalling obscure facts at a whim, and all apparently done via neuronal processes that are very slow in comparison with computer gigahertz speeds. Sometimes people try to explain our abilities in terms of massively parallel computations in the brain, but it is very doubtful whether even this could do the job. However, 'jumping' or 'tunnelling' through a multidimensional structure associated with (or, as a philosopher might put it, 'supervenient on') ordinary 3-D space could account for most, perhaps even for all, of how memory performs in the extraordinary way it does.

A second implication is down to the fact that similar considerations may well apply to the higher level dynamic that encompasses genetic, brain and social dynamics. One effect of an overall dynamic is to modify the attractor landscapes that exist on any particular level, and sometimes to create completely new landscape features — think, for instance, of how the high level dynamic that resulted in the scientific revolution has created a host of new features in social dynamics, the dynamics of individual brains, and is starting to work on genetic dynamics too. Landscape multidimensionality at each level facilitates change, innovation and adaptability, but the overall landscape, to which the dynamics within each level contribute, is likely to add to these effects. Biological forms are going to be more fluid, and new ones will emerge more readily, than traditionalists would ever have predicted. The same should be true of the traits, memes and memories of brain landscapes, and to the structures and organisations of social ones. There will be much more creativity in all these areas than we would expect on the basis of purely '3-D' thinking.

Provided rut formation is kept under control, therefore, attractor dynamics is going to be far more innovative than it would be without its inherent multidimensionality. And the magic, of course, is that the multidimensionality[5] works (as we saw in the case of RNA shape evolution), despite being in a sense an imaginary mathematical concept. Because it has effects, it must nevertheless be regarded as 'real' in the sense defined at the end of Chapter 1. But then lots of apparently imaginary mathematical constructs and ideas turn out to have major consequences for our everyday world, and thus cannot be entirely 'imaginary' after all.

As you'd probably expect if you are any sort of materialist, there is in fact a physical, 'ordinary space' explanation

---

[5] Another consequence of multidimensionality in biological systems is that it greatly increases the 'robustness' of developmental programmes — i.e. it makes particular developmental outcomes a lot less sensitive to alterations in gene expression than they would be in its absence (Wagner, 2005, pp. 152–6). This, too, could possibly have its parallels in relation to mentality. Maybe aspects of mentality like personality traits or even particular percepts, for instance, are more stable in relation to variations in their underlying generators than would be the case in the absence of multidimensionality.

(at least as far as the brain is concerned[6]) for the existence of what we pictured as the 'air links and tunnels' entailed by the multidimensionality of attractor space. I'll be mentioning it in chapter 6, when we've dealt with some of the other concepts that are needed for a balanced view. However, as we'll also be seeing later on in the book, this explanation doesn't wholly lay to rest questions about how something as apparently abstract as an attractor landscape can be so remarkably effective in moulding brain activity. But, before returning to this topic later on, I want to take a look in the next chapter at the concept underlying that of attractor landscapes — that of state spaces — to see whether they, too, manifest in 'real world' properties, and then go on to discuss implications for thinking about the confines of 'mind'.

---

[6] As we'll be seeing, the explanation is to do with scale-free properties of neural activity and thus might also apply to both social and 'overall' dynamics too, though the uncertainties here (about whether there is any multidimensional effect needing explanation, and whether relevant scale-free dynamics occur) are greater than in relation to brain dynamics considered on their own.

Chapter 4

The Boundaries of Mind

Miracles of Perception

Imagine a small boy out for a walk in some woodland. He sees an interesting-looking hole in a tree trunk. Maybe there's an owl's nest inside, or even some treasure! But he's a bit scared there might be a snake or nasty creepy-crawlies. So he finds a stick and explores the inside of the hole with that. What does he experience? We all know the answer. After a bit of poking about, he comes to 'feel' an irregular cavity, roughly spherical perhaps, with hard walls and a squishy floor. What he *doesn't* notice feeling are the varying pressures on the skin of the fingers with which he is holding the stick, or the amount of stretch in the relevant muscles, or indeed any of the happenings in his own body that are transmitting information from stick to brain.[1] It's almost as if the stick has become part of him and he is directly feeling with the tip of that; an everyday miracle of the type we all take for granted when we are driving a car, for instance, but a miracle nonetheless and one that can take quite bizarre forms.

---

[1] The boy's ability to blend tactile and kinaesthetic information to produce a seemingly direct perception of the hole is a particular example of a general characteristic of perception, well-described by McGann (2010) and called by him 'enactive' perception because its development requires active participation of some sort by the experiencer; it doesn't occur if he/she is entirely passive.

To give an example, there is the well known 'rubber hand illusion'.[2] People are placed so that one of their own hands is hidden from their sight, but they can see a similar looking rubber hand in front of them. Then the illusionist strokes the index finger, say, of both real and artificial hands for a couple of minutes. Afterwards, most people will wince if the illusionist pricks the *artificial* hand with a pin, or, if asked to close their eyes and point to their own hand with their other one, they'll actually point to the artificial hand. Somehow, after just a couple of minutes of very simple training, people have managed to 'project' their real hand into the rubber one. And they can pull off the same trick with their entire bodies, too. Here's a user's account by someone who was operating a sophisticated, remote control robot that gave him tactile as well as visual feedback:

> I began to look through the eyes of the robot. The world looked like the world would look if I was located twelve feet to the left of my actual body, where the robot was located … The strangest moment was when Dr Tachi told me to look to my right. There was a guy in a light blue suit and light blue painted shoes reclining in a dentist's chair. He was looking to his right so I could see the bald spot on the back of his head. He looked like me and abstractly I understood that he was me, but I know who me is and me is *here*. He, on the other hand, was *there* (quoted by Tart, 1993).

The very rapid integration of altered sensory inputs with others that are unchanged, produces a new but consistent experience of the world. It's a trick that is hard to understand if you think of your mind as being somehow inside your head, or an expression solely of goings-on in your brain. Agreed, in the case of the 'rubber hand', the brain could perhaps learn to 're-wire' itself so that, for instance, it always perceived its hand as being in a different place from where muscle sense (proprioception) was telling it the hand was positioned. But such re-wirings normally take quite a bit of time. An old favourite of psychologists was to put spectacles on people or, more commonly, on unfortunate animals that turned everything (i.e. their visual worlds)

---

[2] There are excellent video blogs showing this—something else that's well worth googling, if you are not familiar with it.

upside down. Popular myth has it that the people adapted to these 'inverting spectacles' after a day or two and saw everything as normal; so did the animals. However, it appears this isn't quite true of people at least (see Linden *et al.*, 1999). Visuo-motor functioning returns pretty well to normal after two or three days—for instance, people are able to walk steadily without having to use sticks after that period—but the people *don't* actually perceive the world as being the right way up; and of course it's impossible to find out how animals might see things once their behaviour gets back to normal. The myth that vision had been proved to return to normal probably arose from confusing recovery of ability to navigate the world alright with experiencing it as being the right way up.

Be that as it may, the necessary 're-wiring' clearly takes days rather than minutes, and it looks as though it is not always as complete as whatever change resulted in the robot operator seeing himself from twelve feet away or the hand displaced into an artificial one. Some might rightly point out that it is known that sensory inputs inconsistent with any particular preferred interpretation of the environment can be rapidly 'suppressed' or 'inhibited', so as not to get in the way of the inputs regarded by the brain as more relevant. But how does the brain 'know' what to suppress? How can we 'project' ourselves into our tools, etc. so quickly and so completely?

Our remarkable perceptual abilities have been nicely summarized in a recent *Nature Neuroscience* review:

> A conspicuous ability of the brain is to seamlessly assimilate and process spatial and temporal features of sensory stimuli. This ability is indispensable for the recognition of natural stimuli. Yet, a general computational framework for processing spatiotemporal stimuli remains elusive. Recent theoretical and experimental work suggests that spatiotemporal processing emerges from the interaction between incoming stimuli and the internal dynamic state of neural networks, including not only their ongoing spiking activity but also their 'hidden' neuronal states, such as short-term synaptic plasticity (Buonomano and Maass, 2009).

These authors suggest that perception 'emerges from' an implicitly dualistic 'interaction between' inputs and internal brain dynamics, which is a useful stance to take if trying to analyse the detail of what may be occurring. However, as we have begun to see in the last two chapters, there may be no clear dividing line between internal and external dynamics. A somewhat more radical, monistic approach may be appropriate when it comes to getting to grips with the basis of perception.

State Spaces Again

As we saw in chapter 3, the contents of our minds can be pictured as attractor landscapes, while the attractors themselves are features of dynamical state spaces. Let's think for a moment about what contributes dimensions to the state space of our little boy walking through the wood. The first thing to be said is that there won't be a single, unchanging state space, but a whole sequence of different ones as dimensions are added to, or subtracted from, their predecessors. Some of the dimensions are likely to feature in every one of his state spaces, of course, especially those relating to the dynamics of his core awareness of himself (much of which won't be *conscious* awareness) — his position in space and what's going on in his muscles, for example, and all the stuff relating to breathing and emotional tone and general bodily state. Others will put in fleeting appearances, depending on what he looks at, what he hears, what scents reach his nose, and so on.

Then he picks up the stick and starts poking about inside the hole. His overall dynamical state immediately changes due to constraints imposed by the stick itself and the shape of the hole. The new sequence of state spaces will inevitably have a different structure, and harbour different attractors, from the pre-stick ones. Although the dimensional change will be quite small in relative terms, because most of his dynamics will be unaffected by the stick, even a small change is likely to generate or activate some new attractors, and perhaps inactivate others that were previously active, resulting in an immediate reconfiguration of some part of his mental landscape.

This reconfiguration happens fast, beginning very soon after the dynamical state change. While most such reconfigurations are likely to be fairly minor, there's no reason to suppose that they could not sometimes be major — such as representing yourself to be sitting twelve feet away from your actual body, as happened to the man operating the robot. But perhaps the most remarkable aspect of this way of looking at things is that it requires us to view the overall dynamical state space as in some sense fundamental. Goings on intrinsic to the boy's brain merely provide a portion, albeit probably the largest proportion, of the relevant dimensions, and there's no need to give them any sort of primacy when it comes to thinking about how fast changes could happen. That depends on the rate of change of whole situations.

There is a proviso, of course. Our brains do have to be capable of participating in any such 'whole situation'. If they can't participate, they will either not be affected at all by the extra-brain dynamics, or will be reduced to relatively slow processes of learning and adaptation as in the 'inverting spectacles' example. In fact it is mostly previous learning that *enables* brains to participate directly in these wholes. This is true even in the case of dynamics as apparently fundamental as those associated with vision. Babies have to *learn* how to see properly, and it's well known that people born blind, whose vision is restored in adult life, may never learn to see as well as the rest of us.

Reflexive Monism Revisited

Let's see whether state spaces could provide a basis for the 'monism' in Max Velmans' 'reflexive monism' (described at the end of chapter 2). Picture if you will someone who is sitting day-dreaming in a comfortable armchair; nearly all the dimensions of her series of dynamical state spaces will relate to goings-on in her brain with some contribution from mainly vegetative bodily dynamics (mostly sub-conscious awarenesses of posture, breathing, general physical well-being etc.). Then a wasp flies into the room and stings her leg. The dynamic behaviour of the sting itself and the stung leg quickly add a whole lot of dimensions to her previous state space and trigger a large re-configuration of her attractor landscape. However, the post-sting space itself is still a notionally single space even though many of the new dimensions are down to dynamics *outside* of her brain and even, in the case of the sting itself, not part of her own body. There is indeed a sort of 'monism' to the situation, but is it the wrong sort of monism for the purposes of Velmans' theory?

Actually, from one point of view, it is probably just what the theory needs because of the fact, noted in the chapter 2 discussion of 'reflexive monism', that a stereographic picture of the Grand Canyon can look just as big as the real Grand Canyon. This means that the monism can't be any unity grounded in our ordinary 3-D space; if it were, the picture should appear to be the size of a picture, not of a canyon. What seems to be relevant to the size perception is precisely what Velmans regards as relevant; namely that the visual dynamics induced by the picture should be the same, or closely similar, to those induced by the real thing. And that's an identity that fits well with the state space notion.

From another point of view, it might be considered too abstract a notion for Velmans' purposes. After all, our perceptions are the most directly 'real' events in our lives; we can't know anything about ourselves, or indeed about the world out there, without perception of one sort or another. But dynamic state spaces are surely little more than the fevered product of some mathematician's imagination,[3] it might be claimed. How could such an important monism, one alleged to be responsible for how we perceive our everyday worlds, possibly be attributed to something so apparently insubstantial?

---

[3] The mathematician mainly responsible for them was Henri Poincaré.

A possible answer to this objection is to say that the state space picture is nothing more than a means of representing the underlying dynamics, a sort of description of them, and these dynamics are certainly as 'real' as anything else in the world. They are what actually underlie our perceptions, it might be said, and thinking of them in terms of state spaces containing attractors is just an aid to comprehending their essential unity. In its way, this seems satisfactory enough as a reply, but is probably not the full story. As shown in the last chapter, the inherent multidimensionality of these spaces adds, or can add, new features to physical processes; which suggests that the spaces must possess, or at least must represent, some sort of 'reality' peculiar to themselves, according to the definition of 'real' given earlier (in chapter 1).

It's a situation, albeit one perhaps better described as a puzzle, that's been familiar to physicists for a long time. Quantum theory is formulated on the basis of an *infinite* dimensional 'Hilbert' space, and this description adds all sorts of features, some of them unexpected and counter-intuitive, to the behaviour of matter and the world around us. We'll be taking a quick look at a few of these features later on. If the very matter of which the world is composed seems to need an infinite dimensional space for its proper description, it is maybe not so unreasonable to propose that our perceptions have to be put in the context of a multi-dimensional space in order to be properly understood. State spaces, therefore, may well provide an adequate basis for the dynamic aspect of Velmans' 'monism'.

In that case a reflexive model of perception, involving individual objects and experiencers, must be only part of a larger picture. A person's 'mind' while perceiving something encompasses aspects of the dynamics of the thing perceived, as well as those of the person's own self. What if a whole lot of people are both perceiving much the same thing and interacting closely with one another? We have a collection of built-in mechanisms to aid interaction — more or less instant comprehension of speech, gesture and facial expression; the whole 'mirror neuron' system, which is of unknown extent but certainly serves to translate the *meaning* of (at least some) actions from one person to another, in addition to the simple information[4] about actions that people get from other sources.

Provided interactions are not too intense, the majority of each person's state space dimensions will relate to the dynamics of his or her *own* body and brain. But suppose a threshold is passed and interactions become so intense that the majority of each person's dimensions come to derive from the dynamics of their overall situation. How should their 'minds' be pictured then? Clearly one would have to envisage another monism; a single mind encompassing all the people involved; a 'group mind' in other words, but one possessing all the immediacy and apparent reality of relatively mundane monisms like perception of a pain in one's leg.

Let's take a break from abstract discussion and look at some examples of 'group mind' in action. Then, later on in the chapter, we'll need to think about whether mind's boundaries might in fact be even wider than those described hitherto.

Group Mentality

A striking example of a 'group mind' experience happened during a particularly fraught time early on in the history of the Mormons. Their founder was Joseph Smith. Each September for four years, starting when he was aged eighteen, he was visited by an angel who revealed the burial place of golden plates bearing inscriptions in an unknown tongue.

---

[4] Please note that, although people often talk loosely about information and meaning as if the terms were interchangeable, there are sharp philosophical and scientific distinctions between the two, some of which we'll be discussing later. The most commonly used notion of information, as far as information theory is concerned, is that due to Claude Shannon — i.e. our 'bytes' and 'bits'. He specifically excluded any notion of meaning from his definition of these (i.e. a 'bit' of information is the answer to a single yes or no question, regardless of what that answer means). In this book, we're mainly taking 'information' to refer to Bateson information ('a difference that makes a difference'), but that too is meaning free.

When he was twenty-two, he was allowed to take the plates home with him where they were miraculously translated by angels named Urim and Thummim — and the rest is history, albeit a somewhat unhappy history at first. Conflicts with neighbours abounded. 'One way and another, the Mormons [at that period of their history] managed to get on ill terms with anyone, given time,' wrote Wallace Stegner, who has documented their travails. Eventually Joseph Smith himself, his brother Hyrum and one of their companions, John Taylor, were shot by a 'gentile' mob. And the movement was bereft and leaderless for a while.

However, it wasn't long before Brigham Young, a much tougher and more realistic character than Joseph Smith, made a speech during the course of a meeting which was attended by most of the active followers of the movement. Here's Stegner again on the subject:

> In a miraculous manifestation that hundreds attested, his (Young's) pudgy body on the platform assumed the length and beauty of the dead prophet's [i.e. Joseph Smith, who had been a handsome man]: his mouth had opened to send abroad not his own voice but the incontrovertible voice of Joseph. After that speech there was no question who would lead the church ...

There are two striking phenomena here; first, Brigham Young's ability to embody, so to speak, the mind of the group, and secondly the mass hallucination, said to have been shared by everyone present apart, perhaps, from Young himself. He couldn't have seen his own transfiguration of course, but one wonders whether he heard his voice changing into that of Joseph Smith. He should have done so if he shared the 'group state space'. Perhaps, on the other hand, he didn't fully participate in it but merely played a part in creating it, in which case his voice would have remained his own as far as he was concerned.

The basis of this sort of occurrence was described, with characteristic insight, by Gore Vidal (1954) in his novel *Messiah*. Vidal's fictional messiah said of himself:

> Everybody gets ideas about things which he thinks are wonderful but usually nothing happens to the people he

tries to tell them to. With me, it's been different from the beginning. People have listened and agreed. What I know they know. Isn't that a funny thing? Though most of them probably would never have thought it out until they heard me and it was all clear ... but I do get something from those people, something besides the thing I tell them. I seem to become part of them, as though what goes on in their minds also goes on in me at the same time, two lobes to a single brain.

The (also fictional) narrator of the book said of this messiah:

I suspected the fact that this serene mask hid a nearly total intellectual vacuity ... yet I did not mind, for I had experienced his unique magic and already I saw possibilities of channeling that power ... He was indifferent, I think, to everyone. He gave one his attention in precise ratio to one's belief in him and the importance of his work. With groups, he was another creature: warm, intoxicating, human, yet transcendent, a part of each man who beheld him, the long desired and pursued whole achieved.

Guy Claxton (1994), a psychologist by profession, gave a delightful account of what it was like to be immersed in a group as a disciple of the guru Bhagwan Rajneesh. There was a sense of liberation and exhilaration, at least to start off with:

all those 'deep and meaningful' conversations in the coffee bar, all those confrontations, all that sex and all those tears and, above all, the constant injunction to 'be total' ... It was this tyranny of 'totality' more than anything else, I think, that finally started the drift back towards those grey cords [i.e. a conventional life].

The guru himself made a deep impression on Claxton with his 'luminous brown laser-like eyes' and 'spell-binding' oratory:

he might wiggle the tip of his finger at your third eye, and you would come all over funny. Though I never caught him at it, I am convinced that the only way he could have achieved this effect was by simultaneously and surreptitiously sticking the other hand in the mains. Whatever the explanation, no-one could afford to ignore a man with such a finger.

The all-encompassing nature of discipleship can have lasting effects. At a relatively trivial level, most of us have experienced the pointlessness of arguing with Jehovah's Witnesses on the doorstep. The same phenomenon occurs, however, in far more serious contexts. Hannah Arendt (1958) studied one of Hitler's disciples, Adolf Eichmann, when he was brought to trial for his part in the holocaust, years after Hitler's death. She comments that he seemed unable to think in any normal sense; he spoke in clichés and could see no point of view but his own. Yet he was, or had been, an able and intelligent man. When a movement 'takes off' to the extent achieved by Nazism, it sucks in perfectly ordinary people. Taylor (1991) among others has pointed out that even SS concentration camp guards were unexceptional people on the whole, carrying out a job to which they were led by ideology and circumstances. After the war most went back to being ordinary, but those who had been most fully immersed in the group mind, as Eichmann was, might never recover.

These anecdotes can probably be regarded as fairly typical of what goes on in the cults and millennial crazes with which humanity is plagued. It seems that people are drawn, often by some charismatic leader, to interact in ways that create or deepen a few attractors in their 'social' landscapes, which sooner or later appear to dominate the whole landscape. Feedback results in ever increasing modification of their brain landscapes. Their individual state spaces come to share an ever increasing number of dimensions with one another. Eventually some threshold is passed and a significant proportion of the people involved occupy a single state space and thus possess a common mind: a mind which harboured a mass hallucination in the case of the Mormons, caused mass murder by the Nazis and which has led to mass suicide of other cults. Most people's individual brain landscapes are quite resilient, however, and soon bounce back to something like their old configurations. Only a few individuals, Eichmmann-like, retain the once-shared mentality.

Less dramatic, but essentially similar, phenomena occur almost daily for brief periods, somewhere in the world; at exciting football matches, for example, or pop concerts or in outbreaks of mass emotion ('mass hysteria' as some would call it) like that which swept nearly half the population of the UK at the death of Princess Diana. And they can all be attributed to exactly the same circumstance that results in our feeling a pain in our toe, say, as actually *being* in our toe! All these disparate phenomena are, according to the picture we're developing here, down to our mentality being founded in dynamic state spaces with variable numbers of dimensions, some of which are contributed by happenings outside the brain.

So mind can spread its wings far beyond the confines of our individual brains, it appears. Does it have any boundaries whatsoever? There are some who would answer 'no' to this question. We'll take a brief look at their views next and also try to formulate some answers of our own.

Idealism

This is the philosophical position often associated with Bishop George Berkeley (1685–1753), one of the foremost philosophers of his time as well as an influential churchman and philanthropist. He claimed that the only things we can ever directly know about are our own perceptions; the world out there of material 'reality' is, in a sense, apparently secondary to our perception of it; our experience — our 'ideas' — can thus be considered primary. He himself thought that this could be taken to suggest that the material world might be an expression of 'ideas' held in the mind of God. Others however, perhaps influenced by Plato's proposals about 'ideal forms' and also by notions about the illusoriness of the world that percolated into Europe from the East, took the next step and proposed that matter is only a projection or manifestation of mind, which is the truly fundamental reality.

It's a philosophy that has some appeal for some physicists, especially those adhering to the traditional 'Copenhagen' interpretation of quantum theory.[5] But, as

---

[5] The Copenhagen interpretation holds that 'collapse of the wave function' (i.e. the conversion of quantum probability fog into actual

the contemporary philosopher Galen Strawson (1994) has pointed out, it is really no more than the opposite side of the *same* coin as that on which traditional materialism exists (i.e. the view attributed to the classical Greek philosopher Democritus that 'atoms and the void' are all that there is). Idealism does substitute a 'problem of matter' for traditional materialism's 'problem of mind', but that is certainly no step forward as far as the topic of this book is concerned. While Bishop Berkeley's point about what is most 'real' to us is still relevant, the Idealism that has developed since his time seems only to add extra confusion to the puzzles we already face; probably best to avoid further discussion of it!

Panpsychism

A philosophical view with roots than even older than those of Idealism, and one that is currently having something of a revival in (some) philosophical circles is panpsychism. People have probably always been drawn to feel that the nature they see around them—animals, plants, winds, mountains, thunder and lightning—has its own spirit or spirits, and the feeling was almost universally expressed in the animistic religions and Shamanic beliefs of tribal societies. James Lovelock's 'Gaia hypothesis' is a sophisticated expression of the same basic intuition, which is probably one reason why people anxious to get rid of 'primitive' thinking have been so reluctant to acknowledge that there's a lot of evidence in its favour.

Attempts to convert the intuition into an 'ism', however, have often been somewhat confused. The simplest version is to claim that 'consciousness', whatever that is taken to mean, is inherent in all matter. But this runs into the rather obvious problem that a rock, for instance, does not seem to be 'conscious' in any even half-way believable sense of the word; indeed it seems totally unconscious to all appearances. Most philosophical writers on the topic have therefore reverted to some version of what might be called

---

particles or other 'observables') is ultimately down to observation by *conscious* observers.

pan-mentalism. All matter has inherent 'mental' properties, they say, but these don't necessarily always entail, or manifest as, anything that we would recognize as consciousness. The term 'pan-protopsychism' has been used by some, apparently as a sort of half way house between pan-consciousness and views about the universality of information, but I suspect that general agreement as to its meaning is lacking. The arguments are complex and involve a good deal of what can look to outsiders like hair-splitting, so I won't go into them here.[6]

Strangely enough, philosophers with an interest in panpsychism often ignore the physical evidence that matter in general does indeed have attributes that can seem mind-like in some respects. For instance light somehow 'knows' what a straight line is, for it generally travels in straight lines but is also able to change direction (when refracted, for instance, or subject to a gravitational field). How does it do this? Probably the most generally accepted explanation is due to Richard Feynman, that giant of 20th century physics. He argued that light is composed of photons and every photon's (non-material) 'wave function' in fact 'explores' all possible directions that the photon itself could take. But the 'probability amplitudes' cancel out for any direction lying off whichever straight line is appropriate for the medium (air, glass, outer space in the vicinity if a star, etc. etc.) that the photon is traversing. So the photon will always be found somewhere along the appropriate straight line. Thus light travels in straight lines because non-material aspects of its component photons (their 'wave functions') take account of its total environment! Unlike a billiard ball bouncing off the cushion, a photon is not simply under the sway of entirely local conservation laws, although these are involved in other aspects of its behaviour. There's something almost mind-like involved here — a something that might be described as 'knowledge' that a photon appears to possess about its surroundings. And

---

[6] David Skrbina's recent book *Panpsychism in the West* gives a particularly clear account of the relevant arguments, views and issues.

photons, of course, are universal constituents of matter since they are carriers of the electro-magnetic forces that bind our atoms and molecules together. Moreover, other types of particle possess comparable abilities, according to quantum theory.

A more striking example of the 'knowledge' that photons can demonstrate is provided by the Elitzur-Vaidman bomb test.[7] This shows that photons, normally able to take one of two alternative paths at random through an apparatus, have the ability sometimes to demonstrate that the path they *didn't* take was in fact impassable. Indeed, the situation is spookier still because photons can also show whether or not the path that they didn't take *would have become* closed *if they had happened* to take it.

They can show this because the apparatus is so designed that they always emerge from it in one particular direction if *both* paths are open, but they can sometimes emerge in another direction if either one path is actually closed or if it *would have become closed if the photon had happened to take it* (even though, in fact, the photon didn't go that way). That photons can and do behave like this is well-established. The explanation commonly offered echoes Feynman's account of how they know about straight lines; it is that their non-material 'wave-functions' always 'explore' *both* paths through the apparatus (while the photons themselves take only one of the two). However, the actual or even the *potential* closure of one path results in a different directional probability amplitude (i.e. different from the one that would have applied if both paths had been open and not liable to close) applying to any photon that makes it through via the remaining path.

Whatever the merits of this explanation, it's clear that a significant proportion[8] at least of the photons do somehow acquire what appears to be 'knowledge' of the *whole* experi-

[7] See, for instance, two of Sir Roger Penrose's books, *The Emperor's New Mind* and *Shadows of the Mind*, for very understandable descriptions of this.

[8] In the set-up originally suggested by Elitzur and Vaidman, and described by Roger Penrose, the proportion of photons entering the apparatus that were subsequently able to demonstrate their

mental set-up. They not only 'know' about whether the alternative path is actually closed, but also about whether it *would have* closed *if* they had taken it. But is 'knowledge' of this type sufficient to support claims of pan-mentalism? Well, the answer appears to be 'yes and no'; it depends what is meant by the 'mental' in pan-mentalism. My own view is that any 'mentality' recognizably like ours has fundamental features that are additional to the apparent 'knowledge' attributable to photons, but will postpone explaining why I think this till a bit later.

Property Dualism and Dual Aspect Theory

These are two, closely related, philosophical views that are about consciousness itself rather than mentality in general. More precisely they are about 'qualia', which is the word philosophers use to describe the conscious experience of seeing red, or feeling a pain, or having a thought, or whatever. David Chalmers in particular, an Australian philosopher who has had a lot of influence on the 'consciousness studies' movement (especially in the mid to late 1990s), helped to popularize them. They were his means of trying to make some sort of sense of the otherwise incomprehensible, or at least *very* hard to understand, circumstance that we have any conscious experience whatsoever. Why aren't we unconscious robots or zombies? There seems to be no good reason why consciousness should exist as robots could probably manage perfectly well without it. Moreover it is inexplicable, said Chalmers, in terms of any known physical principles. An obvious rejoinder, made by some, was to say that therefore we must possess immaterial souls responsible for our consciousness, as many have believed for millennia. René Descartes, in particular, gave 'soul' a more precise description in the 17th century with his concept of *res cogitans*. This, along with the *res extensa* of the physical world, provided the two components of what is

---

'knowledge' was 25%. However, later modifications of the experiment have increased the proportion to nearly 90%.

now called *substance* dualism (not to be confused with *property* dualism).

Anyhow, the spirit of the times being strongly in favour of some form of materialism, Chalmers wanted to avoid any concept that smacked of 'soul'. So he first of all suggested that matter intrinsically has qualia-like properties, along with its other properties, as a simple 'fact of nature' — i.e. matter is a single 'substance' but has two types of property, qualia and the rest. The qualia property is able to clearly show itself in the special environment of our brains for reasons yet to be discovered. It's a view that has a lot in common with Spinoza's version of 'dual aspect theory', which was used by Max Velmans (see chapter 2). Not entirely satisfied with this formulation, Chalmers later adopted the idea that *information*, as opposed to matter itself, has two 'aspects', thus popularizing the modern version of 'dual aspect theory'. To an outsider, referred to as a 'third-person' observer, information looks like assemblies of Claude Shannon's 'bits' and 'bytes' embodied in words on a page, computer memories, synaptic alterations in brains, nerve impulses, and so on and so forth; seen from the inside, from a 'first-person', subjective point of view however, information manifests in qualia.

In actual fact, although Chalmers took pains to distinguish between property dualism and his version of dual aspect theory,[9] it is by no means clear that they are fundamentally different; if only because, as noted earlier, there have been suggestions that matter itself may derive from information. To me at least, both ideas are strongly reminiscent of the pre-Newtonian 'explanations' of gravity in terms of 'ponderousness' or some similar concept; that is they seem to be pseudo-explanations which merely re-phrase a problem in somewhat arcane language, without actually throwing any additional light on it whatsoever. While Chalmers' emphasis on the difficulty of accounting for

---

[9] It can sometimes be hard to work out what he *did* actually mean as his arguments are often complex and he introduced additional terms, such as 'naturalistic dualism' which may not refer to any underlying unity.

qualia in terms of contemporary scientific concepts was undoubtedly important and worthwhile, I think we can hope to do better than simply accept that his pair of dualities can be taken as the last word on the matter — despite the prominent place they have had in some contemporary discussions of consciousness.

On second thoughts, there is another point that I need to make about Chalmers' version of dual aspect theory, which is that it is probably worse than a pseudo-theory or a fudge, for it is positively misleading in one respect. The two 'aspects' of his theory refer to *information*, which Chalmers seems to have conceived in information theoretic terms. In other words, he implied that the bits and bytes that we use in our computers would possess qualia if they were to be 'seen' from within; though of course he didn't imply that any existing computer could actually take a 'subjective' view of itself.

However, mentality in general and qualia in particular, aren't just about information; they are also essentially about meaning. The consciously perceived quale 'there's a pain in my toe' carries meaning for us; indeed there's a sense in which it *is* its own meaning. Unconsciously perceived happenings and mental processes also carry meaning — for the brain and body that harbour them and often, if indirectly, for our conscious selves too. It has become something of a truism these days to point out that any meaning associated with the activities of computers, which are solely information processing devices, is either designed or projected into them by us. Thus, even if this form of dual aspect theory did point to a useful truth, it would only be a half truth at best since it excludes whatever the ingredient is that must be associated with qualia in order to add meaning to information; information on its own lacks meaning, whether viewed from outside, inside, or upside-down for that matter.

So we need to think a bit about meaning at this stage, and then take a look at any implications for concepts of universal mentality. But this will take us into murky conceptual waters, where there are no good navigation aids. There are no established theories of meaning[10] comparable to information theory, while the philosophical literature on it is fragmented and often contradictory. We need to try to plot our own course, therefore.

Meaning

Evidently there are links of some sort between information and meaning, so the first step is to be clear about what 'information' means. In modern information theory, the term refers to 'bits' of information, each of which is defined as the answer to a single 'yes or no' question when the probability of getting either alternative is 50%, regardless of what the answer means. For the purposes of this book, I prefer to use Gregory Bateson's generalization of this definition, which takes information to be 'a difference which makes a difference', so that a 'bit' of information becomes the difference which results in a pointer moving to 'up', say, instead of 'down' (also when the prior probability of getting either outcome is 50%). Bateson information, too, is meaning free.

This formulation immediately suggests that the following general relationship exists between information and meaning:

- Information is a difference that makes a difference.
- Meaning has to do with what enables a difference to make a difference and/or constrains the type of difference that will result.

For example, if you get a phone call saying 'Congratulations, you've won a million pounds on the lottery', the information is transmitted via sound waves to your ear, then nerve impulses to your brain. Long chains of physical differences propagate (air molecules are displaced, neurotransmitter molecules are released, etc. etc.), but none of these differences carries any intrinsic meaning. That is added only later when the whole context is taken into

---

[10] There have been several attempts to develop mathematical theories of meaning; for instance Keith Devlin's (1991) proposals for a theory of 'infons'. But none of them appear to have taken off or been generally accepted.

account: a context which will include the physical bases of acoustics and neurotransmission, your prior knowledge of language and lotteries, and so on. If, on the other hand, the phone call had said 'I'm sorry to have to tell you you've lost all your money', the informational content would be only a little different from that of the first call, but the different meaning that got attached to it at some stage would result in quite different consequences further down the line.

Melanie Mitchell (2009, chapter 13) has described a computer program, called 'Copycat', that she thinks may provide computers on which it runs with the rudiments of intrinsic meaning—computers generally deal only in information, of course, and any meaning associated with their activities is normally put there by us. Copycat, however, can find simple analogies between groups of symbols and can construct rules for modifying symbols in a way that depends on aspects of their relationships to one another— all *without* any prior, direct instruction. Its activities will often appear sensible and logical to us, but the essential point is that Copycat discovers the logic needed for them without being told about it by any programmer; it finds 'meaning' in the symbols given to it, in other words, relying on a whole lot of semi-autonomous 'codelets' (i.e. small semi-independent programs analogous to applets), which compete and co-operate with one another in probabilistic ways to converge on conclusions. Although Mitchell describes it in rather different terms (she constructed the program and is interested in its details), it's clear that the dynamic interactions of the *whole* system—inputs, pre-existing information given to the computer about the inputs (i.e. 'memories'), the consequent interactions of the 'codelets' and the resultant constraints on their behaviour— are what generate the 'meaning' in the system.

What all this implies is that meaning in the abstract must refer to holistic aspects of systems and their dynamics, including their histories. It must therefore be based upon things like natural laws, memories and attractors. Laws are what allow differences to make differences and they prescribe the form that the outcomes will take. Memories too, whether in brains or other systems, also modify the effectiveness of differences and the results that a particular difference may produce. And the same, to all appearances, applies to attractors, especially to the 'strange' ones in chaotic systems. It's perhaps not surprising that memories and attractors are related in this way, especially since, as far as brains at least are concerned, we regard long-term memories as *being* attractors. But including natural laws along with these two may seem a bit odd, and I had better say something about this.

Unfortunately the status of natural law, and of causation in general, is another philosophical minefield,[11] so I'll simply make some rather general points relevant to the proposal offered above. Like attractors in very complex systems, most so-called natural laws can be regarded as expressions of the regularities that we perceive in the behaviour of dynamic systems. The laws of hydraulics, for instance, are summary descriptions of outcomes of extremely complex interactions between molecules in fluids. The molecules themselves depend for their existence on laws of chemistry, and both the laws of chemistry and those governing fluid dynamics are ultimately down to rules of quantum mechanics. However, in practice at least, it is simply not possible to derive the laws of hydraulics directly from quantum mechanics, just as you can't predict the shape a strange attractor will take from knowledge of the components of a chaotic system.

If there are any truly fundamental laws,[12] they might have a different status from attractors—or perhaps they, too, might be regarded as *being* attractors of a sort! But in the messy and only partially knowable world that we inhabit,

---

[11] See, for example, Price and Corry (2007) for an erudite but readable collection of essays reflecting lack of any contemporary consensus about these topics.

[12] Note that even laws as apparently fundamental as energy conservation aren't necessarily truly fundamental. Energy conservation, for example, is, according to Noether's theorem, a consequence of the fact that the laws of physics must always appear the same regardless of the time at which they are invoked. Similar symmetries underlie many of our 'deepest' laws. It's not known why the symmetries exist. This is discussed further in chapter 7.

both attractors and laws clearly have much the same status. From our point of view they are summary descriptions of how complex systems can behave, and from the system's point of view (assuming it has one), they appear to constrain its behaviour. The main difference is that particular natural laws generally apply to a wide variety of systems, whereas particular attractors are generally confined to one or at most a few systems (except in very simple systems, of course, where 'point' attractors are almost universal; however, systems of this sort are usually so simple that there's no need to think of them in attractor terms).

Similarities notwithstanding, there is one circumstance which implies that natural laws can't in fact be viewed as adding meaning to information in a way that could result in 'mentality' of any recognizably human type. Or at least, they can't do so on their own. The problem is that, so far as we know, natural laws don't change, whereas change is basic to minds like ours. A hypothetical, changeless 'mind', deriving its meaning solely from law, would surely be so different from anything we can envisage that it wouldn't make much sense to call it a 'mind'. Memories and attractors, on the other hand, do share in mind's volatility and are thus well suited to be providers of meaning.

So what conclusions can be drawn from all this about the boundaries of mind? We've already seen that the Idealists and the Property Dualists don't have anything very convincing to offer when it comes to suggestions for the universality of mind. Things don't look too good for Panpsychists either, for the physical evidence that might be taken to support their view (i.e. the 'knowledge' demonstrated by photons, and like phenomena) actually appears not to do so. At best, such 'knowledge' could provide only one ingredient of any supposed panpsychism or pan-mentalism, for the 'knowledge' of photons lacks the extras needed for 'mind' and must be regarded as quantum informational only; (i.e. it is dependent on the same principles that are currently attracting so much research directed towards creating quantum computers). To put it another way, photons lack memories or any other intrinsic potentiality for incorporating the meaning that is central to our experience, whether conscious or unconscious. All the meaning present in experimental or other set-ups has been put there by experimenters or whoever; it's not present in the photons themselves.

Thus Panpsychists may have to settle for what might be termed 'pan-computationalism',[13] which many of them would probably be far from happy about. Ironically enough, a much better case can be made for their predecessor's animistic views. Genetic dynamics, with its attractors and its range of built-in memories (DNA structure being only the most fundamental of these) *does* have what it takes to add meaning to information. It certainly contributes to making our minds and thus can be regarded as possessing mind-like qualities in that context. But there seems to be nothing special, as far as genetic dynamics themselves are concerned, about the human context. Perhaps the whole of biological nature should therefore be regarded as having mind-like qualities. It would be a slow and somewhat vegetable mind for the most part, and there's no obvious reason to suppose that it might be conscious in any way. All the same, maybe the boundaries of 'mind' as such are the same as those of the biosphere.

There is a possible opening for a concept of a wholly universal 'mind', however; which is perhaps best described as an interesting (at least I hope you may think it interesting!) speculation. And it doesn't suggest any form of mind that we could easily recognize, for it would either have no consequences whatsoever for us and our worlds, or would manifest only in obscure statistical effects that would be hard to pin down. With these *caveats* in mind, here it is.

Entanglement 'Dynamics'

This is the 'dynamic' listed at the top of the table at the start of chapter 3; the one sidelined for discussion later. It's in

---

[13] Lots of physicists and science popularisers believe that the universe can usefully be viewed as a giant computer; an idea which also crops up in films like *The Matrix*.

quotes because it is inherently atemporal and you can't have a dynamic without any time to be dynamic in. However, basically because of the fact that we experience time as sequential despite the 'block universe' view of it that is implied by relativity theory (we'll be saying some more about the 'block universe' in chapter 7), the so-called 'dynamic' would indeed appear to be actually dynamic from our point of view[14] if we could view it, which in fact we can't. The possibility that this so-called 'dynamic' may exist is raised by the phenomenon of quantum entanglement, which is a hot research topic at present because it offers hopes of safe encryption and (along with quantum information) of one day building quantum computers. When two or more quantum particles interact (in any of quite a wide variety of ways) they become 'entangled' and subsequently have to be treated for some purposes as a *single* entity, however far apart they may appear to have travelled in the meantime. It's yet another counter-intuitive property, suggested by the mathematics of quantum theory, which has experimental and other consequences for the real world.

Such particles remain 'entangled' until 'decoherence' occurs, which is produced by interaction of any one or more of the entangled particles with the environment. Since the 'environment' includes all the heat and other radiation around, along with atoms and molecules and so forth, decoherence usually happens very fast, within times of the order of a millionth of a billionth of a second. However some particles, photons for instance, are more resistant to decoherence (in the case of photons, this is because they don't interact with one another; hence they are unaffected by thermal or other radiation), while the environmental interactions of other types of particle can be minimized in a variety of ways, especially by lowering temperature to as near absolute zero as possible. Which explains why there are hopes that quantum computation may one day be a

---

[14] The arguments for this assertion are given in more detail in my *From Neurons to Notions* (Chapter 15) and I won't repeat them here.

practicable technology. Be that as it may, the big question for us is 'what does decoherence achieve?'

There are two possibilities; one is that decoherence simply represents destruction of the entanglement unity, so the particles involved regain their status as separate entities. One problem with this interpretation is that they shouldn't usually become separate entities according to entanglement theory itself; they should be regarded as forming new entanglement relations with whatever particle(s) caused the apparent decoherence. Hence it seems much preferable to regard decoherence, not as destroying entanglement, but rather as swamping it in a sea of new entanglements so that the pre-decoherence entanglement, while still existing, is no longer separately identifiable. Another problem with the suggestion that decoherence destroys entanglement is that the phenomenon appears to be inherently atemporal — outside the time of relativity theory, in other words. 'Measurement' of one particle in an entanglement relationship appears, from our point of view,[15] instantly to fix the result of any measurement of another. The time of relativity theory doesn't seem to apply, and any notion of 'destruction' of something outside ordinary physical time seems incoherent. However, if decoherence is indeed a 'swamping' phenomenon, as seems most logical to assume, the implication is that the whole of the visible universe has to be viewed as a vast sea or network of entanglement.

Now it is usually stated in the books and articles on this subject that entanglement relations are no good for transmitting 'information', which always has to travel at light speed or less. However, this is simply not true. If you have a pair of spin entangled particles, say one here on earth and the other on Mars, and the one on earth is 'measured', the result of any measurement of the one on Mars is, to the best of our current knowledge, instantly fixed. Thus, if you get the answer 'up' for spin direction on earth (which, before the measurement you originally had a 50% probability of

---

[15] From an atemporal perspective, of course, questions about which measurement came 'first' or which 'caused the other to become fixed' are meaningless.

getting), you are going to get the answer 'down' for the one on Mars with 100% probability. So clearly, from our human perspective, a single bit of what must appear to us to be 'information' has somehow got instantaneously from earth to Mars, since the answer to the 'yes or no' question on Mars (i.e. 'is the spin up or down?') has become fixed. The same applies in the case of Bateson information as the answer 'down' will make a different difference to measurement apparatus on Mars from the answer 'up'. What the books should say is that *meaning* cannot be transferred in this way because, to extract any meaning from the information, the person on Mars would need to know which answer the one on earth had obtained, and a light-speed-or-less message would be needed for this. By the way, this is fully consistent with the earlier discussion of the meaning of 'meaning', since what is needed to convey meaning from earth to Mars is a record, and thus a *memory*, of the outcome of the observation made on earth.

So far it's looking as though entanglement relations might support 'computation' in some form, but couldn't support mentality for much the same reason that photon 'knowledge' can't support mentality — lack of any capacity for meaning. However, the likelihood that they involve Bateson information suggests that they may have what we would picture from our time-bound viewpoint as a dynamic (since differences that make differences are at the basis of *any* dynamic) — hence, provided 'decoherence' doesn't destroy entanglement but instead adds new entanglements to pre-existing ones as discussed above, maybe the 'dynamics' also harbour equivalents of attractors, memories and thus something mentality-like.

It's just about conceivable, therefore, that a concept of a sort of ghostly pan-mentalism, occurring in the quasi-real world of quantum entanglement, is viable. However it would be spectral indeed, even compared to any supposed 'mentality' that might be attributed to the biosphere, for it would be grounded, not in the definite world of atoms and fields, but in the potential world of quantum wave functions. And *any* sort of 'mentality' that lacks consciousness can be thought of as happening 'in the dark'. It's time to move on now, and grasp the nettle! What is it that lights up aspects of our minds and worlds to create our conscious experience? Do we have any hope of getting to grips with consciousness itself? The story that I shall tell will also give essential roles to shapes and structures, some of them additional to the landscapes of mentality in general that we have looked at so far.

Chapter 5

Turning on the Lights

Ask any two experts on the subject what they mean by 'consciousness', and you'll probably get a slightly different answer from each of them. Occasionally you'll get two *very* different answers. When I lived in the West of Scotland, and was trying to get hold of a suitable Gaelic name for a house, different Gaelic speakers offered a variety of spellings or phrases, all supposed to mean much the same thing. Everybody was their own expert on the language, so naturally came up their own version of it.[1] Similarly, most people who've thought about 'consciousness' at all have their own, idiosyncratic 'takes' on it. A recent survey (Vimal, 2009) of the 'consciousness' literature and of specialist websites came up with 40 distinguishable meanings that get attached to the term.

While most of the meanings either overlap or at least are compatible with one another, some don't and aren't. For instance there are people who use the word to refer to awareness in general, regardless of whether it is an awareness that most of us would call 'unconscious' (e.g. unconscious perception, etc.), or one of what we would normally think of as 'conscious' experience. Some believe the word refers to something transcendental, like a soul or a pervasive property of the universe; others regard it as simply a semi-illusory aspect of brain function. Some think it is a 'suitcase word' (i.e. a word like 'artefact', or 'process', or perhaps 'life', that packs a whole lot of very disparate

---

[1] In case anyone is interested, what we eventually came up with was 'Barfad Beag', the literal translation of which is 'by the small stream little'.

phenomena into a single category); others emphasize the essential unity of consciousness. Given this 'tower of Babel' situation, we evidently need to follow a plan in order to have any hope of making sense of the topic.

The strategy I'll adopt in this chapter depends on taking consciousness to be what I suspect most people ordinarily mean when thinking about it or discussing it. The philosopher John Searle took a similar line when he wrote about the definition of consciousness 'in common-sense terms'.[2] It is introspectible experience; we can look into our own minds, if we are conscious, and say to ourselves 'Wow! I'm conscious and at present I'm experiencing this perception (or thought, or emotion, or whatever—most likely a combination of all of these)'. Of course, we don't have to actually *do* any introspection in order to be conscious; if watching an exciting film, for example, we certainly aren't consciously introspecting[3] but we are nevertheless fully conscious. Provided we *are* conscious, we *could* introspect if we wished or if the thought of doing so crossed our minds. On the other hand, if we are unconscious, we can't look into our own minds, or at least we can't experience looking into them. Indeed, there is no experienced 'us' present who could be

---

[2] Here's what Searle wrote: 'One often hears it said that "consciousness" is frightfully hard to define. But if we are talking about a definition in common sense terms, sufficient to identify the target of the investigation, as opposed to a precise scientific definition of the sort that typically comes at the end of a scientific investigation, then the word does not seem to me hard to define. Here is the definition: Consciousness consists of inner, qualitative, subjective states and processes of sentience or awareness. Consciousness, so defined, begins when we wake in the morning from a dreamless sleep—and continues until we fall asleep again, die, go into a coma or otherwise become "unconscious." It includes all of the enormous variety of the awareness that we think of as characteristic of our waking life. It includes everything from feeling a pain, to perceiving objects visually, to states of anxiety and depression, to working out cross word puzzles, playing chess, trying to remember your aunt's phone number, arguing about politics, or to just wishing you were somewhere else' (Searle, 2000).

[3] Some philosophers, particularly Higher Order Thought (HOT) theorists, might claim that we always have to be doing what might be regarded as unconscious 'introspection' if we are to be *conscious* of anything.

capable of experiencing anything. The lights are out, even though there is usually quite a lot of 'mental' activity of one sort or another still going on in our brains.

Computers, which can 'report' on their internal processes, presumably cannot *experience* their content. And of course there are a whole lot of entirely unconscious routines in our own brains that 'report' to one another about their doings. So I'm not suggesting that the actual or potential introspectibility of conscious experience causes, or can be identified with, consciousness (as we shall see in chapter 7, I'll be suggesting an entirely different origin for it), merely that it is a necessary marker for the presence of consciousness.

A problem with this strategy is that it appears to tie the presence of consciousness of anything to an ability to *remember* the experience, for a brief period at least. Moreover, we have to remember it for long enough to tell others about it if we are to convince them that we had the experience. If we can't remember an experience, maybe we have to say that it must have been unconscious. At the very least, perhaps we should follow Wittgenstein's dictum, *whereof one cannot speak, thereof one must be silent*, and refrain altogether from discussing any supposed but unrecalled 'consciousness'. But that doesn't seem right. What, for instance, is the status of putative conscious experience that we can't recall, such as dreams that showed up on recordings in a sleep laboratory, but which we can't remember on awakening? And what about our pet animals and so forth, who certainly appear to be conscious at times, but can't tell us about it except in indirect ways?

Probably the best way to deal with questions like these is to take a hint from the fact that we don't actually have to do (conscious) introspection in order to be conscious. It therefore seems reasonable to say that consciousness is either experience that is being introspected or experience that could reasonably be assumed to have been introspectible if the conditions had been right. If someone in the sleep laboratory had woken us in up in the middle of the dream, for instance, we probably could have consciously recalled it. If we could talk to the animals, they probably would tell us about their conscious experience.[4]

It's a strategy, therefore, that introduces a certain amount of vagueness into the concept of consciousness, because it makes what is meant by 'consciousness' dependent both on the vagaries of actual introspection and introduces an ill-defined concept of 'in principle introspectibility'. But, given that we don't know for sure what consciousness is, vagueness at this stage in our understanding is certainly inevitable and possibly no bad thing either, as it allows some flexibility of manoeuvre. And the move does have two big pluses, which may more than outweigh any downsides. First, it implies that human consciousness is something that is always reportable, at least in principle. You can only meaningfully think about a thing, or indeed know anything whatsoever about it, if you can either recall it yourself or hear of it from other people (i.e. it has to be self-reportable from your own experience, or reportable to you by others).

If consciousness *wasn't* inherently introspectible, we would not be discussing or writing about it. Indeed, although this comes across as something of a paradox, it's difficult to see how we could be aware of it. We surely have to be aware of awareness in order to know that we have it! Any science of consciousness, too, depends wholly on reports of one sort or another, from people or sometimes from animals, about their conscious experiences. Recognizing that rational discussion of consciousness depends entirely on its (at least in principle) introspectibility helps to provide a sort of anchor for thoughts about it; one which may help us to avoid some of the conceptual tangles that philosophers occasionally get into when they try to deal with it entirely in the abstract.

---

[4] Actually some animals with vocabularies (e.g. bonobos and African grey parrots) can and have discussed their experience, wishes and so forth, according to well-authenticated accounts. Experts disagree about the significance of their accomplishment, while most animals are dependent on more indirect, behavioural 'reports'. Nevertheless experts on the whole seem to be coming round to the view that animals do have forms of consciousness that may often be similar to ours.

The second big advantage of the strategy is actually a product of the same implication that gave us a problem over how to regard the status of unremembered dreams. 'Consciousness' has to be regarded as being tied to the memory process, because you cannot introspect anything if it's not held in some sort of memory[5] for a brief period at least. This implication has all sorts of ramifications that will crop up at intervals throughout the rest of my account.

A consequence of following this plan is that, to start off with at least, we need to think of consciousness as something that brains do, produce, cause, generate, focus, transmit — many verbs *might* apply and you are welcome to take your pick; for it is the neural equipment in brains that introspects and that holds recallable memories. Does this mean that we can forget about all the 'transcendental' meanings that have been attributed to consciousness? In fact it doesn't mean anything of the sort because what becomes introspectible in consciousness has to be a portion of, or selection from, the contents of 'mind'. And we've already seen that mind is surely not limited to the brain alone, even though we were uncertain as to exactly how far it may spread its wings. Mind can't avoid lending some of its wider involvements to consciousness in the course of introspection, so consciousness is bound to gain what can be regarded as a sort of borrowed transcendence of the brain from this circumstance alone. As we shall see later on, other forms of transcendentality may also be associated with consciousness.

However, we do need to start off by a taking a look at biological and neuroscientific proposals about the origins of consciousness. There are a lot of these, and I'm only going to very briefly describe those that seem to me the most interesting, and representative of current or recent thinking. Maybe another writer would pick a different selection, but I hope it wouldn't be very different. It will soon become

---

[5] Robbins (2004) has referred to this sort of memory as 'primary memory'. His paper emphasizes that this is more than the simple 'integration over time' that individual neurons, for example, are capable of.

obvious that most of these proposals are mainly to do with the *content* of consciousness; how the content gets there and why it takes the forms that it does. They begin to struggle, and are a lot vaguer, if they try to account for the *existence* of consciousness. David Chalmers' dictum (see chapter 4) that this can't be explained by present-day science won't be overthrown, but maybe we shall be able to glean hints about what sort(s) of scientific advance may one day lead to an understanding of the fact of its existence.

Let's begin with what is probably the most 'biological' proposal of all, due to psychologist Nicholas Humphrey and beautifully described in his book *Seeing Red*, which is based on a series of lectures that he gave at Harvard.

Seeing Red

Humphrey takes the experience of seeing red — as in experiencing the colour, not as in losing one's temper! — as a paradigmatic example of all perceptual consciousness. After discussing the evidence, and pointing out that experience of this sort always includes emotional components as well as 'pure' perception, he concludes that perception of colour is one thing while (conscious) experience of that perception is quite another; one that involves an active process of 'redding'. But why should there be such an elaborate, seemingly Byzantine, faculty? He proposes that conscious experience is based on systems that evolved to monitor an organism's responses to its environment. These produced precursors of our 'feeling sensations' which, crucially, were about active responses to particular environmental circumstances.

Once formed, there were evolutionary advantages to increasing the separation of these systems from direct stimulus/response ones, in order to allow rehearsal of potential responses and the like. The 'sensation' system, in other words, became increasingly *privatised*, in the sense of internalised and divorced from its immediate environment. Then a whole new selective advantage kicked in, Humphrey goes on to suggest. The internal, private systems developed self-important selves and organisms could treat themselves as special, requiring cosseting, forethought in the interests of their own welfare, and so forth. They needed awareness, especially of themselves, to seem mysterious and ineffable, for it thus motivated them to put extra effort into the survival business.

When it comes to looking at why all this could or should eventually have come to take the form that it does for us, i.e. as the consciousness of our everyday experience, Humphrey hedges his bets. Why, his readers might ask, shouldn't these evolutionarily useful functions all take the form of *unconscious* cognitive assessments or emotional urges, for example? Both are known to occur in us and to influence our behaviour, apparently quite independently of our consciousness. Surely any feelings of 'mysteriousness' or 'ineffability' that might promote self-care could have had equally effective unconscious expression?

On the one hand, Humphrey says that he thinks consciousness is probably nothing more than a lovely, if useful, illusion. He seems to be implying here (though he doesn't say so outright) that it isn't 'real', hence needs no further explanation. However, it is worth noting that, since he has already argued that it does have effects (in aiding forward planning and generally promoting survival), it surely *is* real at least according to the definition of 'real' that we are using (see the end of chapter 1), so perhaps claiming that it's probably an 'illusion' isn't very helpful. On the other hand, he suggests (without going into any detail) that consciousness may have something to do with what he terms the 'temporal thickness' of experience. This refers to the fact that what we mean by 'the present moment', when we are referring to our own experience of the present, is not an instant of clock time but rather what William James called 'the specious present'. This can occupy anything from a minimum about one tenth of a second, if you are very highly aroused, to maybe as much as ten seconds if you are relaxed in a chair listening to soothing music, say. I'll be arguing later on (in chapter 7) that Humphrey's intuition about this may be right and that consciousness may turn out to depend on jugglery with time.

Seeing Red uses themes that commonly surface in the 'consciousness' literature. The most original ideas in it are to do with the detail of the proposals about formation and 'privatisation' of 'feeling sensations' and the evolutionary advantages that may accrue. These certainly come across to me as intriguing and attractive even though, as Humphrey acknowledges, they have to be regarded as 'Just So' stories, given the present state of the art. It's worth identifying the more widely shared ideas, too. Here they are:

- Consciousness is a construct in the sense of being a product of biology/neurology.
- It probably carries evolutionary advantages.
- It has something to do with rehearsing scenarios and/or predicting likely outcomes.
- Self-consciousness is also a brain construct.

That consciousness is somehow produced by brains is almost an article of faith for most contemporary neuroscientists, psychologists and probably the majority of philosophers. Many take the view that therefore it must have evolutionary advantages of some sort, or it would not have evolved (there are a whole range of stories, in addition to the ones offered by Humphrey, about *what sort* of advantages). A few people still claim, in contrast, that it may be 'epiphenomenal', though that's a view that seems to be less popular now than was the case ten or twenty years ago. By the way, 'epiphenomenal' applied to consciousness means that it may have no inherent function or usefulness; it could, for example, be present only because it is what Stephen Jay Gould called a 'spandrel' — a feature which is itself useless but is an inevitable concomitant of something else that *does* have a valuable function.

There's fairly general agreement that one of the most important functions of the brain is to predict likely outcomes from incoming information about body and environment, and then to act in a way predicted to optimize said outcomes; to try to ensure that one eats instead of being eaten, for example. And it seems little more than obvious to conclude that consciousness probably plays a part in the more sophisticated levels of such prediction, perhaps especially those that involve rehearsal of potential responses to environmental inputs as Humphrey and others[6] have suggested. However, as it turns out, any such conclusion has to be hedged around with all sorts of *caveats*, some of which we'll be looking at later on.

When it comes to self-consciousness and ideas about what the 'self' is, there is a huge and confusing philosophical literature (perhaps it would be a little *too* unkind to refer to this literature as 'confused'!), and a rather smaller, often more tentative, neuroscientific one. Many people, however, appear to go along with the outlines at least of neurologist Antonio Damasio's proposals. He says that the 'self' we consciously experience is based on a whole lot of 'vegetative' and other functions which are normally held in the fringes of consciousness, or form a kind of background hum to whatever is at the forefront of awareness; these are things like feelings of fullness or otherwise in one's abdomen, awareness of one's orientation and position in space, and so on. Psychologist Arnold Trehub has a particularly elaborate model in which the *positional* coordinates of a brain representation of the 'self' play the central role. Others like to include more than just basic 'gut feelings' and spatial self-models, and add in extras such as semi-aware memories of one's history and social status. However the 'self' is firmly grounded in goings-on in the brain according to all ideas of this sort.

It's worth pointing out at this stage that the dynamic picture developed in previous chapters puts a slightly different emphasis from Damasio's on the background to any experience of 'self'. Such experience can be regarded as grounded in the set of those state space dimensions that are liable to be relevant to one's 'mentality' at *any* time. They form a permanent, or at least semi-permanent, sub-set of dimensions able to contribute to whatever the total state

---

[6] See, for example, Ellis (1995) for a particularly clear, imaginative exploration of this point of view and its ramifications.

space may be that underlies any *particular* mental happening. Many such dimensions will derive from basic biology and neurology, of course, others from personal history, education and so forth. But there will also be some flexibility about which members of the set come into play in any particular circumstance, thus allowing for the fact that our 'self' at work can be somewhat different from the one we possess at home, for instance. The basis of 'self', according to this view, is a little more abstract, flexible and less brain-bound than Damasio's formulation appears to imply, and is a lot more broadly based than in Trehub's model.

Next up, we need to take a look at what is currently often regarded as the Great Panjandrum among the more neuroscientific theories of 'consciousness'. Strangely enough however, as we shall see, it's not really about consciousness as such, but only about the content of consciousness.

Global Workspace Theory

This theory has been (and still is being) very actively promoted by Californian psychologist Bernard Baars. Other people have proposed variants but, at least in outline, they all say much the same thing. There are lots of 'modules' in the brain, all working away in their own little corners at analysing whatever data they have access to—recognizing faces, parsing grammar, making emotional assessments, and so on almost *ad infinitum*. In addition they all 'compete' for access to a 'global workspace'. Any module that does gain access to the workspace can distribute the results of its own activities throughout the brain, and thus to all the other modules. The stream of consciousness simply *is* the ever changing content of the workspace. It's an attractive theory for all sorts of reasons, the main one being that there's overwhelming neuropsychological evidence that the brain does often[7] appear to work like this. Other reasons include its

---

[7] But not always. Even that early champion of brain modularity, philosopher Jerry Fodor, has changed his mind about modularity being the whole story—see his book *The Mind Dosn't Work That Way*

ability to account neatly for the conscious/unconscious distinction (nothing is conscious *unless* it gets into the global workspace) and for providing an intuitive picture of how attention might work (i.e. through facilitating entry of selected material into the workspace).

Philosopher Daniel Dennett has claimed that there is an 'emerging consensus' in neuropsychological circles that consciousness *is* the flow of what he has called 'fame in the brain'; a fame referring to neural information that both comes to be widely distributed and is effective by virtue of 'reverberating' for a time. Of course the wide distribution part of the package, at least, entails global workspace-like notions.

The theory does have its awkward aspects nonetheless. One is the difficulty of envisaging how the workspace could actually work in neural terms. How does information get disseminated? How are particular modules selected for 'fame' or whatever? After all, it looks as though the information in the lucky modules must *already* be widely known if they are to be 'selected' by attention in any useful way; does this imply that there's a hierarchy of 'workspaces'? Could some unpleasant infinite regress be hiding within the theory? A variety of schemes have been proposed to deal with these difficulties. So far as I know, all of them take the form of those rather clunky flow charts beloved of information theorists and some psychologists; charts with lots of boxes labelled for example 'Visual Features', 'Executive Attention', 'Working Memory' and the like—along, of course, with one labelled 'Global Workspace'.

However, the 'attractor dynamics' picture suggests that there is no 'global workspace' if it is pictured in box-like terms. Instead there is at any particular time, one, or at most a very few, ruling attractor(s) that dominate brain activity. And any particular ruling attractor will have developed

---

(2000). Lots of neuroscientists have described the evidence for widespread modularity. Steven Pinker is perhaps its best known and most active champion. The evidence that he has cited in a series of popular accounts published in the last ten years is undeniable, though he is sometimes accused of over-interpreting it.

from the activities of a group of local attractors at the neural net level ('what we called 'level 1'), often activated as a consequence of addition to the relevant state space of dimensions contributed by environmental dynamics. Sometimes, no doubt, there may be an intermediate stage in which 'level 2' attractors (themselves both created by, and modifying the activities of, level 1) need to combine to create a ruling attractor. Any lesser attractors contributing to the ruler of the moment will *automatically* have some of the information that they contain distributed throughout the brain. Moreover the ruler of the moment can be envisaged as *being* whatever is the overall attentive state of the moment. In other words attractor dynamics suggests that attention and the object of attention form a seamless whole; no need to put them in separate boxes!

One way of looking at the relationship between the attractor dynamics picture and global workspace theory is to view it as analogous to that between general relativity and Newtonian gravitational theory. General relativity includes Newtonian theory as an approximation; one that works well enough in most circumstances, provided one doesn't expect it to explain the mechanisms involved.

Another awkward aspect of Global Workspace Theory, this time one that attractor dynamics can't soothe away, is its simple assertion that what one is conscious of *is* the content of the workspace. Why should the content be conscious as such, rather than unconscious? What is there about widespread distribution in the brain that switches on the lights? So far as I know, the only half-way plausible answer to these questions draws on views like those described in Daniel Dennett's best known work *Consciousness Explained*.[8] His 'explanation' was that it doesn't 'really' exist, so there's nothing to explain. It can be pictured as a sort of illusion, so there's nothing wrong with asserting that the global

---

[8] This book, published in 1991, had a lot of influence. It was very much in line with the thinking of 'eliminative' and other materialists, who tended to dominate academic thought about consciousness at the time. Dennett has modified his views a bit since. He still thinks consciousness is a sort of illusion, but now seems to be saying that it's a real illusion, whatever that means.

workspace just happens to be capable of creating said illusion—there isn't actually anything more needing explanation. And any apparent effects of consciousness, ones that might suggest that it is more than an illusion, are in fact down to the global workspace, not to its illusory consciousness.

Although plausible to an extent, this answer appears far from satisfactory—to me at least. And my impression, judging from the average content of papers submitted to the *Journal of Consciousness Studies*, is that academic opinion generally (including that of Dennett himself!) has shifted away from supposing that this sort of 'eliminativism' might suffice. But claiming that the global workspace is nothing more than a name for a succession of ruling attractors does not in any way help towards resolving this unsatisfactory state of affairs; it merely shifts the problem to the ruling attractors. What could make *them* conscious, while activities described by lesser attractors are mostly carried out 'in the dark'? I'll postpone trying to answer this question till later.

Loops and Re-entrance

Theories in this category can be thought of as focussing on neural mechanisms that might manifest in a global workspace equivalent. Mind and consciousness is considered to emerge, somehow, from these neural goings-on. Earlier on, the so-called 'cortico-thalamic loops' (feedback circuits between brain cortex and nuclei in the brain stem) tended to occupy centre stage. Erich Harth, a physicist based in New York, wrote a particularly clear account of this type of approach, titled *The Creative Loop* and first published in 1993. It described views fairly prevalent among psychologists at the time. Conscious mind is based on ever-changing neural activity fed into circuits looping between cortex and thalamus, Harth wrote. Opinion has shifted to some extent since, and these circuits are now more usually regarded as having something to do with attention and related functions, which may be either conscious or unconscious; the circuits don't seem to have any special or exclusive relationship with consciousness itself.

When it came to the 'why' of consciousness, Harth confessed himself stumped and speculated that 'new physics' of some sort might be needed to account for it. However, he also made an interesting and beautifully phrased point, similar in spirit to the one about 'temporal thickness' made by Nicholas Humphrey. Here it is:

> Consciousness has the capacity to break the causal chains, the infinitesimal moment that is the present, the sliding point in time that separates past from future [it] is like a wedge driven between the whence and the hence, a timeless region where intentionality, volition and creativity are spawned (Harth, 1995, pp. 144–45).

Nowadays, there is more interest in other feedback loops too, including ones within the cerebral cortex. The 're-entrant' variety espoused by Gerald Edelman and his colleague Giulio Tononi looks particularly interesting. 'Re-entrance' can be regarded as feedback on steroids. In the words of these authors, it is 'the ongoing, recursive interchange of parallel signals between reciprocally connected areas of the brain, an interchange that continually co-ordinates these areas' maps to each other in space and time' (Edelman and Tononi, 2000, p. 48). Activity of this sort provides the substrate for consciousness, they say.

When it comes to accounting for 'qualia' (the qualities we experience when we are conscious, such as the experience of seeing red, feeling pain, having an emotion, etc.), they envisage a 'dynamic core', of extensive re-entrant activity between groups of neurons, that is describable in terms of a multidimensional space. This space is a bit different from the dynamic state and attractor spaces that we have been discussing hitherto. It's a neural activity configuration space; each dimension represents one of the 'neuronal groups' that are contributing to the dynamic core at any given time, while points within the space represent particular patterns of interaction between groups. The space is thus analogous to the RNA one mentioned in chapter 3, where the dimensions were contributed by the number of nucleotides being considered, while points within it represented different nucleotide sequences (which were associated with different RNA configurations). It's not a space that could harbour attractors as such, though their consequences might show up in it as clusters of frequently seen patterns of neural activity, for instance.

Anyhow, Edelman and Tononi propose that each 'discriminable' point within their space represents a different quale (the singular of 'qualia'). They also suggest that what distinguishes unconscious from conscious neural activity is isolation from any extensive dynamic core. The concept here is perhaps a little different from a 'global workspace' since, although the 'dynamic core' has a changeable membership of neuronal groups, the picture seems to be that it functions as an integrated unit at all times, while 'modules' contributing to a global workspace are more like individuals being invited into a club that already exists. However, similar questions arise in both cases. Why should extensiveness of neural activity (in the case of the dynamic core)[9] or broadcasting information to all (in the case of the global workspace) bring about consciousness? And the dynamic core formulation seems to raise an additional question: what criterion or other factor makes a 'discriminable' pattern of activity within the core to *be* discriminable? After all, although the number of distinguishable qualia is very, very large, it seems inherently unlikely to be as large as the number of points within the pattern configuration space, even assuming that this latter number isn't infinite,[10] which it probably is.

Balduzzi and Tononi (2009) have subsequently described a formal, mathematical picture of how incoming information might integrate with internal dynamical processes (which would necessarily involve memories) to produce a

---

[9] Tononi has argued that conscious activities are characterized by greater quantitative amounts of information processing, but it's not at all clear why quantity as such should evoke consciousness.

[10] The number of different patterns of neural activity, and thus the number of points in the configuration space, would be finite if the relevant patterns relate to action potentials only, which are in a sense 'digital'. However, if the patterns relate to analogue variables such as electrical field strengths instead of, or in addition to, digital variables, the number of points would be infinite.

'qualia space' in which every quale has its own separate dimension. This concept both avoids the potential infinities of a pattern configuration space and provides a useful visualisation of how the *meaning* associated with qualia might arise from incoming information. Indeed, the authors suggest that the actual experience of 'red', for example, derives from what amounts to its meaning, which in turn derives from the associations and memories evoked by any particular instance of seeing red light.

There are other potential answers to the 'discrimination' problem too, in terms of holography and/or knot theory for instance, which I'll defer discussing till the next chapter. However, so far as I can see, neither Balduzzi and Tononi's suggestion, nor the other answers, can explain why red *is* red and is experienced consciously, rather than unconsciously.

'Quantum Consciousness'

Ideas that tried to tie consciousness in with quantum theory proliferated a few years ago, especially in the early 1990s.[11] They appear to have been motivated from the physics side partly by arguments[12] that 'collapse of the wave function' might ultimately be down to *conscious* 'observation', hence physics needed to explain the nature of this observation. On the neuroscience side, reasons included hopes that quantum theory could solve the 'binding problem' (i.e. the problem of how it is, for example, that the outline, motion and

---

[11] Anyone wanting more detail than is offered here can find an excellent account in the online Stanford Encyclopaedia of Philosophy entry titled 'Quantum Approaches to Consciousness' http://plato.stanford.edu/entries/qt-consciousness

[12] Many of the arguments were based on 'Schrödinger's cat', the tale of which poor beast was recounted in innumerable books and articles of the period. It can be seen as ironic that Schrödinger originally described the predicament of his cat in order to highlight the probable incompleteness of quantum theory. So people seized on an argument intended to show that the theory wasn't entirely right to support using it to explain consciousness! Of course enthusiasts viewed the situation differently at the time; some suggested that a proper account of consciousness might be the key to completing quantum theory.

colour of some object that one is looking at — features which are known to be analysed in separate brain areas — all get combined into a *single* conscious percept), and vaguer hopes that the theory might throw light on other mysterious properties of mind.

The theories fell into two broad categories; first those that postulated the presence of large scale quantum coherence between particles of various suggested types in the brain, based on quite a wide variety of suggested mechanisms; secondly, looser 'field' theories of one sort or another. Probably the most widely discussed, and best developed, theory in the first category was dubbed 'Orchestrated Objective Reduction (OrchOR)' and was due to Stuart Hameroff, an American anaesthetist, and Roger Penrose the Oxford mathematician who had also collaborated with Stephen Hawking. It incorporated Penrose's ideas about a gravitational criterion for wave function collapse, along with detailed proposals about a role for the microtubules in neurons in hosting quantum computation. Although a certain amount of evidence had accumulated, mainly in the 1980s, that quantum effects may occur in biological systems,[13] I think it's fair to say that no convincing and replicated empirical finding has ever surfaced that could be taken to favour any of the 'quantum consciousness' theories.

What seems to have been chiefly responsible for killing wide interest in these theories was not lack of empirical support for them, so much as the advent of 'decoherence' theory plus the effort put into trying to develop quantum computers. Decoherence theory made it possible to calculate, for the first time, how long a coherent state can survive in an environment like that in the brain. The answer was that a few types of state might endure for around a thousandth of a billionth of a second, though most types would be gone more than a hundred times quicker than that. As

---

[13] There's also current excitement over the recent discovery that photosynthesis depends on quantum coherence. It should be noted, however, that the relevant 'coherence' exists on a molecular scale only and lasts for ~400 femtoseconds. (i.e. around one thousandth of a billionth of a second).

consciousness appears to work on time scales of the order of a tenth of a second, it seemed extremely unlikely to most people that coherent states could possibly have anything much to do with it. OrchOR theorists made valiant efforts to overcome the problem by claiming that their coherent states were shielded from the brain environment by 'sol-gel' transitions. But they were unable to overcome the objection that these couldn't shield any coherent state from thermal radiation, which would on its own induce very rapid decoherence. At the same time the 'field' theories that had been proposed, which never achieved as much popularity as the more straightforward 'coherence' ones, were under attack for their realism and consistency[14] and do not (so far) appear to have found effective defenders.

To ram the lesson home, attempts to build simple quantum computers showed only too clearly how extremely difficult it is to maintain quantum coherence involving only a few particles for more than a few microseconds — and the hypothetical brain coherences would have had to involve minima of thousands of particles. Moreover, physically more plausible ways of accounting for the 'binding problem' had surfaced and were gaining empirical support. So the most rational 'neuroscience' motivation for looking to quantum theory had evaporated.

Can this be taken to imply that quantum theory can be forgotten when it comes to thinking about consciousness? My own feeling is that it probably will resurface eventually as it remains our 'deepest' validated[15] theory of matter — and clearly consciousness and matter do relate to one another somehow. There is still some interest in approaches of this sort, though many of the ideas on offer are much the

[14] For instance Chris Clarke has criticized the most prominent type of field theory (promoted by the school of the Japanese physicist Hiroomi Umezawa), which makes essential use of massless, 'Nambu-Goldstone' quasi-particles, on the grounds that Umezawa appeared to use a different definition of the 'equivalence' of vacuum states from that used by Nambu and Goldstone themselves. (personal communication, 2006).

[15] String theory, loop quantum gravity theory, etc., are certainly 'deeper', but are still very much 'work in progress', with no empirical validation whatsoever at the time of writing.

same as those going the rounds in the 1990s (see e.g. Tuszynski, 2006). However, links between quantum theory and biology are in the early stages of being rethought and re-examined experimentally (see, for example, Arndt et al., 2009, for an excellent review of these issues). If and when connections between quantum theory and brain function are established, they will probably take a very different form from current versions, and may turn out to be about relations between the quantum and mind, not about consciousness *per se*.

Neural Correlates of Consciousness: The Evidence

Before going into detail, we need to note something that often passes almost unnoticed. All the most direct evidence hitherto, relating consciousness to neural activity, comes from EEG (or occasionally from MEG[16]) studies. But most research on the brain for the last 15 years or more has focussed on fMRI and (as far as animal research is concerned) on recordings from single neurons. Of course fMRI and single neuron work have both produced a series of dazzling discoveries, many of which have indirect implications for consciousness; but that old faithful the EEG, basically a pre-World War 2 technology, still trumps them when it comes to direct evidence. Why is this?

It's down to what the different technologies can 'see'. The spatial resolution of EEG is very poor; indeed it has been known for over 50 years that it's impossible in principle to pinpoint the source of an electromagnetic field from recordings made on the surface of a volume conductor like the brain. However, its temporal resolution (roughly 1–200 Hertz) appears to be just what the doctor ordered when it comes to consciousness relevance. fMRI, which has excellent spatial resolution, has a temporal resolution of about 1/60 Hertz at best (the machines can create images faster than this, but the blood flow changes they measure take

---

[16] MEG (magneto-encephalography) measures brain magnetic fields. It's thus chiefly a representation of average current flows along axon bundles, whereas EEG (electro-encephalography) mainly reflects electrical fields originating from dendritic plexi.

about a minute to show up, so there's no point in working faster). This is simply too slow to catch anything but quite indirect correlates of consciousness.

Incidentally, the brain oxygen level signals (themselves dependent on local blood flow) that most fMRI studies are tuned to detect are probably an indirect measure of what EEGs show directly and in far greater temporal detail. For a long time there was puzzlement over precisely which aspect of brain activity was showing up in fMRI; many people thought the answer was probably an average of local action potential frequencies, or something like that. As it turns out, however, the fMRI signal appears to correlate best with local electro-magnetic field changes (see Logothetis, 2007), which is what EEGs show directly (with the addition of another, smaller contribution from current flows along axon bundles), albeit from much less well-defined areas.

Single neuron recordings, of course, have excellent temporal resolution, but it appears that consciousness is a relatively large scale phenomenon[17] (or at least its closest neural correlates are large scale), so single records have a 'can't see the wood for the trees' problem. And the bottom line is that, although the favourite modern techniques are good at answering questions about *where* consciousness-associated neural activity is happening, they're of no direct use when it comes to *what* or *why* questions. The main contribution of fMRI to consciousness studies as such has been its role in confirming and refining ideas about the modularity of mind. When it comes to other questions, we are still almost entirely dependent on EEG evidence and there are three principal lines of enquiry that we need briefly to look at.

---

[17] It has been shown that stimulation of a single neuron, or a very small number of contiguous ones, is occasionally sufficient to produce a conscious experience. Indeed the arrival of a single photon at the retina of the eye can, under the right conditions, be perceived consciously. However there's fairly general agreement (with a few dissenting voices) that such very small scale happenings only achieve consciousness via amplification in much larger scale contexts.

Attractors and Rabbits

First of all, there's the work of Walter J. Freeman and his collaborators, which has been on-going for fifty years or more. His most significant studies, from our point of view, were to do with smelling (olfaction) by rabbits. They have large olfactory bulbs, and he and colleagues were able to record EEGs from the surface of these, typically using arrays of 64 electrodes. He then studied the patterns of electrical activity that resulted when the rabbits were given odorants to sniff. A lot of the activity appeared chaotic, but some of it showed a degree of order that appeared to relate to both a rabbit's previous experience of particular smells and whatever smell it was currently experiencing. To cut a long story short, Freeman eventually concluded that the patterns of activity that he saw were best pictured in terms of attractors in a landscape:

> This attractor landscape contains all the learned states ... Each attractor has its own basin of attraction, which was shaped by the class of stimuli the animals received during training. No matter where in each basin a stimulus puts the bulb [i.e. the dynamic state of the activity in the olfactory bulb], the bulb [then] goes to the attractor of that basin, accomplishing generalisation to the class. A new odorant is learned by adding a new attractor with its basin, but ... an attractor landscape is flexible [and changes its conformation to accommodate the new attractor] (Freeman, 1999, p. 83).

As rabbits are presumably conscious of what they smell, this seems like pretty good evidence that attractor landscapes in the brain can and do have a part to play in the 'consciousness' process. The identification of particular attractors with particular memories, and the 'self-organising' properties of the whole system, are features essential to the 'brain dynamics' model outlined in chapter 3.

In an ideal world, I could report that similar findings apply to, say, the visual systems of macaque monkeys. But rabbit olfaction is a particularly simple sensory system and the problems involved in trying to extend Freeman's work to more complex situations are way beyond the capacity of current technology to cope. However, near future technology may be able to do so. As we'll be seeing in the next chapter, there are reasons for thinking that patterns of changing calcium concentration could be even more closely 'consciousness related' than the electromagnetic fields that Freeman looked at, and it may soon be possible to visualise these in unanaesthetized animals (this can already be done with 'in vitro' preparations). There's a good chance that a technique of this sort could provide the temporal *and* spatial resolution necessary for getting to grips with attractor landscapes as complex as those in our own brains.

Synchrony

In the meantime, there has been a lot of interest in 'EEG coherence', meaning synchronisation of phase between EEG activity of particular frequencies in separate areas of the brain. The initial excitement came from finding that 40 Hz, gamma activity in separate parts of the visual system appeared to become phase locked when the system was dealing with some particular percept. Moreover the parts in question matched those that were known or thought to be responsible for dealing with the percept. This finding seemed to many like a perfect answer to the 'binding problem' of how it is that separate analyses of separate aspects of a percept get combined into a single experience. There were even hopes that it would explain the basis of consciousness. 'Neurons that fire together are together', was one catchphrase; the idea being that a synchronously active group of neurons could be regarded as a 'unit' even if the individual neurons were spatially far apart. Of course, since the EEG is only a rather indirect measure of neuron 'firing' (as mentioned earlier, it's mostly a measure of electrical field changes in dendritic plexi), this was a bit too simplistic.[18]

Nevertheless, the finding has stood up quite well. There have been occasional failures to observe a predicted

---

[18] To be fair, single neuron studies have shown that their firing correlates with EEG activity. However, neuron firing is inherently stochastic, so the correlations between separate neurons influenced by a coherent EEG wave are always going to be less than perfect. One suspects that the wave itself has a better claim to be regarded as a 'unit'.

synchronisation (see for example Larock, 2006), but a large majority of studies have confirmed and/or extended the initial result. It's difficult to know what to make of the negative ones; maybe poor experimental technique can be blamed in some cases, but it is far from clear that it can be blamed in *all* cases. Anyhow, it soon became clear that 40 Hz, was not uniquely important and that a range of gamma (30–70 Hz) frequencies can show phase locking in the right circumstances. In one recent study for instance (Colgin *et al.*, 2009), faster gamma appeared to be dealing with information about an animal's location, and slower gamma with information storage. It's been suggested, too, that EEG frequencies below the gamma range also play a part (see, for example Palva and Palva, 2007). And the findings extend way beyond simple object recognition; different patterns of coherence correlate with the alternative perceptions of ambiguous drawings, for instance (see Klemm *et al.*, 2000, who used four different ambiguous drawings including the relatively familiar young lady/old lady and the rabbit/duck) and coherence can extend across sensory modalities (Yuvall-Greenberg and Deouell, 2007); perhaps most remarkable of all, gamma coherence across multiple brain areas is reduced in schizophrenia, an illness characterized by impaired integration of the mind (Spencer *at al.*, 2003).

However, gamma coherence as such does *not* differentiate conscious from unconscious perception. It occurs in relation to both, although there is evidence that the consciousness-associated variety tends to involve more extensive and/or higher amplitude coherence. The initial hopes of some people, that a straightforward relationship between coherence and consciousness might exist, have been dashed. In terms of the view put forward in this book, coherences can be seen as neural manifestations of the attractor dynamics at the basis of mind in general, so we would not expect to see any exclusive association with consciousness. Incidentally, there's no obvious reason to suppose that the attractor dynamics must *always* manifest in EEG coherence, so maybe the occasional negative results mentioned above are exceptions for that reason and their occurrence should be no surprise.

Why should attractor dynamics manifest in gamma coherence, if not always at least more often than not, so it appears? A general answer is that attractors with extensive basins of attraction are going to 'organize' brain activity over large areas. And, in any dynamical process, some of the ordering is bound to manifest in temporal form, which, in the case of EEG, has to show up as coherences of one sort or another — and it just happens that gamma coherence is the form the ordering *does* often take.

A model proposed by Herrmann and colleagues (2004) suggests a more specific possible answer. They use computational rather than attractor language, but note that gamma activity is known to be enhanced by attention and therefore relates also to memory, which in fact has been shown independently to affect gamma activity and its coherence. They conclude that gamma activity, along with its coherence, may initially reflect a matching process between incoming information and that stored in memory, while later coherence is associated with making use of outcomes of matching. In their own words:

> Oscillatory neural activity in the gamma frequency range (>30 Hz) has been shown to accompany a wide variety of cognitive processes. So far, there has been limited success in assigning a unitary basic function to these oscillations ... We propose a new framework that relates gamma oscillations [along with coherent oscillations] observed in human, as well as in animal, experiments to two underlying processes: the comparison of memory contents with stimulus-related information and the utilization of signals derived from this comparison.

They thus give a central role to computational processes involving memory in the genesis of often coherent gamma. But memories *are* attractors and computation *is* a dynamical process, and the two are involved with one another. So their argument implies that attractor dynamics is (sometimes) going to generate gamma coherence. And their suggestion, because it involves memory, provides a neat lead into our third and final category of EEG evidence.

The Timing of Experience

Benjamin Libet (1916-2007) is the name to conjure with in this connection. His work[19] on the timing of conscious experiences in relation to that of neural events extended over at least thirty years, and all his most important results have since been replicated by others. Aspects of his work had been foreshadowed by predecessors (notably Wilder Penfield and William Grey Walter), but his careful, long-sustained enquiries gave us most of what we know about this topic. His methods involved various EEG techniques and sometimes direct stimulation of the brain (the latter in people requiring neurosurgical operations, who had consented to additional research investigation). The findings fell into two categories; firstly ones relating to what it takes, in terms of type and duration of stimulus, for a stimulus to become conscious; secondly, ones to do with the relationship between brain activity and a conscious decision to perform an action. The latter results, in particular, attracted wide attention because of their apparent implications for 'free-will'.

We've known for a hundred years or more that we live a little behind the times, because it takes a while for information about the outside world to get to our brains. There's a very short delay in the case of visual information, but pain, for example, can take a second or more to get from finger to brain cortex—as all of us have noticed after injuring ourselves. What Libet found was that, even after information has reached our brains, there's a further delay before we become conscious of it. Direct stimulation of the sensory cortex, he observed, has to last for one fifth of a second or more before a subject becomes aware of any sensation. He then found that, if he stimulated a subject's finger and *later* gently stimulated the appropriate part of the subject's sensory cortex, the subject would never be aware that the finger had been stimulated provided that the 'later' was not more than about one fifth of a second. However, if subjects were

---

[19] Reports of his research are scattered throughout the literature. I've given only one reference to it in the 'bibliography', selected for offering a fairly complete overview of his work.

asked to report on *when* they became aware of the stimulus (if they did), those whose sensation was down to direct cortical stimulation reported a time of around 200–300 msecs after the onset of stimulation, whereas those whose sensation was due to finger stimulation (that hadn't been blocked) reported a time corresponding to the onset of stimulation.

These findings may sound a bit confusing, but what they boil down to is that it takes 200 msecs or more to become conscious of anything sensory that impinges on the brain. If the 'anything' is interfered with before consciousness of it has 'gelled', so to speak, there may never be any conscious awareness that it has occurred. However, provided the 'anything' originates outside the brain cortex, the brain will take note of when information about it first arrived and will later incorporate that time into its consciousness of the 'anything' when, in due course, such consciousness develops. There's an analogy to be made here with an old-fashioned Polaroid camera. You snap the shutter to take the picture, then pull the film out of the camera so that it can develop. Snapping the camera shutter corresponds to information getting through to the appropriate sensory cortex, then something happens in the brain corresponding to pulling out the film and the picture developing. But the time the 'shutter snapped' is displayed as part of the picture in both conscious experience and holiday snapshots.

Interestingly enough Libet also found that, if he directly stimulated sensory nerves or sensory tracts in the brain stem, what he called this 'backward referral' of awareness of the timing of the onset of awareness also occurred. It was absent only with direct cortical stimulation; a plausible explanation being that the brain normally uses the initial waves of cortical evoked responses as time markers for sensory awareness, and direct cortical stimulation doesn't adequately mimic this marker — i.e. it doesn't, in terms of the analogy in the last paragraph, snap the camera shutter. It thus appears that we always live 200 msecs or more behind the times, but our brain normally 'tricks' us into thinking we're fully up to date. Findings like these led Gerald

Edelman to title one of his earlier books on consciousness *The Remembered Present*. The very fact that consciousness takes a while to put in an appearance means that it *must* be intimately linked with early stages of memory processes, because information has to be stored in some format or other during the 200 msecs or thereabouts that is needed for its 'development' into consciousness.

And the propensity of conscious awareness to put in late appearances on the scene is not confined to sensory stimuli alone. Grey Walter discovered nearly sixty years ago that, if someone is waiting to perform an action of some sort, an electro-negative potential builds up over the front of the brain, which can be visualised if successive EEGs are taken and then averaged to remove the clutter. He called it an 'expectancy wave', though it now goes by the considerably less pithy name of 'contingent negative variation' (CNV). Libet added an important twist to this observation. He asked people to flex their wrists *at a time of their own choosing*, while they were watching a large clock with a fast moving hand. He, meanwhile, was watching their EEGs for CNV-like activity, which duly appeared. The subjects (who couldn't see their EEGs of course) then reported on the time they first became aware of a 'decision' to comply with the previous instruction and bend their wrists. The onset of the CNV-like wave always preceded subjects' conscious experience of decision-making by an average of about 350 msecs.

Consternation resulted in some circles when the finding became widely known and had been confirmed by other researchers (first reactions were sometimes to blame Libet for making mistakes with either his experiments or his conclusions). Clearly, it was inferred, these results show that our brain make decisions for us; consciousness only registers the outcome. As consciousness doesn't make the decisions, any notion of free will has to go out of the window! Such an inference not only seems like an implied assault on our dignity as conscious beings, it was felt, but also undermines the rationale for many of our social structures, especially the criminal justice system. It's worth making a short digression to look at these issues.

Free Will

Libet's finding certainly suggests that tactical decision-making precedes conscious awareness of it. People were quick to point out that his subjects had already made a strategic, voluntary decision to comply with the experimental protocol, so maybe that was where 'free-will' came in. Others countered that the strategic decision, too, was probably down to unconscious brain processes, albeit ones inaccessible to EEG visualisation. Libet himself argued that, while the time between onset of the CNV-like wave and awareness of a decision to move was about 350 msec, the actual movement took another 200 msecs to commence, so maybe consciousness could somehow use this interval to veto movement.[20] We may have 'free won't', in other words, even if we lack 'free will'. This loophole seems to have been closed recently, as it has subsequently been shown that conscious awareness of a decision *not* to move is also preceded by EEG changes (Hughes, 2008).

Moreover there's plenty of evidence from other sources that the feeling of 'I did that; that's my action' is based on the output of a brain module that can be fooled or coerced into feeling responsible for things the brain *didn't* do and vice versa (i.e. not feeling responsible for things the brain *did* do). Daniel Wegner, a Harvard psychologist, has described all this with admirable clarity in his book *The Illusion of Conscious Will*. The module may make its estimates of responsibility for action by comparing what actually transpires with what it had predicted to happen from knowledge of both environmental circumstances and brain motor outputs (e.g. Frith, 2007). If actuality and prediction match, then it was me that did it; if they don't, it must have been someone or something else. But, whatever the precise mechanism, consciousness appears to have no role in the 'I did it' experience other than as observer of a probability estimate, made by 'its' brain, that the brain was responsible for some happening.

---

[20] The actual window of opportunity for a veto is only around 150 msecs, as it takes about 50 msecs for commands from the brain to get to muscles.

Other findings, too, pointed to the ineffectuality of consciousness. For example, it is possible to trick people into perceiving an object to be larger or smaller than its actual size, given the right setting. However, if the person is then asked to grasp the object, her fingers will automatically adjust to the *correct* size for holding it, not to the perceived size. The explanation usually given is that the perceived size is down to so-called 'what is it?' visual circuits, but there are also, more rapidly acting, 'where is it?' ones (including, it has to be assumed, information about where 'its' boundaries are). The rapid reaction circuits are the ones used by the brain to adjust grip size, but are so fast that consciousness doesn't have time to get to grips with them — as usual, it appears to be a passive latecomer and, in this case, one liable to misreport the facts.

Suffice it to say that, from the standpoint of orthodox, late 20th century neuropsychology, 'free-will' was looking pretty much a dead duck.[21] Brains appear to be responsible for conscious decisions, not vice versa, and even the feeling of responsibility for action merely reflects the output of a neural computation. But, bring in the link between consciousness and memory/attractors, and the picture looks quite different. Moreover, it looks different independently of whether the consciousness-memory link is considered to be an identity between consciousness and an aspect of the memory process, or whether the link is thought to be mediated by a mechanism. Any mechanism is bound to be reciprocal in some way. Neural mechanisms would involve feedback of some sort, however indirect, while extra-neural ones, if any are conceivable, would be constrained to obey more fundamental reciprocal ties, such as those necessitated by energy conservation. Whichever option one

---

[21] Of course the deadness of the duck is relative to what 'free-will' is taken to mean. I use the 'common-sense' meaning here — i.e. a supposed ability of consciousness to influence the behaviour of 'its' brain and thus to have a say in its own future.

chooses, therefore, consciousness has to be regarded as able to influence the memory process.[22]

Since new memories contribute to brain attractor landscapes, it follows that consciousness can affect the form of these landscapes. And what the brain can and will do is moulded by the landscape. Thus consciousness has to be regarded as able to influence 'its' brain, not via any direct causative process, but by modifying the constraints under which all those neural causative links and computations operate. This view is fully consistent with the neuropsychological findings, but casts them in a very different light. As noted in chapter 4, consciousness deals in meaning and it exercises free will through the inherent ability of meanings (which, we argued earlier, refer to natural laws, attractors and memories) to affect the behaviour of physical systems like brains.

It's surely true that, if 'free will' is taken to refer to the feeling of 'I did it', then it has to be regarded as a sort of illusion because that feeling actually means 'my brain has made the estimate that it was probably responsible for the action'. But, if free will is taken to mean 'my consciousness, including my awareness of goals, intentions and choices, had a part—often a rather "strategic" part—to play in determining this action', then it surely does exist. Our choices and behaviour are not solely down to deterministic or random neural events, because these events (sometimes) dance to consciousness's tune. However, it's worth noting that questions of freedom from *social* determinism raise much more difficult issues, if only because the 'us' that we perceive in consciousness—the 'us' that we conceive of as exercising free will—is partly a social construct. But discussing these issues would be too much of a digression here.[23] Let's move on to ask which bits of memory are linked to consciousness.

---

[22] Provided one keeps within the materialist paradigm. Step outside that, and this conclusion doesn't necessarily hold. In that case, however, all bets would be off and there would be no good reason for accepting the neuropsychological anti-free-will arguments in the first place.

[23] I have tried to deal with them in my book *De la Mettrie's Ghost*.

Memory

Memory comes, if not in a thousand guises, at least in an uncomfortably large number of manifestations. For psychologists, it appears in ultra-short (sometimes described as 'iconic'), short-term and long-term varieties. Working memory, which is short-term, refers to what one holds at the back of one's mind for use in on-going mental processes. Famously, its capacity is often said to be limited to holding only about 7 'items'[24] at any one time, which is true for things like telephone numbers though visual short-term memory is even more restricted — to about 4 'items' in the case of humans (Todd and Marois, 2004) and less for animals. In fact there are probably a whole range of working memories, relating to specific mental functions. However, a lot more than working memories alone is held in short-term storage because *anything* that eventually gets into long-term, consciously recallable, memory has to be held in short-term format first.

Types of long-term memory are equally various. They range from learned perceptual and motor skills, through 'conditioning' to episodic and declarative memory; the last two overlap, though the former is about ability to recall 'I saw such and such' or 'such and such happened to me', while the latter is about 'I know Paris is the capital of France' for instance. Rare varieties have also been given separate names, for example 'flashbulb' memory which is the ability to recall details of some events, particularly emotionally charged ones such as seeing the Twin Towers attack on television or hearing of Princess Diana's death, with extreme clarity[25] and perhaps for a lifetime. A few individuals, especially when young, have 'eidetic' memory — the ability to accurately visualize, or otherwise recall, nearly every detail of past experiences, or at least some types of past experience.

[24] An 'item' is any memorable unit; it may be a single number from 0 to 9, or some mnemonic representation of a single book or single aspect of a visual scene, etc.

[25] I find it fascinating that memories of this sort don't have to be about events in the world out there. Some Near Death Experiences, of being transported to what appears to be the suburbs of Paradise for example, have all the characteristics of 'flashbulb' memories.

If things are difficult for psychologists because of the nebulousness of memory, they are even more difficult for neuroscientists although you might not think so from reading some of the current literature. This tends to focus on memory as a form of Hebbian learning due to processes of long-term synaptic potentiation (LTP), the chemical basis of which has been worked out in admirable detail (see e.g. Bickle, 2003). And it's true that LTP does appear to have an important, maybe central, role in many longer-term forms of memory. However, it originates from antecedent 'memories' in the form of protein conformational changes, and is maintained by protein synthesis dependent on gene activation, which can also be regarded as a type of memory. And there are other, less well understood, sorts of synaptic memory, such as long-term depression (LTD).

Then there are a whole lot of memory mechanisms that don't appear to have any direct relationship to the functioning of individual synapses. There are reverberating circuits, for example, or structural changes such as alterations in the shape of dendritic spines (which affect how much influence they will have on their parent dendrites and ultimately their parent neurons), or the connectivity of dendrites, or that of entire neurons, or the brain as a whole for that matter. The brain is constantly remodelling[26] its own anatomy at all scales, both spatial and temporal, and the changes of course are equivalent to memories. No doubt all these separate mechanisms co-ordinate and relate to one another somehow, but in most cases the 'how' remains unknown.

Despite all the complexity, it is possible to say a little about the relationship of consciousness to memory processes. For instance, it must relate to processes that are active while it is present, which means ones commencing at around 200–300 msecs after an initiating event and lasting for at least the duration of the 'specious present' (which is

---

[26] Professional interpreters provide a particularly striking example of this. Most of us have our language centres in our left hemispheres of course, but they have shifted their native language to their right hemispheres and use the left for their other languages (van Hemmen and Sejnowski, 2006).

an ill-defined period, but is usually a few seconds at most). This narrows the field down to the shorter end of 'working' memory in particular and short-term memory in general. The figure usually given for the duration of most short-term memory is based on the time for which people with Korsakov states can remember things (these unfortunates have brain damage that renders them unable to transcribe their short-term memories so as to make new long-term episodic memories, though they are able to learn new motor skills). The time for which they can remember what has happened to them[27] is usually about ten minutes. That it is as long as this presumably implies that consciousness can't be identified with short-term memory as such, but relates to goings on during its initial stages. We'll try to come up with some specific ideas about what these 'goings-on' could be in the next chapter.

When long-term, episodic or declarative memories are consciously recalled, they must first be transcribed back into a consciousness-friendly, short-term format. But the process is nothing like what goes on when a computer accesses permanent memory for use in its RAM, for the accessed memories have to be *re-transcribed* back into long-term format after use, if they are to be retained. This fascinating fact was discovered because forming a long-term memory involves protein synthesis, and it was found that such memories could be lost after they had been recalled if an animal was given a protein synthesis inhibitor at an appropriate time. Animals given the protein synthesis inhibitor, but not asked to exercise their memories, were later found to have retained long-term memory in the normal way. The re-transcription process is thought to differ in some respects (there's debate over precisely *which* respects) from the one that originally established whatever memory

---

[27] If asked, 'what were you doing yesterday?', for instance, some people with Korsakov's state will simply reply 'I don't know', but many will construct (objectively, but not subjectively, false) accounts based on old memories of their doings before their brain injury, or even on stories or films that they had come across earlier in their lives. This is called 'confabulation'.

it was, but nevertheless it is needed if the memory is to be retained. (see e.g. Alberini, 2005).

This finding is especially fascinating from the attractor dynamic point of view because it implies that consciousness has the ability and the opportunity to directly edit even well-established features of its brain landscapes. There's no need for consciousness always to put 'its' brain through long learning or training courses in order to remodel the landscape (although of course it often does use this method); it can do some remodelling through 'thought' alone. That it can and does make use of this ability is strongly suggested by the existence of 'false memory syndrome'. Such 'memories' appear to be just like genuine episodic ones, except that they are the constructs of conscious or semi-conscious thoughts and fantasies; constructs that often appear to be based on distortions of, and/or additions to, genuine memories. When self-initiated, false memories are probably usually or always unintended, by the conscious mind at least. In those cases, the conscious fantasies that lead to falsity probably well up from unconscious mind. However they can also result from repeated rehearsal of what was initially an incomplete but genuine memory, as when a witness is repeatedly questioned by the police for example. They then sometimes come across as the semi-intended consensus of a conscious dialogue.

Conclusions

We've seen how consciousness provides a window onto aspects of mentality, while mentality itself is a broadly based dynamic that can usefully be pictured in terms of state spaces and attractor dynamics. In this chapter, we've been trying to take a look at the window itself and that's not easy; hard to see the glass when you are looking through it! Hard, but not impossible. The problem is that we may not have some of the essential concepts needed to understand the nature of the glass, and we certainly don't have anything better than primitive tools for probing its nature—except for consciousness itself, of course; but trying to use that in any direct way brings us back to the inherent difficulty of seeing what you are using for the faculty of sight. All the same, a range of insights and hints have been surveyed in this chapter, many of which probably are relevant to the nature of the 'window'. I list them below and give each my own estimate of their 'star' rating; 4 stars for almost certainly right and likely to stand the test of time, down to 1 star for possibly a useful hint although I wouldn't bet a lot of money on its enduring value.

- Any form of 'consciousness' that we can meaningfully discuss has to be introspectible, at least 'in principle', and thus linked to early stages of memory processes. ****
- Consciousness is associated with extensive neural activity and information distribution on the brain. ***
- The links that consciousness has with memory mediate its 'efficaciousness', in relation to 'free will' for instance.***
- Consciousness plays odd tricks with time. It involves both prediction and recall, while the subjective present differs from the objective one and is elastic. ***
- Consciousness has something to do with 're-entrant', coherent neural activity. **
- Consciousness developed from primitive, cellular 'awarenesses'.**
- We're likely to need new physics in order to understand consciousness.*

We'll be making use of these insights and hints, along with the dynamic picture of mentality, to see where they can lead us. The next chapter will be basically about the possible 'shape' (i.e. topology) of consciousness-associated neural activity, while the following one will take a look at what those odd tricks with time might conceivably imply.

Chapter 6

The Shape of Consciousness?

To get a handle on this topic, let's start off by going along with the popular 'global workspace' view, which regards consciousness at any particular moment as simply *being* the 'information' that occupies a workspace and is widely distributed throughout the brain in consequence. We needed to modify that picture (see the previous chapter) by regarding the so-called 'workspace' as a term for the ruling attractor(s) that happen to be dominating brain activity for some (usually brief) period of time. Although we could not say *why* ruling attractor(s) should be consciousness-associated, any more than traditional global workspace theorists can tell us why the contents of their spaces are conscious, we'll just assume that this is so for the moment as what philosophers like to call a 'brute fact'. The question then arises, what must these ruling attractors look like in concrete terms? Remember, they exist in a notional, multidimensional state space, while brains exist in ordinary 3-D space; indeed, since the brain's sheet-like cortex is probably often the most relevant part of it in this connection, we have to refer to an effectively 2-D space a lot of the time.

The attractors have somehow to 'map' their dimensions onto ordinary space. To get a feel for what this involves, assuming that you don't already have one (as I didn't), I suggest looking up Wikipaedia's entry on 'tesseracts', 4-D cubes. There's even a nice animation of a tesseract, drawn as if it were rotating in 3-D space. Then remember that this is an object with a relatively simple shape and only two dimensions up from the sheet of paper or computer screen on which it can be represented. Attractors are unlikely to have simple shapes and they are millions of dimensions up from any 2-D surface. So far as I know, the only form of mapping able to represent the necessary complexity is fractal. The implication is that, when looking for the representation of consciousness in the brain, we need to be looking for something with a fractal structure; something that is self-similar on all scales like an ever branching tree or, more aptly, like those 'Mandelbrot sets' that appeared on so many posters and T-shirts a few years ago. Incidentally fractals are known to occur in various forms in the brain, and the idea that they—along with the strange attractors that they often represent—are relevant to mind is far from new (see, for example MacCormac and Stamenov, 1996).

There are in fact many potential candidates in the brain that definitely or probably have the right (i.e. fractal) structure, but we can narrow the field down a bit. Whatever it is has to work on time-scales consistent with the time-scale of consciousness (i.e. somewhere in the range of about one tenth to one or more seconds, judging by the durations of what we experience as 'present moments') and, as we also saw in the previous chapter, it has to be intimately involved with early stages of the memory process. This pretty well rules out what was the favourite candidate for a close correlate of consciousness of many 20th century neuroscientists —i.e. information in the form of action potentials. Action potentials are too ephemeral and too indirectly memory-related to fit the profile. Diffuse electro-magnetic (EEG) fields are a better bet. They work on the right time scale and there is evidence that they often have a fractal structure, both spatially and temporally. A good many authors have proposed that they are at the basis of consciousness, or indeed *are* consciousness (e.g. Pockett, 2000; McFadden, 2002). Stuart Hameroff too, who was an originator of the quantum 'OrchOR' theory (see chapter 5), has recently proposed that consciousness relates to large scale gamma synchronous EEG activity, mediated by ever changing 'dendritic webs' whose connectivity and evolution depends mainly on the opening and closing of gap junctions[1] between dendrites, also possibly involving the astroglial cells that support neurons (Hameroff, 2009). He refers to this 'mobile, gamma-synchronized web' as the 'conscious pilot'. It can be regarded as a possible physical instantiation of 'ruling attractor(s)' and is an appealing suggestion in many respects. However, the concentration on EEG fields alone leaves the problem that their connection with memory processes is rather indirect. By themselves, they don't have the intimate relationship with early stages of memory processes required by any plausible candidate for the immediate basis of consciousness.

I think a somewhat different candidate is probably a better bet (Nunn, 2003; Pereira and Furlan, 2009), though it is one closely involved with EEG fields. In fact its relationship with these fields can be viewed as incorporating a sort of 're-entrance' at the cellular level[2] as well as at a range of super-cellular scales. Unlike Edelman and Tononi's 're-entrance' of reciprocal, information-bearing spike activity,[3] however, it involves a yet more intimate inter-relationship; namely one between between the fields and some of the ions that contribute to generating them, especially calcium ions.

Perhaps I should offer a disclaimer at this stage: please remember that my proposal is intended only as an illustration of the sort of neurology that *might* be most relevant to

---

[1] Gap junctions are direct connections between the cytoplasm of one cell and that of another so that, especially in the case of neurons, electric currents and their associated ions can flow without impediment from one cell to another. They are formed by proteins called 'connexins' and 'pannexins'. Although a lot less is known about them than about synapses, they are thought to be dynamic structures capable of opening and closing and of appearing and disappearing. Astroglia, too, have them in abundance.

[2] A suggestion which fits in with Humphrey's intuition that consciousness may ultimately derive from rather basic biological phenomena.

[3] Incidentally, Edelman and Tononi's emphasis on highly *accurate* reciprocal mapping being at the basis of conscious neural activity, if correct, suggests another reason for thinking that spike activity cannot be directly involved. Neuron firing is stochastic, so mapping dependent on it is always going to be blurry to some extent.

consciousness; one able to fit the constraints we have identified. The brain is full of surprises however, and is inordinately complex. Quite possibly it actually does things in a different way from the one I'm going to suggest. Nevertheless, a concrete model helps with conceptualizing the general type of neurology that seems to be needed, and with visualizing relevant structures and dynamics. Moreover, Hameroff's 'conscious pilot' also gives an essential role to calcium ions albeit with rather less emphasis on the necessary fractality of the overall structure than I'll suggest in what follows. Our arrival at similar pictures, by very different routes maybe suggests that there is something right about them: so here goes.

Calcium Waves and Their Concomitants

Calcium ions have a large number of roles within cells in general and neurons in particular (see e.g. Koch, 1999); some fairly well understood, others not. They play an essential part, for instance, in triggering neurotransmitter release when an action potential arrives at a synaptic terminal. Cells, including neurons, have stores of calcium from which ions are released when needed, and there are a range of proteins around to mop them up afterwards. There are special calcium channels in cell membranes and 'calcium currents' can be found in nerve cells, which contribute to modulating their activity and can occasionally appear to be a primary cause of spiking. In brief, these ions have an essential part to play in many aspects of neuron functioning, including the generation of EEG activity.

However, I'd like to focus for a moment on another aspect of calcium ion activity. Release occurs in bursts, mainly in dendritic spines. Changing calcium concentrations can thus be thought of as calcium ion waves, not entirely confined within dendritic spines (Hering and Sheng, 2001), which are highly dynamic structures. The actual calcium concentration and degree of confinement following synaptic activation (i.e. the amplitude and spread of the waves) depend on how much is released within spines, of course, but also on the shape of the spines, which is constantly changing. The dendrites themselves form a sort of mat, their interiors directly linked in places by gap junctions, while they also connect with the interstitial fluid in which they are bathed via a range of channels, including voltage dependent calcium channels. The calcium channels can respond to voltage changes smaller than those involved in spike activity, so they can open and close in synchrony with local EEG fields; fields that the calcium flows themselves help to create.

What this boils down to is that the dendritic 'mat' permeating grey matter areas of the brain harbours calcium waves on scales ranging from that of dendritic spines up to, in all probability, quite sizeable chunks of 'mat'. On small scales, the 'waves' are generally referred to as 'calcium currents', but the two terms are equivalent since both refer to changing calcium ion concentration. Whether these waves are fractal in the formal sense of possessing a single Hausdorf dimension that applies at all scales is not known, but they are bound to be fractal-like and are perhaps sufficiently so to be capable of instantiating ruling attractors..

You might suppose that calcium waves occur only in the interior of neurons or adjacent interstitial fluid, but more extensive ones are supported by astroglia[4] too. These cells can show whole-cell changes in calcium concentration, and groups of them are known to support the existence of inter-cellular calcium waves (Haydon, 2001; Pereira and Furlan, 2009). In their case, the spatio-temporal size distribution of inter-astroglial calcium waves *is* known to follow

---

[4] Astroglia are brain cells that surround neurons and synapses. At one time they were thought to be of little interest, except as 'housekeepers', but are now known to be capable of influencing synaptic transmission, and generally appear to have important, but little understood, parts to play in what the brain does (see Fields, 2010, for a comprehensive account of the many parts they may play). For instance, their activity is now thought to be primarily responsible for the BOLD signal of fMRI. Just like neurons, they are organized into networks although astroglial network connections are via gap junctions between cells (Giaume et al., 2010), not via the synapses that play the major role in connecting neurons (though gap junctions between dendrites belonging to different neurons are quite plentiful).

a power law, i.e. is fractal (Jung *et al.*, 1998). Furthermore, these waves appear often to be initiated by activity of neuronal NMDA synapses[5] (Harris-White *et al.*, 1998), particularly one of the specific sub-types of such synapses (Fellin *et al.*, 2004). Astroglia therefore seem well suited to supporting larger calcium waves[6] in the hierarchy of scales needed for 'mapping' attractors into brain activities and thus for providing the neural basis of consciousness. To quote Haydon (*op. cit.*, p. 192), 'Perhaps it is no coincidence that the ratio of glia to neurons increases through phylogeny. For example, the nematode ... has about one glial cell for every five neurons, whereas the ratio in the human brain is thought to be at least ten glia per neuron'.[7] The 'coincidence', of course, refers to the fact that nematodes presumably have little, if any, consciousness, whereas humans have a lot. Just maybe it isn't the number of neurons we possess that makes the biggest difference in this connection, but rather the number of astroglia.

So it looks as though calcium waves *could* provide a medium for mapping attractors in general and ruling

---

[5] I.e. synapses of the type that are thought to play a major part in memory, particularly long-term memory. Astrocytes themselves possess receptors for both glutamine and D-serine, agents released in NMDA synapses..

[6] Calcium wave spread between astroglia may partly depend on gap junctions, especially as a consequence of ATP diffusion through gap junctions which triggers release of calcium ions within astroglia. But it also appears to be a consequence of sodium entry upsetting normal sodium/calcium exchange (Jung *et al.*, 1998). The sodium entry itself may be mediated by some unknown chemical transmitter; it is possibly relevant, in this connection, that tetrodotoxin, which blocks voltage gated sodium channels, abolishes single glia calcium oscillations and attenuates larger scale waves (Harris-White, 1998). This finding suggests that there may also be coupling between diffuse e- m fields and calcium waves in astroglia.

[7] It is now thought that this may be an over-estimate. Although most textbooks cite between 5 and 50 astrocytes per neuron in higher mammals, the more likely ratio in our brains is actually between 1 and 2 astrocytes per neuron (Hilgetag and Barbas, 2009), but Haydon's point about the proportionate increase through phylogeny is still relevant. The astrocyte/neuron ratio in leeches has been estimated at 1:25, in rats as 1:3 and in humans as 3:2. Moreover human astrocytes are considerably larger than those of rats (Oberheim *et al.*, 2009).

The Shape of Consciousness? 121

attractors in particular, but then so could a large number of other structures or occurrences in the brain. What makes me think them a particularly attractive candidate is the existence of a protein called CaMKII, which is widespread in the brain. This protein has truly remarkable properties; ones which allow calcium waves to link directly into the memory process. And the existence of the right sort of link(s) with memory is a *sine qua non* for any model purporting to represent the neural basis of consciousness.

So what is this amazing protein? 'It' is actually a family of related proteins with similar functional capacities, which constitute 1–2% of the total amount of protein in the brain (see Lisman *et al.*, 2002, for a clear survey of what is known about 'it'). It is particularly associated with excitatory synapses and, when activated, is thought to play a vital part in initiating and/or maintaining long term potentiation of the NMDA type of glutamine neurotransmission. There's good evidence that potentiation of this type underlies some forms of memory and learning. Activated CaMKII may influence other types of synapse, too. And that's not the last of its remarkable properties, for it has recently been shown to also influence the connexin protein of gap junctions when activated (Alev *et al.*, 2008). In other words, it appears to be capable of affecting the opening of these junctions, thus allowing direct spread of currents and ions between cells. But what is it that activates this versatile performer?

The answer is 'calcium', specifically calcium ion concentration. As concentration increases, the time for which CaMKII remains in active form initially increases in a graded manner; eventually, however, a threshold is reached and it remains in active form indefinitely, regardless of the ambient calcium ion concentration. Of course proteins in the brain tend to have a short half-life and that of CaMKII is around one month. However there is evidence that, when replaced, the replacement adopts the same activation state as its predecessor. The calcium concentration → CaMKII link thus has *exactly* the right properties to fit the consciousness→ memory link that we identified. It initiates at a very early stage of the memory process, but then may have effects that can last indefinitely.[8] Moreover, even if the calcium concentration doesn't exceed the threshold for triggering long-term activation of the protein, lesser increases still leave their traces for a time; traces likely to trigger further memory-related changes in the brain.

Whether or not consciousness is actually associated with calcium waves remains to be seen. We won't know until techniques are available for visualizing them in real time and in conscious subjects.[9] But they do appear to have the right characteristics, and maybe they can tell us something about the 'architecture' needed by any neural basis of consciousness. So what do they look like? We pictured mentality in terms of attractor 'landscapes', as viewed on a geological timescale in which they heave and move and reshape themselves. Does our putative 'consciousness' fit a similar image? As it happens, the answer is no! Viewed overall, it is more like a choppy sea, with waves of all sizes coming from all directions, sometimes reinforcing one another, sometimes cancelling out. Every now and again epochs of more ordered, synchronized activity might occur, corresponding with the organisation imposed by some 'ruling attractor'. But on average, if 'frozen' for a moment, it would look fractal or approximately fractal; the dynamics would appear chaotic most of the time for they reflect an order in multidimensional space that would only occasionally be visible in our everyday world. Looked at more closely, however, some of the 'sea' would appear to possess a sort of 'stringiness' (fractals can be stringy; e.g. tree branches or frost patterns on a windowpane) because waves can travel more easily down the length of dendrites than through gap junctions or voltage gated calcium channels, while calcium ions get bound to the stringy microtubules that all cells contain. Astrocytes, too, have

---

[8] Incidentally, calcium dependent activity in single astrocytes can also affect LTP in synapses belonging to large numbers of neighbouring neurons via serine release (Wiedeman, 2010). This provides a Ca ion/long term memory link additional to the CaMKII dependent one.

[9] There are already techniques for visualizing calcium waves that have excellent temporal and spatial resolution. However, they can't be used in conscious subjects.

long stringy processes, and presumably similar considerations apply in their case.

Both of these aspects — the choppy 'sea' and the underlying stringiness — have implications that are worth exploring. We'll take the 'sea' first.

CaMKII Holography?

Calcium waves interfere with one another. If the peak of one wave coincides with the trough of another, they will cancel out; two peaks coinciding add up to give a 'higher' wave. Now this at once suggests that some form of holography might be on the cards. The essence of holography is recording information about phase relationships between waves. By the way, there is some ambiguity in the term 'hologram' as it can be used in three different senses. It may refer to the 'image' generated from a holographic record, or to the wave interferences that allow formation of holographic records, or to the records themselves. In what follows, I'm going to be a bit pedantic and use 'holography' for the process of making 'holographic records' (i.e. the registers of the wave interferences that are at the basis of 'holography') and will avoid using 'hologram'.

In the optical holography that we're all familiar with, if only from the antifraud holographic records on our credit cards, what happens is that a light sensitive medium is more affected where light waves from different sources (typically those reflected from a scene and others from a 'reference' source) have constructively interfered and is less affected where they have destructively interfered. If using old fashioned photographic film, the film responds to more light by precipitating a greater density of granules. It's a characteristic of these records that they have a fractal structure (self-similar at all scales), which is what allows the well-known fact that you can recover the *whole* of a holographically recorded picture from *any* part of the record (albeit with increasing loss of fine detail as the area of record used gets smaller). Recovery of an image involves illuminating the pattern of deposited granules with light having similar characteristics to that from the original 'reference' source. These optical holographic records also work the other way round in that, if re-illuminated with light reflected from exactly the same scene as that originally recorded, they will generate a replica of the 'reference' beam.

It's clear from the properties of CaMKII that it can't avoid playing a role in relation to calcium waves just like that of the granules in a photographic film in relation to light. In addition to responding to waves as such, it is bound to record information about their phase relationships since it will be converted to its permanently, or at least longer lasting, active form where the waves 'add up', but will remain inactive where they cancel out. Given that holographic record formation has to occur, holography looks like being a possibility—provided an equivalent exists for the 'reference beam' of optical holography. And that, maybe, is where the coherent gamma activity that was discussed in the last chapter could play a part. Because of the close, reciprocal coupling between EEG and calcium ions, the gamma waves are inevitably reflected in calcium waves which provide, potentially at least, a suitable 'reference' background. If there's anything at all to the picture of conscious 'architecture' that we've been developing in this chapter, holography is pretty well certain to be part of it.

We're still no nearer to accounting for consciousness as such, of course. Gamma activity has no exclusive association with conscious, as opposed to unconscious, mental events. But, sticking with the 'brute fact' assumption used in this chapter, it is looking as though 'conscious' memories, those destined for long-term storage as episodic or declarative memories, are holographic records and presumably are later stored in similar format. Which is something that Karl Pribram, one of the all-time neuroscientific 'greats', has been trying to get us to understand for over 40 years (e.g. Pribram, 2000). Although the idea is still controversial to some extent, the mere fact that long term memories of this sort don't appear to have any well defined storage location in the brain, often degrading with diffuse loss of detail when brain damage occurs, strongly suggests that they *must* be in a holographic format of some sort.

Incidentally, rather as optical holographic records can be viewed in ordinary daylight, recall of an holographically stored memory would not necessarily involve re-creating 'reference' waves identical to those associated with its creation. A range of ambient activity would suffice. But perhaps the fact that exact replicas of the original reference waves aren't usually available could account for some of the blurriness of long term memory recall as compared to 'immediate' experience which is, of course, itself a form of (very short-term) memory. One might even speculate that, if precisely matching reference waves *are* available for some reason, you get memories that are as vivid as the originals, such as flashbacks or eidetic memories.

Viewing consciousness-related neural activity as a choppy sea thus leads fairly directly, thanks to the properties of CaMKII, to the idea that episodic and declarative memories are likely to be holographic records. But what might the small-scale 'stringiness' suggest? Teasing out interesting implications is a bit trickier here, but still potentially worthwhile.

Knots, Braids and Seifert Surfaces

Where there are strings there are almost bound to be tangles, and very likely there will be knots or knot equivalents too. Indeed, a look under the microscope at dendritic plexi, which house at least some of the relevant stringiness, shows that there *are* complicated tangles. Knot theory is one of those slightly obscure branches of mathematics liable to put in an appearance in all sorts of rather unexpected situations. Presumably because of this surprising tendency, a *Journal of Knot Theory and its Ramifications* has been going since 1992. Many of the 'ramifications' are connections to other branches of mathematics, but some extend beyond mathematics to aspects of quantum field theory, computation and statistical mechanics, among other apparently independent topics. Knots are best described by polynomial equations;

indeed the reef knot[10] that you may have tied recently can be regarded as an instantiation of a polynomial! Given the tangles we've identified, it's maybe worth seeing whether the theory could also be relevant to the neural basis of consciousness. Just very basic knot theory will do for our purposes. Two aspects of the theory may be especially relevant and a third is quite intriguing.

The first property is simple; knots are formally equivalent to braids, and braids of course are simply tangles, containing some degree of order, that can't be untangled by any simple procedure. It thus appears almost certain that some at least of the 'stringiness' that we are interested in can be viewed in terms of knot theory, though whether this could have any relevance whatsoever to consciousness remains to be seen.

A second property that could possibly turn out to be relevant is more surprising. Knots are exactly like the natural numbers in the sense that prime knots exist which are entirely distinct from one another, and from which all other knots can be constructed by simple addition. A prime number, of course, is a number divisible only by itself and 1. A prime knot is a knot which cannot be decomposed into a sum of other knots.[11] The number of prime knots is very large, perhaps infinite. Knots can be classified according to the number of string crossings they contain. That reef knot you tied earlier has 6 crossings. There are 552 prime knots with 11 crossings and 9998 with 13 crossings. For knots with 100 crossings the number of primes is known to be at least 10 with *twenty-seven* noughts after it!

What could all this have to do with consciousness? Well, I find it deeply puzzling that one bit of consciousness can be

---

[10] For a long time, the polynomial description that allowed mathematicians to distinguish a reef knot from a granny knot proved elusive, though it now exists. I confess to sometimes having the same problem with distinguishing the two, when trying to tie a reef knot.

[11] Mathematicians do refer to what they call the 'unknot', which is basically a loop; it may be a very tangled loop, but can always be straightened out into a simple loop without having to be unknotted. It plays the same role in relation to prime knots as 1 to the natural prime numbers.

distinguished from another. There's nothing obvious about neural activity in my auditory cortex, which allows me to experience the ringing of a bell, to distinguish it from activity in my visual cortex allowing me to perceive a particular shade of red. Agreed, the two bits of cortex are in different areas of my brain, but their intrinsic activity, whether viewed in terms of neuron firings, EEG, calcium waves or whatever, appears much the same in both cases. 'But surely the relevant dynamic state spaces are different in the two cases', someone might point out; 'one involves the acoustics of the bell and the other the reflective properties of the red surface. They are bound to have some different dimensions, so why shouldn't the experiential differences be down to that?' The problem with this answer as a stand-alone one is that the dynamic state spaces are relevant to *mental* activity, whether conscious or unconscious, but we're specifically concerned with conscious experience in this connection. Conscious experience is a feature which the brain appears to add to a small selection of the available 'mentality' from its own resources. Presumably, therefore, it has to be something within the brain that is responsible for the different qualities of differing experiences.

As we saw in the previous chapter, Edelman and Tononi attribute different qualities (qualia) to 'discriminable' points in a neural activity configuration space. This solves one part of the problem, for the different state spaces relevant to bells ringing or seeing red will no doubt be reflected in different neural activity configurations. But it still doesn't tell us what makes for 'discriminability' between two points in the space. You can't appeal to some little man inside the brain looking at the configuration space and saying 'this point is here, and that point is there', because doing so would merely shift the problem to the little man and leads to infinite regress. There has to be something intrinsic to the different configurations; something that entails discriminability. Balduzzi and Tononi's suggestion (see chapter 5) for a 'qualia space' in effect provides only a circular 'solution' to the problem since they *define* different qualia as different from one another (because they allocate its own 'dimension' to each separate quale). That, however, is where the prime knots could come in. They are inherently different from one another; any brain activity that generated, or could be described in terms of, one prime knot would be different in a very deep sense from activity describable in terms of another prime knot. Could the differing qualities of conscious experience be down to differential 'knotting' of some neural activity? There are certainly more than enough prime knots available to allow allocation of one prime to each distinguishable conscious experience.

An obvious objection to any such notion is suggested by our previous argument that any neural basis of consciousness must have a fractal structure. The 'stringiness' is inherently small scale, involving only smallish volumes of dendritic plexus at most. Larger volumes are pretty well ruled out, according to the calcium wave model, by the rather slow diffusion rates of calcium waves if not coupled to EEG fields. Although EEG fields are stringy at the smallest scale, because at that scale they are simply trans-membrane potentials and thus elongated like the dendrites themselves, they surely lack stringiness at larger scales. So it's looking as though knot theory may not provide a possible solution to the qualia discriminability problem because it could only work at small scales and thus clashes with the fractal (self-similarity at all scales) requirement.

This is where the third knot theoretical consideration, the one I described as 'intriguing' earlier in this section, might just possibly come to the rescue. There are *surfaces*, called Seifert surfaces, the boundaries of which are topologically equivalent to particular knots, retaining all their prime-ness or otherwise. In other words there are Seifert surfaces to match, or in a sense to *be*, the entire range of ordinary knots. And clearly surfaces in the form of wave fronts, whether calcium waves or EEG, can and do occur over a wide range of scales—in the case of EEG up to the size of the entire brain. Might such surfaces provide the larger scales of 'knottedness' needed if this is to have any chance of providing an answer to the discriminability problem?

There's no way of knowing at present. However there is a quite literal twist to the tale which suggests that it may be possible one day to find out. Seifert surfaces have to be 'orientable' and this means that, where separate parts of the surface are connected by a twisted band, the number of twists must always be even, never odd. If future research were to discover that ribbon-like structures in the brain show a strange preference for having turns that are integer multiples of 360 degrees, as opposed to integer multiples of 180 degrees, it would be a strong indication that the brain may indeed make use of these surfaces.

Conclusions

This chapter has shown, I hope, that one can build on contemporary ideas and findings about the neural basis of consciousness to construct a model that has interesting properties. It's likely that some at least of these properties will be part of any final picture of what goes on, when eventually we have it. The model shows how a rather complex process, involving calcium waves in a 're-entrant' relationship with EEG waves, plus a recording medium in the form of CaMKII, could meet the criteria identified earlier as probably necessary to any viable picture of the neural basis of conscious experience — i.e. fractality, operating times in the appropriate range and close links with early stages of the memory process.

Incidentally, the 'fractality' part of the picture, if applied to unconscious as well as to consciousness-associated brain activity, can be used to account for the 'small world' character of brain attractor landscapes, which we noted in chapter 3 and pictured as 'tunnels and air links' joining landscape features. Fractal networks, being self-similar at all scales, are said to be 'scale free'. And all scale free networks have 'small world' properties[12] which, in the case of the brain, have been discussed by for example Sporns and Honey (2006). However, the type of fractality underpinning this

---

[12] The reverse is not true — many small world networks are not scale free.

property is unlikely to be the same as the calcium wave fractality that occupies centre stage in this chapter. Intuitively at least, it is more likely to involve the anatomical network of cell connections throughout the brain, distributed fractally in terms of numbers and distances. The anatomical network no doubt influences the wave patterns, and perhaps sufficiently so to account for their 'small world' properties (which are required because the waves are 'mapping' contents of a multidimensional attractor space). But the relationship between the two is probably best pictured as one of semi-independence — a circumstance mirrored in the relationship between unconscious mind and consciousness.

Getting back to the main theme of this chapter, the model offered two somewhat unexpected bonuses. It strongly suggests that long-term declarative and episodic memory is stored in holographic format; an idea for which there is good suggestive evidence, though it has never become entirely 'mainstream'. And it suggests a rather 'way-out' answer to the discriminability of qualia problem for which, as far as I know, there are no better explanations on the table. Moreover, it's an answer that is testable, at least in principle (are even numbered twists selected for in brain pathways?), which is always a point in favour of taking this sort of speculative suggestion seriously.

But we seem to be no nearer to getting a grasp on why qualia, the constituents of consciousness, should occur in the first place. The model does have a possibly relevant implication, however. We pictured all the fractal, wavy activity as 'mapping' the occurrence of a succession of ruling attractor(s). And the basins of each of these successive ruling attractors must encompass, for short periods of time, a significant proportion of the brain — perhaps all of the brain or even the entire nervous system in some circumstances. This inclusiveness was the property that allowed us to identify the succession of ruling attractors with the more traditional 'global workspace' notion. When looking for the 'why' of qualia, therefore, we need to be thinking quite large scale.

Large scale thinking may appear to run counter to all the fMRI evidence that particular sorts of conscious experience are often associated with increased activity in relatively small brain areas. However, it has to be remembered that there is a 'figure-ground' situation here. The increased activity is visible only against a background of constant or reduced activity. But this ground may equally be included in the attractor basin, and be equally significant when it comes to the genesis of particular qualia. To put it in terms of Edelman and Tononi's neural configuration space, to get different configurations you have to have holistic groupings of varying neural activity. It's the overall pattern that matters, not solely the particular part of it that happens to 'light up'.

The model also has a rather curious feature overall, which you may not have noticed. It appears to attribute at least as much 'reality' to the attractors as to the brain activity. We pictured the brain activity as 'mapping' the ruling attractors, which rather implies that the primary reality lies with the attractors. After all, a map is only a simulacrum of what is mapped. Of course you may say, to some extent rightly, that the attractors in turn are no more than a representation of brain dynamics. But maybe that would not be completely correct. After all, as argued in earlier chapters, the actual dynamics represented by the attractors can include a whole range of events *outside* the brain as well as endogenous neural events. The relevant state spaces generally include dimensions that have nothing directly to do with neurology as such.

There is thus a sense in which the brain dances to the tune of attractors that encompass a reality larger than a purely neural one. In fact, to put it crudely, we have a sort of 'which came first, the chicken or the egg?' problem here. There's an ambiguity, as far as the model is concerned, about whether attractors cause brain dynamics or brain dynamics cause attractors. I suppose a majority of people nowadays would have little hesitation in saying that it's the brain dynamics that are 'real' and the attractors are nothing more than a fancy way of picturing that reality. However, as we shall be seeing in chapter 8, there are phenomena that make any majority view of that sort appear simplistic at best.

As with all 'chicken and egg' problems, we're not going to get anywhere by arguing the toss about which came first or which causes which. Larger concepts are needed. In the case of actual chickens and eggs, of course, it takes the idea of evolution to resolve the difficulty and we then see that it was always a pseudo-problem. What larger concepts are needed to resolve the attractor/brain activity ambiguity? Could they also help with the existence of qualia problem?

As you would expect, I have no idea what larger concepts *are* needed, but it may be interesting to take a look at what sort of concepts *might be* needed. As brains are material, while attractors, as pointed out earlier, share commonalities with natural law, a good place to start in the search for useful concepts is with what we know about matter and law. And that's what the next chapter is mainly about; as it turns out, the concepts that we'll be identifying suggest a quite specific speculation about what may put the fire into the neurology to produce conscious experience.

Chapter 7

Of Matter, Laws and Time

The plan in this chapter is to start off by looking at some rather general features of what we actually know, or think we know, about matter, natural law and temporality. Then we'll try to work out where conscious experience could possibly fit in. I won't be discussing inherently unobservable bubble universes, or the number of dimensions in M theory, or the alleged invisible 95% of the universe comprised of 'dark matter' and 'dark energy', or anything like that. I'll simply be taking a look at what some of our best-confirmed results and theories either say or imply. And I need to do that because, although many of the so-called 'new' ideas about matter in particular have been around for fifty years or more, they have often been poorly assimilated by people who think of themselves as 'materialists'. The picture of the world that lots of non-physicists still appear to have at the back of their minds owes quite a bit to Democritus's 2500 year-old concept that it consists of 'atoms and the void', updated a little by 18th century notions of a 'clockwork universe'. In fact our situation turns out to be far less confined and far stranger than those ideas suggested, albeit still apparently based on underlying order that we can sometimes glimpse.

Our world is comprised of particles and fields, subject to rules (often dubbed 'natural laws') which constrain their behaviour, set in a 4-D, spatio-temporal framework and 'observed' by us through a faculty of consciousness that appears to be quite different in character from that which it experiences. However, as many have commented, one of the most remarkable things about both the world and us is that we are able to understand it to some extent. This surely implies that our minds must share its properties, or some of its properties. The materialists have to be correct about that. People have also remarked on the 'unreasonable effectiveness' of mathematics when it comes to understanding the world. I've never quite grasped why they should be surprised at the usefulness of maths, for science is basically all about elucidating patterns that occur in nature while mathematics can be regarded as the abstract study of patterns in general; so it seems only to be expected that some maths should turn out to describe aspects of nature. Perhaps the remark has something to do with surprise over the fact that any discernible patterns whatsoever exist in nature, obeying rules that can often be expressed mathematically. Is that surprising or inevitable? Who knows? But, moving on, what do we know about where these rules come from? Let's first take a look at what can be said about the origins of law—and save up matter and time for later.

Natural Law

Emmy Noether (1882–1935) was a hugely creative mathematician. In 1915 she published a theorem that, arguably, deserves as much fame as Einstein's general relativity, published in the same year. Few outside specialist circles, however, know of it. It needed no dramatic confirmation—as Einstein's theory was confirmed in 1919 by Sir Arthur Eddington's much publicized expedition to view star shifts during a solar eclipse—because it was a self-sufficient, watertight proof. It was its own confirmation. But Noether's proof probably would be better known if it could be fitted to some catch-phrase like John Wheeler's 'matter tells space how to curve; space tells matter how to move' (referring to general relativity). What she proved was that *'any differentiable symmetry of the action of a physical system has a corresponding conservation law'*.

Our lives are certainly constrained by Einstein's gravity, but they are equally constrained by conservation of momentum and conservation of energy, plus a whole slew of less familiar conservation laws. Conservation of momentum is the ultimate cause of fatal car accidents, for example, while energy conservation is what prevents us from solving all our energy problems by building perpetual motion machines. What Noether's theorem tells us is that conservation of momentum is a consequence of the fact that identical physical systems will always behave identically, whether they are sited in New York or Madrid, Timbuktu or Cape Town. Similarly, conservation of *angular* momentum is down to it not mattering to the physics whether the spin of an apparatus, or a football, or anything physical, points to the North or the West, vertically or horizontally (except for physics carried out in a vector field, of course!), while conservation of energy is a reflection of the fact that it makes no difference to the basic physics involved whether you do your experiment at lunch-time or tea-time, or any other time of day or night (obviously timing does make a difference to experiments on physiology or whatever, but it won't affect the quantum rules, underlying chemistry or anything else of that sort).

Suitable catch-phrases to explain the idea could be '(temporal) symmetry stops changes in total energy', or 'before and after sums of momentum are always equal because of (spatial) symmetry', but I have to admit they are not very catchy. On the other hand a simple 'symmetry rules!' would convey the general idea. We tend to think of energy conservation, for instance, as being a fundamental natural law. As it happens, though, it is an almost trivial consequence of the circumstance that the behaviour of physical systems is unaffected by temporal displacements. And that circumstance appears, in the present state of our understanding, to be simply a 'brute fact'.

Special relativity, with all its weird spatio-temporal effects and its equation of mass with energy, depends on a similar principle for it is founded on the fact that physics always looks the same to all observers, however fast they may be moving relative to one another. General relativity depends on the inability of any local physical measurement to distinguish between accelerations due to gravity and those due to other causes.

The rules of quantum theory are a bit more 'iffy' as far as symmetries are concerned, though extensions of Noether's theorem do have applications in quantum field theory. For instance, the rule that energy (the technically correct term here is the 'action', but 'energy' is more easily understood) is always to be found in multiples of Planck's constant does not appear to be a manifestation of a symmetry. Feynman's dictum that 'anything not forbidden in quantum theory is compulsory', which is responsible among much else for the ability of light to 'know' what a straight line is (see chapter 4), is a sort of borderline case. Most of what is 'forbidden' is forbidden by conservation laws,[1] and perhaps there is some sort of hidden meta-symmetry between what is ruled by symmetry and what isn't. And of course quantum theory can't be the full story, as shown, for instance, by its deeply puzzling incompatibility with general relativity.

Another good reason for thinking quantum theory incomplete is that calculations of the 'vacuum energy' based on standard quantum rules give an answer which is too large by over a hundred orders of magnitude, or possibly by infinity (Wilczek, 2008, pp. 109–10)! At one time physicists were not too worried about this because they thought that some 'hidden symmetry' might cancel out the vacuum energy, leaving it at zero. However, there are now grounds for believing that a small, positive vacuum energy exists after all. If so appeals to 'hidden symmetry' won't work because, if that were responsible for the vast discrepancy between theory and observation, the cancellation would be exact. You don't get approximate conservation of energy or momentum; every single last Planck unit has to

---

[1] Pauli's exclusion principle, that no two fermions can occupy the same quantum state, is the most obvious exception to this. However, it appears to involve what can perhaps be regarded as a broken symmetry since it depends on the fact that fermions have spin ½, whereas bosons, which do like to occupy the same state, have integer spins. There's thus a sort of overall symmetry involved.

add up correctly. When symmetries are involved, they are strict taskmasters demanding account of every jot and tittle. Actually, in the case of quantum theory, what can be said about *broken* symmetries is of more interest from our point of view than the symmetries themselves. We'll see why when we get to discuss the origins of matter. In the meantime, something needs to be said about rules or 'laws' more superficial than the very basic ones we've looked at so far.

There's a sort of hierarchy of natural law, curiously reminiscent of the medieval concept of 'The Great Chain of Being' (from God, through archangels and angels, down to us, then the animals and beyond). The conservation laws, and possibly some of the quantum rules, are at the 'angelic' level.[2] But there are lots of 'human' and 'animal' level laws, too, in principle perhaps dependent on those higher up the chain but in practice almost always appearing to be autonomous. Laws like those of thermodynamics or hydraulics, for instance, are often taken to be manifestations of quantum rules, but they don't seem as if they are. Laws of physiology are yet further along the chain, dependent on thermodynamics, chemistry and the like, but they too have usually to be treated as though they were emergent properties that are not reducible in any simple way to laws further up the chain; and so it is, also, with the more complicated (strange) attractors.

There's a loss of generality as one goes down the chain; conservation of energy applies to all systems everywhere, thermodynamics only to macroscopic ones, hydraulics only to fluids – and particular strange attractors only to precisely defined dynamic systems. But the apparent emergence of what often appears to be (and perhaps sometimes actually is) new, unpredictable and apparently irreducible 'legislation' is also a feature of progress down the chain, shared as much by the more complicated attractors as by 'laws' of physiology or the like. Thus the most general natural laws, so far as is known at present, seem often to be consequences of symmetries in nature, while more specific laws are fre-

---

[2] We don't know why the symmetries themselves exist or are so important. That has to be put down to God!

quently assumed to be emergent consequences of general ones. Whether specific laws are sometimes irreducible to general ones in principle, or whether they are irreducible only in practice, is unknown and hotly debated. Indeed the whole topic of 'emergence' is fraught with philosophical and other difficulties (see e.g. Clayton and Davies, 2006), so the question of whether specific laws, including complex attractors, ever embody true novelty has to remain open.

Matter

This consists of particles and fields, the first example of which (the electro-magnetic field) was discovered by Michael Faraday in the 1830s. Both are manifestations of 'energy' as shown by Einstein's most famous equation — the one involving energy, mass and the speed of light. But what sort of relationship do the particles and fields have with one another? Fashions swing. A generation ago particles were often given primacy and the fields usually treated as derivative; now physicists often discuss 'matter fields'.

Maybe there's something comforting about putting 'particles' first. It harks back to Democritus's 'atoms' — good, solid things that are kind of understandable. But of course the particles of quantum theory are nothing like that. When 'observed', they have the properties of 'wavicles'; when not 'observed' they have no defined properties whatsoever; only a probability that a particular value of a defined property will manifest as an apparent consequence of being 'observed' in a way that is capable of eliciting the property in question (e.g. the particle's position, or momentum, or spin). That last sentence is something of a mouthful, and I should apologize for it; my excuse being that there is no easy way of describing entities with such very counter-intuitive properties.

Particles pop in and out of existence with promiscuous abandon. The so-called 'vacuum' is thought to be a seething sea of 'virtual' particles that evade energy conservation by 'existing' for hardly any time.[3] And these 'virtual' particles are 'real' according to the definition given in chapter 1 for they not only play essential roles in quantum theory but are responsible for an experimentally observed phenomenon called the Casimir effect. But I'm getting dangerously close to being drawn into a discussion of the interpretation of quantum theory. And that's something to be avoided at all costs, for it usually generates far more heat than light, and leads to envisaging monsters such as Schrödinger's famous cat or David Bohm's 'pilot waves'. The greatest monsters of all, so far as I can see, are surprisingly popular at present — i.e. the 'many worlds' and/or 'many histories' approaches to solving the conundrums.

Despite all the interpretational problems, the mathematical picture, so far as it goes, is reasonably clear in some respects. For instance the particles that carry force fields (apart from gravity) can be precisely described as the 'generators' of 'symmetry groups'.[4] And this description matches reality for it allowed physicists to predict the existence and properties of previously unknown particles. The simplest of these groups describes the electromagnetic force and has only one 'generator' — which manifests as the photon — and I'll stick with that in what follows. The two 'nuclear' forces (the 'weak' and the 'strong') are relatively complicated and are confined to atomic nuclei.[5] They are irrelevant from our point of view except insofar as they provide evidence of the value of the 'symmetry group' model.

---

[3]   They can do this thanks to Heisenberg's uncertainty principle, which is often described as saying that the more accurately you measure the position of a particle, the less you can know about its momentum, and vice versa. However a similar relationship between energy and time applies.

[4]   The groups model the electro-magnetic force, the weak force and the strong nuclear force. They are referred to as $U(1)$, $SU(2)$ and $SU(3)$ respectively and describe rotational symmetries of complex numbers. The first group has only one generator, the second three and the third eight.

[5]   Incidentally, according to Wilczek (2008), some 95% of the mass of ordinary matter comes from the energy of the 'colour' force (the effects of which we see as the 'strong' force), as manifest in its particles ('gluons') and their interactions. The remaining 5% may be down to the famous Higgs field, he says.

And symmetry appears to play a more remarkable role still in these force fields, for not only can it be used to describe the particles carrying the force (i.e. photons in the case of electromagnetism), but also appears to have some responsibility for the very fact that they exist.

The (Schrödinger) 'wave functions' that define the probability that a particle will appear in a particular position, or possess a particular momentum or spin when 'observed' have an intrinsic property called 'phase'. It's like the phase of an ordinary wave in most respects, which can be at a peak or a trough or somewhere in between. If you happen to be swimming with friends far from the beach, for instance, with ocean rollers coming in but not yet breaking, phase makes a difference to you because your companions will disappear out of sight if you are in a trough and the crest of a wave separates you from them. When you are on a crest, on the other hand, you'll be able to spot nearly everyone (some at the bottom of a trough may still be invisible). However, 'wave function' phase has no observable consequences whatsoever. It makes no difference to anything.[6] So, like the unicorn, it can't be 'real', you may say. But wait a moment! Phase only makes no difference if it's the same everywhere — if it has 'global invariance' or is symmetrical everywhere, in other words. What could break its symmetry and what would be the consequences of doing so?

Well, according to special relativity, nothing can travel faster than light, and a consequence of this is that the wave functions shouldn't be able to maintain the same phase everywhere. They could only do so if instantaneous propagation of causes was possible. Since it isn't, some bits of wave functions ought to start lagging behind others, thus altering the phase locally. Special relativity, in brief, ought to break phase symmetry. And that would never do because

---

[6] The reason it makes no intrinsic physical difference is that 'phase' for a Schrödinger wave refers to angle of rotation on a complex plane, which doesn't affect the probability amplitude. And that amplitude (when squared) is what gives the probability that you'll find a particle here, say, instead of there. Waves on the sea, in contrast, are phasic displacements of water molecules in 3-D space so they have plenty of effects.

it would throw the Schrödinger wave equation into chaos, altering predictions that are known to be perfectly good into others which wouldn't match what nature does.

In the mid-1950s, two American physicists (Yang and Mills) were worrying about this and related problems.[7] They played with the Schrödinger wave equation by making additions to it that would cancel out the effects of any local phase alteration caused by special relativity. And they came up with a term that did exactly this. The surprise was that this term also precisely described the electromagnetic field! Electro-magnetism exists, so it appears, in order to prevent breakdown of global symmetry of an otherwise totally invisible property; the disruptive factor tending to cause local asymmetry being consequences of special relativity. It seems totally weird that something of such fundamental importance to our everyday world as electro-magnetism, the force behind molecules, chemistry and life as we know it, should be down to a need to maintain the symmetry of something that otherwise has no effects whatsoever on the material world. Yet nature does appear to work like that. The Yang-Mills equation is now at the basis of the 'gauge' theories that successfully describe all the fundamental forces of nature (except gravity). Incidentally, the global phase invariance implies, via Noether's theorem, that something must be conserved. As it turns out, the 'something' that's conserved is electric charge.

The idea of symmetry breaking proved so useful in the Yang-Mills context that people have looked for lots of other applications. There is even speculation that the universe as a whole arose from a sort of broken symmetry, resulting in the appearance of 'positive' mass-energy balanced by 'negative' gravitational energy. But following these fascinating

---

[7] I've described a very simplified version of what really happened, using understandings that took another 20 years to 'gel'. What Yang and Mills were actually after in 1954 was an explanation of the strong nuclear force. Their original equation completely missed the mark, for it actually turned out to be relevant to the weak nuclear force. However, it built on ideas previously offered by Hermann Weyl and others to provide a foundation for the whole concept of 'gauge fields', which has proved hugely fruitful.

threads would take us too far from the purpose of this chapter, which is to take a look at nature and try to see where consciousness might fit in. The next topic we need to look at is even more of a puzzle than is the nature of matter.

Time

While the picture that physics has painted of what matter is 'really' like is simply weird and often counter-intuitive, its picture of time runs directly counter to our everyday experience. Actually, I shouldn't refer to a scientific 'picture' of time in the singular, for there are at least two very different ones, neither of which offers much more than an impressionistic outline sketch.

In our experience time is a one-way ticket on a journey that can sometimes flash by and at others seems to move at a snail's pace. And, as long as we are conscious, there's always a present moment separating the unknown future from a partially remembered past. The present is where it all happens for us, but is very hard to pin down. Its perceived duration fluctuates wildly. If one is very aroused (due to a sudden realisation that you've hit black ice when driving, for instance) a 'moment' of time can be as little as a tenth of a second. Relaxed but not asleep on a sun-soaked beach, one's experienced 'moment' can occupy five seconds or more according to the clock. And it's not only arousal that makes the difference, but also context. When listening in one way to music, entire phrases several bars long can be experienced as being in the present; listen another way and each note has its own present moment. Our time is flexible, organic and elusive; science times are not.

Indeed our conscious time is more than flexible; it can be very odd indeed. For example, there's a well-known moving dot illusion; a dot of light is flashed on one part of a screen, followed about 200msecs later by another dot flashed on another part of the screen. One's conscious perception is of a single dot that moves from the first position to the second. If the first dot is red, and the second green, one's perception is of a moving dot that changes colour around half way between the two positions. But the green dot does not actually appear on the screen until about 100msecs *after* the time one apparently perceives the colour as changing to green! It looks at first sight as though the brain has some marvellous precognitive ability to foretell the colour change. In fact, however, it's probably down to Benjamin Libet's 'backward referral' (see chapter 5). Consciousness of the first (red) dot doesn't 'develop' until the second dot has already appeared, but then the experienced timing of its appearance is re-assigned to when it was actually flashed on the screen, and the experienced timing of the subsequent change of colour is presumably an expression of some sort of probability estimate by the systems involved of when it 'ought' to have happened. But, even though the apparent precognition is an illusion, it is still a little uncanny. Discussing this, psychologist Jeffrey Gray commented:

> The first, temporal, inference is that, on a sufficiently fine-grained temporal scale, it is impossible to allocate a precise time to a conscious experience (Gray, 2006, p. 153).

He points out that a similar tactile illusion exists, so the inference is not confined to visual experience only. His second inference by the way (he only discusses two inferences), has to do with the difficulty of allocating any precise spatial position in the brain to a conscious experience — something that we would expect given that we pictured it (in chapter 6) as relating to fractal/holographic mapping of events in 'attractor space'.

Moving on to the two types of science time, time (a) is basically Newtonian time with a few added wrinkles. Newton envisaged time as a universal succession of instants, existing everywhere simultaneously and each of infinitesimal duration. It was the foundation for his (and Leibniz's) differential calculus, which has provided such an enormously useful tool in so many areas of science and technology. The present instant, for Newton, is a universal 3-D interface between an unreal or unrealised future and a defined past. The more modern additions have chiefly had to do with working out what determines the direction of time's arrow (i.e. what differentiates past from future). The answer is entropy,[8] which increases in the future direction. This conclusion is reinforced by the quantum theoretical concept of 'wave function collapse', for it too is said to be associated with entropy increase and is irreversible in principle as well as in practice. However, Sean Carroll's (2010) 'quest' for the origins of time's arrow shows that this is still very much 'work in progress', involving concepts that are far from adequately understood. Nevertheless, the overall picture is that time's ever rolling stream, the universal succession of instants, is heaved along by a kind of irreversible entropic ratchet. Yes, the metaphor is horribly mixed; a ratchet wouldn't work on a stream! But I hope the mixing both conveys the general idea and suggests that it needs further work.

Science time (b) is the Minkowski 'space-time' of special relativity, where time is regarded as a dimension analogous to a spatial dimension except that it is given the opposite sign to the spatial dimensions (i.e. if space is regarded as positive, time has to be negative—or vice versa; it doesn't matter to Minkowski which way the positivity and negativity are assigned, although Penrose advises that it may be preferable to assign negativity to time). The different sign given to time has consequences 'responsible' for many of the apparent paradoxes of special relativity, so it is important. One of the big problems with this formulation from a human point of view, of course, is that time doesn't behave anything like a spatial dimension as far as we're

---

[8] Entropy is the measure of the amount of disorder in a dynamic system, referred to in the 2nd law of thermodynamics which says that entropy in closed systems always stays the same or increases. Actually this 'law' isn't entirely true as stated above, since there is never anything better than an enormously overwhelming *probability* that entropy will follow the 'law'. Entropy led gloomy thermo-dynamicists of the last century to write jeremiads about the coming 'heat death of the universe'. It now has a somewhat better image, for increasing entropy is associated with increasing (algorithmic) information—and information is a good guy in most people's estimation.

concerned, and hopes of being able to move about in it are likely to remain science fiction for the foreseeable future.

The idea of infinitesimal 'instants' does retain a sort of tenuous foothold in time (b), but all universal simultaneity has of course gone. The nearest equivalent to 'simultaneous' is that two separate events should be sited on the surface of the same Minkowski 'light cone'. Thus an event on earth 'simultaneous' with one on alpha centauri according to the light cones would be regarded as having happened four years apart by Newtonian standards (since alpha centauri is 4 light years distant). Even in this case, however, third parties who were moving differently from one another, relative to the two events, would not agree about any assignation of simultaneity.

The best evidence supports Einstein and Minkowski against Newton. There is no universal time, except ... well, except that entanglement relations (see chapter 4), so far as we know, do involve Newtonian simultaneity. There's great reluctance to accept this, naturally enough, and we can't be certain about it; but experiments have shown that consequences of entanglement do appear to propagate at considerably more than light speed over macroscopic distances. Which is not something that can happen in the post 'decoherence' or post 'wave function collapse' world (identifiable entanglement is a feature of the pre-decoherence world). Clearly further work is needed here too but, whatever the ultimate conclusion may be, the time of special relativity nevertheless does have a huge amount of evidence in its favour, plus the remarkable ability described earlier to magically bring electromagnetism and the other gauge fields into existence.

One implication of time (b), as philosophers have been quick to point out, is that it appears to support the 'block universe' view of time. This says that past, present and future are all equally real,[9] and appear different to us only

---

[9] Some people have worried that such a view rules out any possibility of 'free will', but in fact it doesn't. Inching across the 4-D surface as we do, we may still at times have what appears to us to be a 'choice' of which route to take and thus which bits of the 'surface' we will

because of our particular perspective on the 4-D whole. We're kind of inching across its surface so it looks to us as if time is passing, rather as it looks as though the landscape is flowing past when you're sitting in a train. The catchphrase often offered here is 'time is what stops everything happening all at once'. But the 'time' referred to in the catchphrase is a sort of semi-illusory by-product of our perspective on 'real' time.

What is particularly interesting from our point of view is that both time (a) and time (b) embody symmetries. In time (a) the universal, simultaneous instant is a bit like a perfect wave advancing everywhere to turn future into past. Although that picture is almost certainly wrong, time (b) also has symmetries (from the perspective of any particular individual): namely those between past and future light cones. Moreover, if the block universe implication is correct, it blurs past, present and future into a (symmetrical) whole. Now our brains, with their 'remembered present' and their predictions, retrodictions and re-assignments of temporal events, are effectively messing with time. They are creating local eddies in time (a) and are introducing biases into aspects of time (b) that are peculiar to brains. In other words, they are causing local disruptions to the symmetry of science time. Maybe this accounts for why subjective time, especially the subjective 'present', is so very different from both times (a) and (b). But could the local disruptions have other consequences? Could they generate a field analogous to a gauge field? Any such field would not be universal like the electromagnetic one, of course, since the universality of that depends on global quantum phase plus universal relativity. Any hypothetical brain field of the sort I'm suggesting would depend on universal temporal symmetry but only localized disturbances of it, so would pre-

---

encounter in our own personal futures. From the block universe point of view, our 'choices' can be regarded as creating parts of its structure — the overall structure would have been different if we had 'chosen' differently. Calvin was thus wrong to suppose that God's knowledge of the future implied predestination by Him! In fact God simply sees whatever future *we* create for ourselves.

sumably be restricted to brains while they were acting in a time-messing manner.

Could such a field exist and, if it does, could it be equated with consciousness? It certainly looks as though brains can be said to break temporal symmetry, and we've seen that the consequences of restoring a threatened break in phase symmetry are responsible for an essential feature of our material world, namely electromagnetism. By analogy, maybe it's not unreasonable to think that consciousness might be what restores broken temporal symmetry. There don't seem to be too many other loopholes in the causally closed world of physics that could conceivably allow consciousness a look-in. Indeed, other than vague appeals to an unspecified 'quantum consciousness', I don't know of any other loopholes. So I'm going to run with the possibility that the answer to both of the above questions is 'yes'. At least Erich Harth and Nicholas Humphrey might approve since the possibility is consistent with their intuitions (see chapter 5) that consciousness has something to do with temporal 'thickness' as Humphrey put it. We'll take a look next at field theories of consciousness in general and this suggestion in particular. Then, in the following chapter, I'll describe some of the phenomenological evidence that may offer some support to field theories.

Fields and Consciousness

I should confess first of all that field theories of consciousness have a somewhat wacky, New Age reputation. Taking them seriously can damage your credibility both in academic circles and elsewhere, at least partly because extravagant claims are often made for them that owe much to pseudo-science and wishful thinking. However, they do have a very long history, particularly in Eastern cultures, and have attracted the interest of eminent Western thinkers more recently. Alfred North Whitehead, for instance, argued that reality is composed of 'actual occasions of experience' which he seems to have envisaged as field-like in a way, albeit non spatio-temporal. Moreover, as we shall be seeing in the next chapter, some of these ideas appear better able to account for unusual types of conscious experience than are the more 'respectable', neuro-scientific concepts. Indeed, entirely brain-bound concepts don't seem able to account for *any* conscious experience, as we saw in chapter 5; they can't do more than explain aspects of the *content* of consciousness.

Field theories come in various flavours and can be categorized in a variety of ways. Perhaps the most basic distinction is between those that take consciousness to be a universal field that our individual brains tap into, and the rest. The field analogy often given for the 'universal' type is with television. Consciousness is like all the broadcasts from television stations everywhere and our brains are the sets that tune into and display some of it. It's just as much of a mistake to attribute consciousness to the internal workings of our brains, say supporters of this view, as it would be to attribute the content of a television programme to the electronics of the set in our living rooms. Idealists (see chapter 4) often hold views of this sort,[10] and it crops up in some Eastern philosophies too.

An especially popular notion in some circles at present is that of the *akashic* field. The word 'akasha' is apparently the Sanskrit for 'sky' or 'aether', and some of the concepts associated with the supposed field have Indian origins. It owes much of its current popularity in the West to Dr Erwin Laszlo, an indefatigable writer and founder member of the Club of Rome who has published over 40 books, many of them mainly about this alleged field. As I understand it, he pictures the field as a scalar[11] one that permeates the universe and constitutes a universal memory. It has been variously described by various other authors as a universal collective *un*conscious, or as a universal consciousness or ground of consciousness. So far as I can judge from his latest

[10] Amit Goswami is a physicist, based in Oregon, who holds this sort of view and has written particularly clear accounts of it. See, for instance, his book *The Self-aware Universe*.
[11] Scalar fields are characterized by quantities only at each point — unlike vector fields, such as the electromagnetic one, which are characterized by quantities and directions at each point.

edited collection (Laszlo, 2009), Laszlo himself still thinks of it as a universal memory field that consciousness is able to access, but which is not itself conscious, responsible for '... artistic visualisations and creative insights to non-local healings, near-death experiences [NDEs], after-death communications, and personal past-life recollections' (Laszlo, 2009, p. 1). Very much a 'one size fits all' concept, it appears.

Since Laszlo seems to conceive of it as an informational field, the idea is likely to have implicit problems in relation to accounting for the *meaning* encompassed by all the rather disparate phenomena that he lists. As noted in chapter 4, quantum entanglement on its own can't deal with meaning, and Laszlo does at times seem to suggest that his akashic field has something to do with entanglement. My suggestion (also in chapter 4) that an 'entanglement dynamic' might allow a sort of ghostly meaning to emerge could maybe help here, but would still leave major questions as to how something which would probably have no effect on the material world, or could manifest only in almost certainly minor statistical effects at best, could be responsible for anything so precise as the neurally retained memories of an NDE 'life review' for instance, which I'll be discussing in the next chapter.

Local field theories, on the other hand, have mainly centred on attempts to apply quantum field theory to the brain. Possibly the most fully developed of these theories has been described by Jibu and Yasue (1995). To try to put a very complicated story into a nutshell, they suggest that rotational symmetries of water associated with the innards of nerve cells spontaneously break and generate quasi-particles called 'Goldstone bosons'. These have a low energy, thus a long wavelength, and create a type of long-range order in the water,[12] which in turn has consequences for brain function.

---

[12] They state: 'The Goldstone boson [in our theory] is nothing but a long-range correlation wave of the water rotational field created in an ordered vacuum state in which all the electric-dipole-moment vectors of [water] molecules are aligned in one and the same direction' (1995, p. 171).

Non-local field theories have great appeal to some people, but it's never very clear how *consciousness* arises in them unless it is included as a sort of axiom, which doesn't seem very satisfactory. As speculated in chapter 4 (especially the 'entanglement "dynamics"' section), *mentality* could perhaps be present universally, but consciousness, so far as we can see, is linked somehow to brains. Saying that brains simply 'tune into' universal consciousness as a television set tunes into the broadcast program doesn't work, it seems to me, because the analogy leaves out the viewer who watches the programme. Television sets don't know anything about the picture on their screens but, if you try to say that the viewer who is aware of the picture is included in the television set somehow, then the set must be the source of consciousness after all. If one were to say, on the other hand, that the viewer is actually the universal field, then it is not at all clear why the field shouldn't experience itself as such. Moreover, I can't personally see any point in consciousness entering this 'vale of tears', unless it has to, which implies that it may be created here or at least that brains contribute something essential to it.

My own feeling, therefore, is that, if one wants to consider field theories of consciousness (as opposed to field theories of mentality in general) at all, they have either to be strictly local or at least ones that start off local. How does the temporal symmetry-breaking suggestion measure up to quantum field proposals? It seems to have two big relative advantages and one major drawback. The drawback is that, if not exactly 'new physics', it is certainly an unexplored slant on old physics, albeit one based on analogy with some of the best-established mathematical and physical ideas available. And, because it's not an idea that has had attention hitherto, there is no accepted view on how it might work. Exactly which re-entrant processes or circuits create eddies in time?[13] How could the new field be pictured mathematically?

---

[13] As time's arrow is thought to be correlated with entropy increase, it's obviously tempting to suppose that 'eddies' in time are created by

The main advantage of the suggestion, indeed the whole reason for making it in the first place, is that it links consciousness directly to memory and our experience of temporality, the first of which, as we saw in chapter 5, is just about a *sine qua non* for any viable theory of consciousness. The existing quantum field theories, on the other hand, don't do this, or at least they don't do it in any direct manner. Indeed it's often not clear how they could possibly link in with conscious experiences (qualia) of any sort. They are at least as 'bad' as mainstream neuroscientific theories in this respect. The other advantage of the temporal symmetry proposal is the flipside of its disadvantage. Unlike the quantum field theories of consciousness that have been proposed hitherto, it is not tied to extensions of existing field theories; extensions which can seem contrived at best and which appear to lack both empirical support and general acceptance by the community of physicists. All the same, I can offer a suggestion as to how the 'temporal field' suggestion *might* be quantized.

Quantizing the Temporal Field

The idea that I'll describe here depends on a suggestion made by Tal Hendel (2009). The Schrödinger 'wave equation' at the basis of quantum theory incorporates an energy function called a 'Hamiltonian'. Hendel pointed out that, whenever the wave function collapses in circumstances leading to the manifestation of some particular energy state, the equation of the associated Hamiltonian can be written either as an 'operator' acting in time or as an 'operator' act-

---

entropy *decreasing* processes. Equally obviously, this could not be the whole story as many open systems decrease entropy locally (by exporting it to the environment), but they are not all conscious so far as we know. One type of event that may directly decrease entropy, however, is the formation of a Bose-Einstein condensate, a popular candidate for the basis of consciousness in many of the now largely discredited 'quantum consciousness' theories. Some types of condensate are known to 'mess with time' in the sense that they can slow light down to a snail's pace. But the difficulty of envisaging their instantiation in the brain probably rules them out as plausible mechanisms in this connection.

ing in space. Here they are — 'H' stands for Hamiltonian and the circumflex above it shows it is a quantum 'operator':

First, equation (1), the Hamiltonian expressed as an operator acting in time:

$$\hat{H}_t = i\hbar \frac{\partial}{\partial t} \qquad (1)$$

whereas in equation (2) the Hamiltonian is expressed as an operator acting in space:

$$\hat{H}_r = \frac{\hbar^2}{2m} \nabla^2 + V(\mathbf{r}) \qquad (2)$$

Hendel suggested that the second equation, the 'spatial one', represents the objective energy that we measure or perceive, while the temporal equation represents a *subjective* experience — a sort of quantum of subjectivity that he dubbed a 'qualion'.

This seems to me a wonderful idea, since it depends on equations at the very heart of quantum theory, not on fanciful or questionable extensions of the theory. Of course the 'temporal' equation may not reflect any aspect of reality, but long experience with quantum theory has shown that, if a legitimate equation *can* be written, it often *does* turn out to mean something profound. And what this equation may possibly imply is that 'subjectivity' could be associated with every manifestation of energy everywhere. The idea endorses and accounts for the 'pan-experientialism' that philosophers have discussed (see chapter 4). But how could one get from a universal 'subjectivity' of the sort implied to any human-like consciousness?

An answer to this question involves another circumstance that has been central to quantum theory for more than eighty years, namely Heisenberg uncertainty. The usual way of stating what this means is to say that the more accurately you know the position of a particle, the less accurately you can know its speed (momentum) — or vice versa. However a similar relationship exists between energy and time; questions about what 'temporal uncertainty' might actually mean have never received any conclusive answer. According to Hendel's proposal, however, the temporal uncertainty must be a *subjective* one, manifesting in what might be called a subjective temporal fuzziness of 'qualions'. If an objectively observed energy state (an energy 'eigenstate' to use the technical term) is very precisely defined (e.g. a change in the energy level of a hydrogen atom) the associated 'qualion' will be of almost infinite (subjective) duration. If an energy state is poorly defined (as when a raindrop falls on one's head, say), the associated 'qualion' will be of infinitesimal subjective duration. However, 'objective' energy states must also occur with a precision entailing subjective qualion durations of the order of 100 msecs. Energy states with this characteristic are very likely to occur in the brain — they might be energies associated with binding of neurotransmitters to receptors, for example, or changes in protein conformations such as the change accompanying activation of CaMKII (see chapter 6).

What this means is that 'wavy' energetic processes in the brain — maybe those associated with calcium waves, for example, or with EEG activity — could be associated with modulated 'qualion fields', provided that the frequency with which the energetic processes occur is of the same order as the subjective, 'Heisenberg uncertainty', duration of the associated qualions. Each spatio-temporal pattern of energy manifestation in the brain is associated, according to this picture, with a tempero-spatially modulated *subjective* field. The claim is thus that objective brain processes associated with experience have an equally complex, but subjective, shadow-side or reflection which *is* the sort of consciousness that we experience.

But why in that case, one may ask, is so much brain activity *unconscious*; why is it apparently only processes associated with 'ruling attractors' that generate 'qualion fields'? There are two possible answers to this question. The first is to say that all 'wavy' brain activity is indeed conscious, but only the activity associated with ruling attractors has the right characteristics to allow its recall; so that is the only type that we can subsequently remember having experienced. The second possible answer is to say that only energetic processes associated with ruling attractors have temporal uncertainties of the right magnitude to produce modulated qualion fields. Other brain processes, with different temporal uncertainties, will have nothing more than the sort of 'pan-experientialism' attributable to ordinary energetic processes everywhere — which is presumably not at all like our structured experience. These two answers are not mutually exclusive of course; if 'qualion fields' do exist, both factors probably contribute to the conscious/unconscious distinction.

And the whole idea is *testable*, which is a big plus in favour of taking it seriously. The Heisenberg 'temporal uncertainties' associated with different energetic processes in the brain can be calculated (in principle at least; so far as I know, this has not actually been done). Only those processes having temporal uncertainties of the order of a tenth of a second should turn out to be associated with our sort of consciousness. As suggested a couple of paragraphs back, the relevant processes might prove to be binding energies of some type for example. Any interference that sufficiently altered the degree of temporal uncertainty (by making the relevant energy eigenstates either more or less well-defined) should abolish the sort of consciousness that we experience. An obvious prediction to be made here is that energetic processes with the right 'temporal' characteristic to be candidates for the basis of consciousness will be found to be affected by anaesthetic agents in a way that considerably alters the definition of their energy eigenstates.

Does the 'qualion' idea link in with my earlier suggestion about 'consciousness fields' being down to broken temporal symmetry? The implication of the first suggestion was that symmetry breaking is due to memory-related re-assignments of timings by neural processes associated with consciousness. The 'qualion' idea, however, depends on a sort of automatic symmetry breaking, dividing the Hamiltonian into two separate components whenever an energy state manifests. The role of neurology in this second case is to bring about energetic processes with objective frequencies matching their associated qualion durational uncertainties. To put it another way, the first suggestion is that neurology may *cause* broken temporal symmetry, while the second is that neurology allows an already broken symmetry to *manifest*. Although these two suggestions appear very different if thought of in terms of classical physics, there may be a lot less distance between them from a quantum-theoretical point of view since the distinction between 'causing' and 'allowing manifestation' is not nearly so clear-cut in quantum physics as it is in classical physics. My earlier suggestion could, therefore, turn out to have been an imprecise way of expressing the second.

Another question worth asking is whether the consciousness field that we have pictured would have any conserved quantity associated with it, via Noether's theorem. If it did, one's imagination could run riot picturing the form that the quantity might take—conservation of consciousness itself would surely be one possibility, in rather the same way that electric charge turns out to be the conserved quality in electro-magnetism. Here's the theorem again:

> Any differentiable symmetry of the action of a physical system has a corresponding conservation law.

It's that word 'action' that creates a difficulty, for it refers to a type of energy function called a 'Lagrangian'. Noether's own proof of her theorem works only for physical systems that can be defined by Lagrangians. However, Lagrangians are actually very similar to Hamiltonians and, according to Baez (2002), extensions of Noether's theorem can and do apply to at least some systems describable by Hamiltonians. Maybe it *is* possible that some sort of 'conservation of consciousness' law exists. Hendel (personal communication, 2009) thinks that some such law would follow directly from conservation of energy, if his 'qualion' proposal is valid. I am not so sure because conservation of energy is down to physics being indifferent to temporal displacements, while 'qualions' *are* (subjective) temporality; extending conservation of energy to cover them therefore seems 'iffy' at best.

However, the fact that they too incorporate Hamiltonians makes it quite likely that *some* conservation law applies in their case—it might have much the same relationship to energy conservation as conservation of angular momentum has to conservation of momentum. Since conserved quantities are 'substances' from a philosophical point of view, this raises the interesting possibility that *both* monism *and* a form of substance (Cartesian) dualism are true—and hence that centuries of philosophical argument about *which* view is correct have been entirely past the point!

Conclusions

The last two chapters in particular have been heavily theoretical, and it's worth pausing at this stage to sum up where we've got to so far with the overall argument. After some introductory material aimed at showing that our minds are rather fluid entities with indistinct boundaries, we introduced a picture of mentality based on dynamic state spaces and their associated attractor landscapes. The relevant state spaces, we found, often extend beyond brains in a manner that accounts for both the fuzzy mental boundaries between individual people, their societies and their environments, and for the very rapid adjustments to experience that can occur when the overall dynamics change. The picture implied a certain ambiguity, we noted, over whether attractors manifesting in brain, or the brain processes themselves, should be regarded as primarily responsible for experiential outcomes. The ambiguity arose because we saw that the multidimensionality of 'attractor space' probably contributes to mental and neural function, thus suggesting that it may have a 'reality' all of its own. That took us from chapters 1 through to 4.

Then, in chapter 5, we took a look at current ideas about consciousness, and identified themes likely to feature in any future understanding of the topic. As a reminder, here they are again, with their star ratings referring to my estimate of how likely they are to survive as our ideas develop:

Of Matter, Laws and Time 157

- Any form of 'consciousness' that we can meaningfully discuss has to be introspectible, at least 'in principle', and thus linked to early stages of memory processes. ****
- Consciousness is associated with extensive neural activity and information distribution in the brain. ***
- The links that consciousness has with memory mediate its 'efficaciousness', in relation to 'free will' for instance.***
- Consciousness plays odd tricks with time. It involves both prediction and recall, while the subjective present differs from the objective one and is elastic. ***
- Consciousness has something to do with 're-entrant', coherent neural activity. **
- Consciousness developed from primitive, cellular 'awarenesses'.**
- We're likely to need new physics in order to understand consciousness.*

Chapter 6 was about how the contents of the dynamic state spaces of mentality could translate into patterns of neural activity. Fractal, holographic mappings appeared to be the best bet, indeed the only adequate bet so far as I know. We suggested that these might take the form of reciprocally interacting calcium and EEG waves, partially dependent on and recorded by alterations in CaMKII activity, which initiates further memory processes.

All this was undoubtedly speculative, but consistent with current neuroscientific thinking and empirical evidence. We then added the further speculation that knot theory might provide an answer to the problem of conceiving of what could possibly distinguish different patterns of neural activity from one another, in the way needed if qualia are to be thought of as arising from these patterns. However, we noted that neither knot theory, nor any of the other considerations or ideas discussed hitherto, could convincingly account for the existence of conscious experience in the first place. And there was no resolution of the ambiguity over whether attractors should be regarded as steering dynamics in a manner analogous to the role of natural laws, or are no more than notional representations of dynamics that are, in principle, entirely explicable in terms of fundamental natural laws.

The present chapter 7 has mainly been about identifying some plausible niche or gap in established physics that might provide a home for the existence of consciousness. A good bet, albeit a highly speculative one, appears to be the idea that consciousness might arise from a threat to temporal symmetry, in a manner analogous to the origin of electro-magnetism in the threat posed to phase symmetry by the demands of special relativity. The reason for favouring the idea is that it fits in with the associations of consciousness with memory and 'tricks with time' that were identified in chapter 5, and with the intuitions of a number of other people who have thought about the problems. Moreover, any 'temporal field' originating in broken symmetry may turn out to be describable in terms of Hendel's 'qualions'. Earlier in the chapter, we also looked briefly at reasons for supposing complex attractors to have a lot in common with the more specific types of natural law, though without coming to any firm conclusions about the actual status of either attractors or 'local' natural laws.

Thus the overall picture that we've arrived at suggests that the dynamic state spaces representing 'mentality', with their associated attractor landscapes, link via brain processes (and I've offered some concrete suggestions in chapter 6 about the sorts of brain process that might be up to the job) to local consciousness fields. It would be good to have some evidence for all this and, if we can find any, to see whether it helps us to refine the picture. In particular the ambiguity over the status of attractors has to have empirical input of some sort if we're to get any further with sorting it out.

We need to turn to the phenomenology of experience and especially to unusual phenomenology. Why 'unusual'? Well, let's take yet another analogy with electro-magnetism. It wasn't till Michael Faraday demonstrated the very unusual physical phenomenon of patterns of iron filings formed under the influence of a magnet that he could get far with understanding magnetism in terms of fields. We need to try to find experiential equivalents of iron filing patterns to help us get to grips with consciousness and its underpinnings.

But there's a final question to ask before moving on: does the picture that we've built up explain *why* consciousness is like what it is like? And the answer has to be, 'yes to an extent, but there's still quite a way to go'. As far as the *content* of consciousness is concerned, the 'ruling attractor' notion encompasses all the explanatory power of global workspace theory (GWT) and then adds some extras. It shows, much more clearly than 'traditional' GWT, how all experience is dependent on the activation of memories of one sort or another and why attention is an integral part of conscious experience; it offers an intuitive account of the fluid, organic quality of our consciousness that largely escapes the somewhat clunky 'information processing' imagery of GWT. Moreover, it shows how and why experience often appears to be in charge of the neurology (i.e. because attractors appear to have, and may indeed actually possess, a law-like relationship to neural events), which is something that GWT doesn't deal with adequately. And our ideas about the neural instantiation of ruling attractors threw up an indication of what might possibly differentiate one experience from another (i.e. knot theory); GWT has nothing inherent to offer in this connection, though 'add-ons' such as Tononi's 'qualia space' have been proposed.

The 'temporal field' suggestion provides a basis for explaining our experience of the 'specious present', plus accounting for temporal binding (i.e. the problem of how it is that temporally distinct neural events can be tied into *single* experiences). But, when it comes to 'explaining consciousness' in the sense of accounting for why it 'lights up' its content in the way that it does, the suggestion doesn't get us very far (yet). Essentially, the claim is that a 'temporal field' modulated by brain events *is* consciousness, and the fact that it is like what it is like is simply a 'brute fact' — just as an electro-magnetic field is like what it is like as far as we observers of it are concerned. However, thanks to the development of quantum electro-dynamics, we are now able to say quite a bit about why e-m fields are like what they are like; why they are vector fields, for example, and why charge exists and why photons are the force carriers. Maybe, one day, we shall be able to do as much for the temporal fields that are consciousness, if indeed that idea should turn out to be true. So let's move on and see what the evidence can tell us about these attractor and temporal field issues.

Chapter 8

The Wilder Shores of Experience

It would be great if there was an accepted, overall classification of unusual conscious experiences, showing where they fit in relation to one another. But there isn't. There are just a whole lot of, usually separate, literatures on various types. Search through categories in a bookshop and you'd almost certainly have to go from A to T (Anthropology to Theology) to be sure of covering most of them, though they do cluster to some extent under P (e.g. Psychology and Psychedelics). One category that I won't be discussing here is N for neurology and neuroscience. Strange experiences in those categories have had quite extensive coverage from a number of marvellous writers[1] over the last three or four decades. My reason for passing them by is that, although experiences of that sort are indeed often bizarre and fascinating, they mainly tell us about the modularity of the brain; about what modules do and how they inter-relate. I doubt if they can throw much additional light (over and above issues addressed in chapter 5) on questions to do with overall dynamics or putative consciousness fields. Just to give a reminder, the questions we're enquiring into are to do with whether attractors have the sort of apparently independent 'reality' (by the chapter 1 definition of 'real') that we attribute to natural law, and whether we can find any evidence relevant to local field theories of consciousness such as that proposed in the last chapter.

[1] Writers such as Oliver Sacks (e.g. 1986) or Ramachandran and Blakeslee (1999).

For similar reasons, I'm also going to ignore one of the Ps—Psychopathology. Many of the weirder experiences there, for example 'Capgras syndrome' where people believe that their nearest and dearest have been replaced by imposters, are almost certainly neurology in disguise; i.e. down to the misbehaviour of particular 'modules' and/or their connectivity. Others, such as depersonalisation and the like, float in a limbo somewhere between neuropathology, social pathologies and experience that isn't pathology-related at all. The complications are such that conditions of that sort are more likely to confuse than to help us. We need to search for relatively uncluttered examples.

Lacking any clear chart, we're going to have to try to find our own way through the jungle of phenomena that might be most relevant to our questions. And I'd like to make a start by looking at what can be regarded as a sort of baseline; an example that shows how what can be regarded as 'ordinary' brain dynamics can manifest in extraordinary experiences. It's not going to tell us anything much about whether attractors do possess an independent reality analogous to the reality of natural law, nor will it throw any light on 'consciousness field' questions. But it will be of use when we get on to more directly relevant examples, as an aid to distinguishing between significantly strange experiences, i.e. ones that may help with our enquiries, and those that are merely strange in the sense of statistically unusual, which are unlikely to tell us anything new.

The Story of Ruth

This is an account by psychiatrist Morton Schatzman of one of his patients, the eponymous 'Ruth', published in 1980. It's a tale that is remembered by few people nowadays, but is worth re-telling for its own sake as well as for any light that it may throw on other types of story when we get to them. And it's not about psychopathology, I hasten to add, despite the psychiatrist/patient aspect. Once Ruth had got her remarkable experiences under control, there is no evidence whatsoever that they were in any sense pathological.

The Wilder Shores of Experience

Her relationship with Schatzman quickly became like that of a star sportswoman with her coach. She had a rare and wild talent, and he helped to train her in its use. Maybe he also contributed to its growth and development, but questions about how much of it was hers alone and how much was a joint effort aren't relevant to the phenomenology; and it's the experiences themselves that matter to us.

Indeed the analogy between a sportswoman and her coach is closer than Schatzman himself could probably have appreciated, because views about the nature of memory have changed since his time. Many of us still tend to think of the memories that we can consciously recall as sitting in our brains in much the same way as photographs sit in an album, waiting to be looked at; but in fact they are more like the unconscious ('procedural') memories of things we can do, such as playing tennis. Just as the memory of how to play consists of a set of instructions for making the correct movements, so a memory of one of our friends, for instance, consists of a set of instructions for creating, usually in a rather shadowy sort of way, an *experience* of her face, or voice, or whatever. With a little bit of help from Schatzman, Ruth was able to create experiences, presumably memory-based, that were equivalent to finals at Wimbledon performances.

Ruth's special talent was for experiencing extremely realistic hallucinations of people that she knew. At the time she first met Schatzman, she was twenty-five years old, an American woman living in London where she and her husband had moved because of his work. They had been married for eight years (teenage marriages were more usual in the 1960s and 70s) and had three children. Although she had occasionally smoked pot, she was not a regular user of drugs of any sort. She had originally gone to her doctor with symptoms of anxiety, distress, nightmares and the like, and he had referred her on for psychiatric assessment. Schatzman, too, was an American expatriate working in a psychotherapy clinic, and the two of them seem to have 'clicked'. Ruth soon confessed that she thought she must be going mad because she kept seeing involuntary, frightening and unwelcome 'apparitions' of her abusive, if mostly absentee, father — who had never left the USA.

Her general distress settled down with a bit of emotional support, reassurance and what would now be called 'counselling', but the 'apparitions' continued. Schatzman became ever more interested in them, both for therapeutic reasons and because they were so unlike the usual run of hallucinations that psychiatrists hear about in clinical practice. Were they a factitious or even fictitious ploy by Ruth to keep herself in the limelight? Schatzman considered this question at length and in depth and, after a certain amount of wavering, decided that the answer was 'no'. He thought that her accounts of the 'apparitions' accurately reflected her actual experiences, and he certainly comes across from the book as being an insightful, probably reliable, judge of Ruth's truthfulness or otherwise. Moreover, as we shall see in due course, objective evidence of her truthfulness was eventually found.

What Ruth found particularly frightening about her father's apparition was that it seemed to have a mind of its own and could apparently intrude on her at any time. It looked absolutely realistic and fitted in perfectly with wherever she happened to be; it would sit on chairs or open and close doors appropriately, for instance. Moreover it held conversations with her that matched her real father's somewhat snide and aggressive personality, but which didn't seem to be replays of remembered conversations. On a few occasions it 'superimposed' itself on her sleeping husband while they were in bed and then smelled like her father, so she reported, not like her husband.

Schatzman had the very bright idea of getting Ruth to get the apparition under her voluntary control. If she were able to summon and dismiss it at will, it would no longer seem so frightening, he considered. With encouragement, she was soon able to do exactly that and did indeed lose most of her fear. And once she had learned the knack, there was no stopping her. The next step was to produce apparitions of her best friend 'Becky' whom she had not seen for a couple of years. She was soon having regular chats with Becky, who always appeared quite real and fully integrated with the real environment. For instance:

> Once, while taking a bath at home, she asked an apparition of Becky to put some toothpaste on her toothbrush ... She watched Becky pick up the toothpaste tube, remove the cap and squeeze some toothpaste onto the toothbrush. Becky squeezed the middle of the tube ... and Ruth wished [she] had squeezed it from the bottom ... from the moment she hallucinated Becky's hands picking up the toothbrush and tube, the real toothbrush and tube disappeared from view. Ruth was sure of this because [she looked where they had been to check] (Schatzman, 1980, p. 107).

The next development was that she started producing apparitions of Schatzman himself, sometimes when the real Schatzman was also present. The apparition often behaved or moved differently from the real man, and was not a mirror image. It looked totally realistic, Ruth claimed, and could even cast its shadow on the real Schatzman when the lighting was arranged appropriately. On another occasion, Schatzman got Ruth to position the apparition next to him with both of them facing a full length mirror. She reported that both reflections looked equally real, both wore their wrist watches on the same side and both blocked out reflections of what was in the room behind them.

Then she began, with Schatzman's encouragement, to produce apparitions of *herself*. She found this exhausting at first, and they were not always so clear as the ones of other people. But she soon got into the swing of it and started holding regular conversations with 'herself'. Interestingly enough, she did not see herself as a mirror image either. The apparition looked like her as other people would see her — and of course, except for photographs, her own visual memories of herself would have been of her mirror image. Which seems to imply that the dynamic behind the apparition of herself was not down to visual memories alone but to 'deeper' aspects of her self-image.

To cut a long story short, she discovered how to use the apparitions, especially the ones of herself, to explore aspects of her history. It emerged, for instance, that the imaginary playmates that many children have were unusually numerous and realistic her case. Her strange talent went back a long way, it seemed. She also learned how to merge with apparitions, allowing them to 'take over' her own body. Schatzman was thus able to interview her 'father' for instance, and also to interview 'her' at seemingly any pre-chosen age.

The latter phenomenon, her ability to regress to any age without being hypnotized (though perhaps it might be claimed that she hypnotized herself), was tested for realism in a number of ways by independent psychologists. Her responses on a range of personality tests matched her claimed ages, as did her hand-writing and behaviour in general, including the personal and other facts that she claimed to be able to remember. Perhaps most remarkable of all, her reaction times on the Stroop test[2] differed appropriately according to the age to which she had regressed. Another finding was that she had an excellent visual memory in her normal adult state but, when regressed to age 7, appeared to have eidetic memory for pictures shown to her.

But all good things come to an end. Ruth's husband was recalled to the USA, and her association with Schatzman was over. Before she left, however, she agreed to co-operate with some neurophysiological testing. The following observations were made:

- Her visual (EEG) evoked responses to a reversing chequer board pattern disappeared when she hallucinated an apparition between her and the pattern, but her electro-retinogram responses remained normal.

---

[2] The Stroop test involves measuring how quickly people can report the colour of colour names flashed on a screen, when the colour name is printed in the same colour and when it is printed in a *different* colour from that named. This sounds more confusing than it is! For example, if the word 'red' flashes up in blue print, it takes you longer to say 'that's blue' than it would take to say 'that's red' if the word had been printed in red. But obviously you have to be able to read quickly and automatically for the effect to manifest. Ruth showed the effect if she was being her normal adult self, but not if she regressed to an age when she couldn't read or could read only with difficulty. She showed no Stroop effect at 'age 3' and a *reverse* one at 'age 7', which is not something that you could easily fake without a lot of practise—and Ruth was given no advance warning of the test.

- Her auditory (EEG) evoked responses to clicks disappeared if she hallucinated her 'daughter' putting her hands over her (i.e. Ruth's) ears.
- Her skin showed red marks in appropriate places if an apparition 'slapped' her.
- If she hallucinated sucking a lemon, she salivated more than if she simply 'imagined' sucking one, though less than if citric acid granules were put on her tongue.
- If an apparition of her 'daughter' placed an imaginary heater in front of her hand, the skin temperature of the hand increased
- Types of hallucination that would have done so had they been 'real' did *not* influence her pupillary diameter or enable smooth pursuit eye movements.

These results certainly provide quite good 'objective' evidence that her reports of the apparent reality of the hallucinations were accurate. I guess the most appropriate conclusion to draw from all this is that Ruth had or has[3] a superb talent for controlling the perceptual dynamics within her brain, but was unable to influence automatic routines like retinal responses, pupillary reflexes and reflex eye movements. Her talent was, in its own way, at least equal to that shown by Olympic class gymnasts for controlling their motor dynamics. Thanks to Morton Schatzman's care and insight, we can see clearly how Ruth's extraordinary perceptual phenomena are expressions of very rare, but essentially normal, psychodynamics.

And the whole story provides an object lesson in how what appear to be normal dynamics, with nothing 'spooky' about them, can generate very remarkable phenomenology. Brain dynamics can produce amazing effects — but they are just brain dynamics, so far as one can see. We'll need to remember that when we come to look at some of the other evidence. People, it seems, can produce what seem to them to be perfectly realistic 'apparitions' on the basis of normal,

---

[3] Schatzman was admirably careful to protect Ruth's anonymity, which is perhaps one reason why we know less about her husband than one might wish from the point of view of constructing a clinical and family case history. The chances are she's still alive, of course.

common or garden brain mechanisms behaving in an unusual way. Moreover, as Ruth showed and good hypnotic subjects who are 'age regressed' continue to show, people can re-create dynamic states that existed in their distant pasts with quite astonishing accuracy.

So Ruth's story can be viewed as a demonstration of how very far out of the ordinary what appear to be ordinary brain dynamics can stretch ... except — actually, there were a couple of possible exceptions in her story that might point to an incursion of something not so easily explained on any mundane basis. They don't amount to enough to get excited about, but maybe they shouldn't be dismissed altogether. One concerned her much-loved Grandmother. After Ruth had learned how to control her apparitions, Grandmother became ill and was expected to die fairly soon, but not immediately. Ruth booked to go home, hoping to get there in time to say her goodbyes. However, before she could leave, an apparition of Grandmother appeared without Ruth having had any say in the matter, apparently to say *her* goodbyes, at a time that roughly coincided with Grandmother going into a coma six hours before her death. And when, after the death, Ruth tried to get the apparition back, she couldn't.

The other hard to explain (but not *too* difficult to explain away) episode happened when Ruth was practising producing apparitions of herself at home. She was sitting in a chair and had put the apparition on a sofa. Allegedly her husband then came into the room and both saw and heard the figure on the sofa, mistaking it for the real Ruth until he noticed her sitting in the chair. He was subsequently quite 'twitchy' about the whole episode, she said, which is perhaps understandable! Is there any chance that he may have been right to feel spooked, or was it all a simple mistake down to poor lighting and maybe a fraught atmosphere at home with all the talk of apparitions and Ruth's preoccupation with them? Perhaps other sources of evidence may help us to decide.

Throwing a Spanner into the Works

If I were to spray the processor and RAM of my laptop with water from an atomiser, it would very likely stop working and I'd have to buy another. One thing it certainly would not do is switch from displaying the page I'm typing at the moment to showing an excerpt from *Othello*, for example, or *The Merchant of Venice*. Yet brains can and do behave exactly like that. Put certain drugs into their blood supply, drugs which alter synaptic activity and thus disrupt their normal patterns of connectivity rather as water in an Intel processor short-circuits its internal connections, and the owners of those brains can enter wholly different realms of experience.

Many of the drugs with the most dramatic effects (e.g. LSD, psilocybin, mescaline) mainly affect synaptic receptors for the neurotransmitter serotonin. They have complex effects which haven't been fully worked out, boosting some serotonin receptors and blocking others. In any case, drug effects don't seem to be all that closely dependent on the precise neurochemical details of their actions; for example Salvinorin A, some of whose effects are not unlike those of LSD, is a booster of kappa-opioid receptors, while phencyclidine (angel dust) is mainly a blocker of glutamine receptors of the NMDA sub-type. You can throw quite a wide range of different types of spanner into the works and, instead of grinding to a halt, they switch to making new experiential products. That ought to be capable of telling us something about how the works are controlled, so it's worth going into a bit more detail.

The 'spanner' I want to look at more closely is *Ayahuasca*, originally a South American brew but now popular (in some quarters) throughout the Western world. It's a good choice for two reasons; first, its effects have been described in meticulous detail by psychologist Benny Shanon (2002); second one of its active ingredients is dimethyltryptamine (DMT), a molecule that we all synthesize for ourselves, although it doesn't normally reach more than trace concentrations in our brains as it is quickly destroyed by enzymes called MAOs. It is structurally very similar to serotonin and LSD, and its pharmacological properties are similar to those of LSD. We'll get to why containing DMT makes ayahuasca a good choice for discussion in *this* section when we get to the *next* section. The other active ingredients in ayahuasca are harmaline alkaloids, which both block the MAO enzymes that would normally destroy swallowed DMT before it got anywhere near the brain, and have some hallucinogenic properties of their own. Perhaps we should think of ayahuasca as more of a neural sledgehammer than a spanner! But, unpleasant though it is to take,[4] it isn't known to cause long-term damage.

In his book, Shanon describes data from some 2500 ayahuasca imbibing sessions — 67 of them his own and the remainder elicited in the course of structured interviews with other participants. The sessions were held in a wide variety of settings, albeit mostly South American ones, and participants were from a wide variety of national, racial, social and educational backgrounds. Hallucinations under the influence of the drugs were predominantly, but not exclusively, visual. Their content was very varied, and the frequency of particular types varied between groups of participants. Overall, however, the five most frequently hallucinated types of phenomena (from the 27 categories that Shanon identified) were, in order of frequency: 'objects of art and magic'; 'mammals' (especially black panthers and jaguars); reptiles (especially snakes); 'divine beings'; 'royal and religious figures' (taken from Shanon, 2002, Table 7, pp. 428-9). Other categories of particular interest included 'ancient civilisations', 'history', 'mythology', 'scenes of light', 'personal biography'.

The scenes are often dreamlike, though allegedly far more vivid and realistic than most dreams; for instance:

> A scene in Europe in the sixteenth or perhaps the eighteenth century. Knights are riding. They are mounted upon magic motorcycles full of colour and light. All is like a cartoon and enchanted. It is all part of big [sic] procession.

[4] *Ayahuasca* is said to taste absolutely disgusting, and commonly causes vomiting and diarrhoea. Partly because of this, it's apparently best to take nothing but water for at least 24 hours before swallowing the brew. And of course it should only be taken under experienced supervision, as short-term risks to the 'spaced out' are high.

> There are also small dwarfs there. Two of them are holding a banner with the insignia of the sovereign (Shanon, 2002, p. 139).

However, the states in which they manifest are not sleep-like — or so at least the following report suggests:

> All during this walk [across the hall where the session was taking place] I saw myself passing through a celestial palace of incredible beauty... Noblemen wearing pointed, steeple-like mitres roamed around... With my gaze forward and upwards I was fully immersed in the celestial palace, which was experienced as totally real. When I lowered my head I saw the hall of the session as it was (*Ibid.*, p. 80).

The main appeal of ayahuasca sessions doesn't lie in seeing wonderful hallucinations, according to Shanon, so much as in the feelings of cosmic understanding, love and universal beauty that are often achieved during them. A regular participant in sessions is said to have described them as 'divine banquets', and Shanon tells us that he himself experienced them as spiritually educational and mentally cleansing.

While some sense of personal identity is usually retained in these sessions, there can be distortions of body image; for example a feeling of limbs becoming detached, or of one's whole body floating above the ground. A general weakening of boundaries is apparently quite common, with feelings of unusual 'connectedness' with surroundings. Shanon comments that sometimes, when singing in a group during an ayahuasca session, 'the group becomes a kind of a single organism that acts in a precise and highly concentrated fashion' (*op. cit.*, p. 201). In terms of the ideas set out in chapter 4, it looks as though the brew affects the 'core' state space dimensions that contribute to the sense of 'self', weakening or eliminating some of them so that a 'group mind' can more easily form. Occasionally, people have reported loss of all sense of self, though consciousness remained — could that be a state in which all the bodily dimensions that usually contribute to dynamic state spaces are temporarily absent? It's tempting to think so, at least.

There are alterations in the experience of time, which aren't easily described but seem to fall into three main categories. The first sounds like the sort of experience we all have when a whole lot of exciting things are happening in quick succession. We pack a lot into each moment and are surprised when we check with our watches and see how little time has passed. Ayahuasca often produces this effect, presumably mediated by all the action-packed hallucinations and cognitions that it induces. The second alteration is to retain a normal temporal frame of reference oneself, but to feel that one is observing events taking place in a different time — the visions of 'ancient history' and the like. People apparently feel that they are still anchored in their own 'now', but are viewing a quite different 'now'. It's not altogether clear from Shanon's account whether this is any different from the experiences we all have when watching some historical drama in the cinema, but he seems to feel that it is not quite the same in a way that's hard to explain; as I read him, he suggests that the viewed 'now' is stronger and more real in some sense for the ayahuasceros than for a cinema audience.

The third type of altered time is definitely not like anything that we ordinarily experience. It's a feeling of being 'outside time', in a realm 'beyond past, present and future', where 'everything that has ever happened, as well as everything that will ever happen, has an equal temporal status'. The latter phrase sounds to me like a pretty good description of the 'block universe' implied by special relativity (see chapter 7)! Nevertheless, perceptions of change are still present while in this state, says Shanon. Aldous Huxley's friend, Christopher Mayhew, offered an analogy for the experience — induced in his case by peyote — that Shanon thought 'illuminating':

> When we take off from an airport at night, we are aware of individual runway lights flashing past in succession. But when [we] look down a little later, we see them all existing together motionless. It is not self-contradictory to say that the lights flashed past in succession and that they exist

The Wilder Shores of Experience 173

together motionless. Everything depends on the standpoint of the observer (Mayhew, 1961).

Overall, the ayahuasca experience comes across to me as a lot harder to explain than Ruth's stories. She was dealing in essentially normal percepts, memories and behavioural predictions. There *was* some remarkable jugglery with time, shown especially in the resurrection of long past dynamic states, but we know from hypnotic regression in general, and from the phenomenon of 'flashback',[5] that that's something within the behavioural repertoire of many people's brains. Her main talent seems to have been an unusually well-developed ability to exclude, from the relevant state spaces of her mentality, dimensions that would normally have been contributed from the environment; substituting for them ones provided by her own brain and memories. And that ability can be seen as an emergent property of her brain dynamics; there seems no need to infer that her attractors might have taken on a life of their own, or that her consciousness was up to anything totally weird.

But the ayahuasceros are plunged into worlds of experience that are often way outside anything in their own past experience. Amazonian Indians have no experience of visiting Russian cities; Europeans who stay in Europe don't meet jaguars prowling in their surroundings; nobody has ever transformed into an animal or a bird. All the same, they can and do have these experiences under the influence of the brew. Dreams occasionally provide pale reflections of similar experiences. But for most of us they rarely, and for some people probably never, have the creativity, novelty, vividness and apparent reality of experiences available to nearly all participants in ayahuasca sessions, who can sometimes, as in the example given earlier, combine worlds

---

[5] 'Flashback' refers to when someone suddenly 'relives' some past, usually traumatic, event. Psychiatrists of my generation sometimes tried deliberately to bring about this sort of re-living in the course of a treatment named 'abreaction'. The intensity and vividness of the reliving were often extremely impressive.

of fantasy with awareness of the real environment.[6] As Ruth showed, it is quite possible to integrate hallucinations seamlessly into the real world, but to combine immersive awareness of a fantasy environment with an independent awareness of the real one seems a different order of achievement.

The drug 'sledgehammer' appears capable of triggering the appearance of a whole lot of new attractors that operate in a surprisingly well integrated way. Could the remarkable creativity of the hallucinatory and other experiences be down to the multidimensionality (see chapter 3) of attractor space and its instantiation in fractal patterns of neural activity (as mentioned earlier, fractals possess 'small world' properties)? If so, there would be a case for regarding the new attractors as being in a sense 'real', or at least as describing an aspect of reality able to drive the brains that harbour them. Similarly, the sophistication of the stories told in some of the experiences suggests that the new attractors are dancing to the tune of hierarchies of (also new) 'ruling attractors'. What enables the remarkable integration of all these dynamics? Perhaps the 'small world' properties of brain networks are sufficient on their own to account for the phenomena, but it's not obvious that they could do so. They would surely be more likely to generate chaotic incoherence than beautifully crafted, out-of-this-world experiences. Hard to believe that stuttering neural circuits, struggling to cope with drug-altered synaptic weightings, could be up to the job without some additional organizing principle. And the only candidates for the role of organizing principle are the attractors themselves.

These are no more than hints that attractors may share the sort of independent 'reality' that we allow to natural law — i.e. the ability to constrain the behaviour of physical systems

---

[6] I don't know of any reports of dreamers doing this. Environmental inputs that get through to them, a bell ringing for instance, generally either cause awakening or get incorporated into a dream narrative. So-called 'lucid' dreaming involves no more that an awareness that one is dreaming and sometimes an ability to choose what one wants to dream about. It doesn't include awareness of one's real environment.

while apparently having some sort of existence that is independent of the systems in which they manifest. And, apart from the hints that attractors have a 'life' of their own, there's also a puzzle. What does the experience of being 'outside time' signify? It doesn't seem to be the same as the loss of the sense of self (for which we could offer a tentative explanation—i.e. exclusion of state space dimensions from brain/body 'core' dynamics). But perhaps it could be a feeling that arises from consciousness getting disconnected somehow from body clocks, rather as loss of self may arise from consciousness getting disconnected from proprioceptive and other somatic inputs. On the other hand, if consciousness is a product of 'jugglery with time', maybe the experience is telling us something more profound. So far as I can see, there's not even the slightest hint in what has been described so far as to how one might begin trying to decide between these and related alternatives. Let's move on to the next topic, therefore, in the hope that it may get us a bit further.

Near Death Experience

This is a topic which has been battered almost to death over the last thirty years, one is tempted to feel, by a torrent of popular books, magazine articles and the like. The finding oneself out of one's body, the tunnel, the ascent into the light, the encounter with 'spirits' of one sort or another, followed by the return, have become almost as much of a cliché in popular culture as were Mesmeric 'passes' and their consequences a hundred and sixty years ago. However, it does raise fascinating questions, nearly all of which remain unanswered.

There is now fairly general agreement about a number of important points:

    a) the experience is quite common—some components of it are reported by around 10% to 20% of people who have needed intensive care, though a 'full house' of phenomena, including 'life review', is less common at maybe around 4%;

b) it can happen at all ages from childhood on, but no-one has yet identified any pre-disposing factors that make it more likely to occur — sex, education, religious belief, etc. don't seem to influence the probability of getting an NDE;

c) it has been reported from all periods of history and all cultures for which we have records, so is clearly not a product of Western culture or medical practices;

d) although the experience overall appears to be independent of culture, particular details are culture related — e.g. how the 'tunnel' stage is pictured, which mythical figures are encountered;

e) seemingly identical experience has been reported by people who have not been near death or even unwell.

The biggest puzzle of all, I'd say, is to do with how it gets remembered so vividly. Recall of NDEs is often reminiscent of 'flashbulb' memory — i.e. the experience gets burned into people's memories and remains long after many associated memories have faded. It's a quality attested by the fairly well-established fact that having an NDE is likely to produce a long lasting shift in people's attitudes and values; more of a shift than is produced by simply having a life-threatening illness by itself. This fact alone more or less rules out traditional, soul-based explanations. In order for an NDE to be remembered and reported to others, it must have been recorded in neural memories. Whatever one's views about the nature of subjective memory, the reporting at least must certainly depend on neural machinery. But, if the 'soul' was far from its body wandering in some empyrean realm, how could the recording have taken place? If attached enough to record memories, it must presumably have been in the same spatio-temporal continuum as its brain after all. Maybe it was only partially detached from its body, someone might suggest; the 'silver cord' connecting soul and body that is occasionally reported by NDEers carries the memories from one to the other, it might be claimed. But then how come the memories conveyed through this tenuous connection are more vivid than when the 'soul' is still fully attached? The dualistic 'soul' concept doesn't seem to make much sense when memory of NDEs is taken into account, but neither do the more neuroscientific suggestions that have been offered, and partly for much the same reason.

There are a whole range of suggestions about what 'causes' NDEs. Lack of oxygen to the brain, endorphin release, temporal lobe disturbances, and so on and so forth. All can account for some aspects of many NDEs, and maybe they do often play significant parts. No-one knows which causes are most often relevant, nor exactly which aspects of an NDE they are responsible for. Obviously oxygen lack is unlikely to be relevant in people who have the experience but aren't near death; similarly it's not easy to see that temporal lobe disturbances could be a primary cause in many cases (they are surely more likely to be a secondary consequence, if they occur at all). To save profitless debate, I'll assume here that Rick Strassman's[7] (2001) hypothesis is correct and that the immediate cause of NDEs is DMT accumulation in the brain—for whatever reason. According to this theory, an NDE is basically an 'acid trip' caused by the same chemical that is the main active ingredient of ayahuasca. Ayahuasceros get it from the brew they imbibe, whereas NDEers simply up their own normal production of it or fail to destroy it as they normally would. As the phenomenology of ayahuasca experience does overlap with NDE,[8] though there are some differences, the theory seems to me to account for more of the phenomena than others,[9] and of

---

[7] Strassman is an American psychiatrist who, in the 1990s, studied the effects of injections of varying doses of DMT on sixty volunteers; the volunteers were already experienced drug users and curious about DMT.

[8] For example, ayahuasceros frequently see animals, but NDEers don't. Ayahasceros often see visions of cities populated by strangers, but NDEers typically encounter people known to them. Generally, NDEs seem more 'personal' and stereotyped in their overall form than ayahuasca experience.

[9] It is only a theory. So far as I know, no-one has ever checked brain DMT concentrations in intensive care patients to see whether those with higher levels are more likely to have an NDE. It would be a

course does not preclude endorphin release or whatever from also contributing. How complete is a theory of this sort when it comes to explaining the phenomena? As it happens, not very complete.

The first problem is with the 'out of the body' state when people realise that they have left their own bodies and are witnessing events at the crash scene or in the emergency room, as if they were bystanders. Out of body experiences are not that uncommon and can be spontaneous, or due to trauma, or drug induced. Indeed they can be artificially induced in 'virtual reality' set-ups. Ordinary brain dynamics are quite good at producing them, it appears. The trouble with NDE-associated ones is that they occur in severely traumatized, sometimes apparently unconscious people, but they nevertheless often integrate the experience remarkably well with what is *actually* going on in the emergency room or wherever. Use of equipment is described in realistic detail; nurses actions and conversations are reported accurately; the behaviour of relatives is described. There are far too many authenticated accounts of this sort to dismiss. Although ayahuasceros can integrate out-of-body experience with the actual environment, it has to be remembered that they have full, if not normal, use of all their faculties while doing so. How can someone lying comatose on a hospital trolley manage the same trick?

Wonderful, heavenly lights are perhaps understandable in terms of an 'acid trip', and so is meeting mythical figures in beautiful surroundings. Ayahuasceros often do this, even though they rarely or never traverse a 'tunnel' in order to get there. They meet deceased relatives and the like less often than NDEers, but maybe that's something to do with the very different settings in which the two types of experience occur. What about the 'life review' that a proportion of NDEers report? Shanon found that 'personal biography' was a theme that cropped up in ayahuasca sessions; it was not among the most frequent themes, but wasn't too far

---

difficult study to organize, but might be possible in people with brain trauma, for instance, who were having lumbar punctures for other reasons.

down the list. Apparently it often seems to take the form of brief 'snapshots' of past experiences, while the typical NDE 'life review', in contrast, covers pretty much the *whole* of a person's life; and some reviewers claim to have experienced events, not from their own points of view, but from the points of view of people with whom they had interacted.

It is worth re-emphasizing that ayahuasceros are generally in good health when they take the brew, but many NDEers are severely traumatized, confused or even comatose to all appearances. Yet the latter suddenly switch to a state in which they claim to have experienced unusual *clarity* of consciousness, and which they remember when most of the rest of their traumatic episode is either totally forgotten or has faded into a blur. So there seem to be at least three, probably related, questions about NDEers that don't appear to be covered by the analogies with ayahuasceros and thus, by implication, cannot be put down solely to DMT accumulation — or probably to any other purely 'physical' factors :

- How do they get hold of the information needed to integrate their out of body experiences with goings-on in their actual environments?
- How do they sometimes manage to achieve such remarkably well-organized experiences as those exemplified by 'life review', while apparently confused or even unconscious?
- How do they experience unusual clarity of consciousness and memory while having an NDE, especially when this occurs along with confusion and poor memory immediately before and after.

So far as I can see, there are two stock responses to questions of this sort. One is to say that Descartes must have been right after all with his claim that *res cogitans* is a separate 'substance' from the *res extensa* of our brains. But this is merely a variant of the 'soul' hypothesis, that the spirit of the NDEer must have left its brain and visited the suburbs of paradise. As we saw earlier, that is hardly a tenable position. Another response is to either ignore the questions altogether, or blame the messenger and say that reports of these experiences are untrue. The problem here is that reports keep coming in; they appear to be as reliable and well replicated as any other reports of experience of any type. Prejudice aside, there is no more reason to doubt that the reports accurately reflect an NDEer's experience than there is to doubt someone's account of what they experienced during their last holiday in the Caribbean. There is a more sophisticated version of the 'untrue' response, however, which is to say that the reports represent a type of false memory syndrome.

Could false memory provide the answer? In other words, could the alleged NDEs be constructed later when a person came to ruminate and fantasize over their experiences while ill? No such theory is adequate. The 'flashbulb' clarity of NDE memories is there right from the start and is not a gradual build-up. People, including children who have never heard of NDEs and therefore couldn't fantasize about them, still get them; atheists and materialists are as likely to get an NDE as people who believe they have a soul.[10] Maybe, a diehard might object, there is a type of 'false memory' that forms pretty well instantaneously; maybe you don't need a lot of time and day-dreaming to construct every type of false memory. Well, I think one would have a hard time distinguishing hypothetical 'instantaneous false memory' from consciousness itself, which takes us straight back to the questions listed above. There doesn't seem to be any legitimate way of avoiding them.

Might the questions relate to the picture of mentality and consciousness we've been drawing and, if so, how? We've found quite a lot of hints, hitherto, that dynamic state spaces and what goes on in them have some sort of independent reality, and even an appearance of primacy at times, when it comes to mentality. And, according the view that we took of Velmans' 'reflexive monism' (see chapters 2 and 4), the ones

---

[10] Some Christians who get NDEs are said to be surprised by them because they apparently conflict with the doctrine that resurrection won't occur till the last trump sounds. However, I think it's reasonable to suppose that, if NDEs were a product of fantasy, they'd still be more likely to occur in those who expect an afterlife than in those who don't.

relevant to conscious mentality include dimensions contributed by the environment.

It's possible to speculate therefore that, in the early stages of an NDE, environmental dimensions become predominant, displacing those normally contributing to the bodily 'self' (proprioception, 'gut feelings', aches and pains, etc. etc.). This might happen for all sorts of reasons; the ayahuasca experience shows that drugs can produce similar effects, so it could be down primarily to DMT and/or endorphins, or maybe to some sort of 'shock' reaction or protective neural reflex. The outcome is that the 'self' loses any bodily distress and appears to displace into the environment—finds 'itself' floating up near the ceiling or wherever. And the awareness of what's going on comes from a sort of hyperacuity of residual sensation. Remember the people are not actually dead; there's still information getting through to their brains. Without all the normal clutter from somatic inputs, any environmental information that does get through, plus whatever the brain constructs and predicts from it, is going to have a much better chance of making it into conscious experience. To put it another way, the conscious 'channel' can deal only with a minute proportion of the total amount of information reaching the brain and, when it is less occupied with its own body, it is presumably going to be a lot more sensitive to any remaining environmental inputs.

Despite perhaps appearing to be comatose, therefore, people may actually be *more* sensitive than normal, for a time at least, to what is going on around them, and thus able to construct conscious representations of it from apparently insignificant clues. But this suggestion implies that people can retain a sense of 'self' when relevant aspects of their mentality are deprived of what normally seems to contribute most to the sense of self—i.e. all those 'core' somatic inputs. That people can be aware of 'themselves' in the absence of the normal bodily background hum of sensation seems to be another 'brute fact'. Presumably memories, habitual thought patterns, habits of emotional evaluation and the like contribute more to the sense of self than we commonly suppose. Indeed, judging by the NDEers claims, our sense of self can become enhanced in some respects when we lose the somatic clutter.

So the answer to the first question, I suggest, is that NDEers get the information they need for producing an integrated picture of themselves floating in a realistic environment, via an enhanced ability to make conscious use of those sensory clues that still reach their brains.[11] However, this suggestion makes sense only if we regard the 'state space' picture of mentality as having its own, at least semi-independent, reality (according to the definition of reality given at the end of chapter 1). Something other than basic neural machinery is surely needed to maintain a sense of self and to give that self such an unusual, but coherent, point of view in a realistic environment. Moving on to the next questions, what about the remarkable coherence and clarity of the later stages of (some) NDEs?

An explanation for these features that may make some sort of sense involves proposing that the attractors in an NDEer's brain, all those memories and habits contributing to the sense of self, take on what is to all appearances a life of their own that is entirely independent of their environment. They self-organise into producing the remarkable experi-

---

[11] I'm a little uneasy about this explanation because there are occasional reports of people gaining access to information, while 'out of their bodies' that couldn't possibly have reached them by any normal means. However, these reports, especially the one about the shoe spotted on an outside window ledge that is so often quoted, seem to have quite a bit of 'urban myth' about them. Attempts to prove paranormal access to information, by hiding pictures above the ceilings of intensive care units for instance, have so far come to nothing. Charles Tart's much quoted case of a 'Miss Z' who once spotted some hidden random numbers while having one of her frequent Out of Body Experiences (her health was good and they were not NDEs), is the only similar one I know of that's half-way convincing, and that dates from the 1960s I believe (Tart, 1997). But maybe there's more going on than the explanation suggests. There have also been fascinating claims that people born blind are able to see 'normally' during NDEs which, if true, would require extensions at the very least to the explanation I offer. Some of the ideas that we shall be looking at soon might be consistent with 'add-ons' of one sort or another, but in the absence of compelling evidence, I prefer to stick with the explanation as it is for the time being.

ences, and they do so with a purity and clarity unimpeded by all those messy somatic and environmental inputs that normally get in the way of such qualities. And, since the experiences *are* (early stages of) new attractor/memories, they get remembered with a corresponding clarity.

That people tend to have broadly similar types of near-death experience can be put down to the fact that we all share broadly similar types of attractor[12] because our brains are built along similar lines and human nature is much the same everywhere. The personal stuff, on the other hand, concerning encounters with people one knows and the detail in any 'life review', originates from personal attractor/memories acquired over a lifetime. The coherence of the self-organisation is remarkable, however; especially the ability some NDEers have shown to represent past happenings from *other people's* point of view. Ruth demonstrated that this is something within the repertoire of normal brains when she let herself be 'taken over' by her father's apparition, or indeed her own past selves (for childhood selves are very different from adult ones). All the same, I find it very hard to conceive that traumatised brains could manage to produce any such degree of integration from the bottom up, so to speak. The normal result of trauma is confusion and inability to follow any single line of thought or imagination clearly or in detail. How could shocked brains possibly display such a rare and unusual talent for what amounts to total empathy, if it were all simply down to the physics and electro-chemistry of neurons? The experiences really do seem to be telling us that, at least in the NDE context, 'attractors rule'!

To sum up, the ayahuasca experience certainly hinted that attractors and their associated state spaces have a 'reality' of their own, and NDE seems to reinforce the hint. Although a lot of the latter can be explained by analogy with ayahuasca, this does not appear to apply to all of it. And the parts that couldn't be explained by analogy imply a quite

---

[12] In this sort of connection such attractors can be thought of as Jungian archetypes— features of our mental landscapes shared by the whole of humanity.

strongly realistic role for attractors. But none of this seems to have implications for our other quest; the search for evidence for the existence of consciousness fields which could perhaps, so we argued earlier (chapter 7), be local products of brain function in ordinary 4-D space-time.

Because consciousness definitely relates to 4-D space-time, maybe one should say that hypothetical 'temporal fields' comprising it must be entirely separate from attractors 'existing' in their multidimensional spaces, so we shouldn't expect evidence about the latter to tell us anything about the former. However saying that would be wrong. We can expect the two to relate to one another because we viewed brains as 'mapping' attractor space into fractal/holographic neural activities (chapter 6). But any mapping is a two way process. Memories formed in brains become part of the overall 'attractor landscape', and we regarded the neural machinery associated with very short-term memory as either responsible for the existence of the 'temporal field', or at least responsible for its manifestation. Therefore attractors and the type of consciousness field proposed, if it exists, must be linked despite occupying conceptually different sorts of space. How might their relationship manifest itself; what sort of evidence should we be looking for?

The difficulty we have in answering these questions is due to having pictured our consciousness field as associated with a broken temporal symmetry. There was no reason to expect it to manifest in objectively observable particles ('qualions' are purely subjective) or some new force of nature. Given such origins, it's probably reasonable to suppose that the field might show up in temporal anomalies of some sort, although there is no obvious way of predicting *what* sort. Maybe the experience of being 'outside time', occasionally reported in both ayahuasca and near-death experience, has something to do with it, or maybe not; there's no way of knowing. We need to explore a bit further and see if we can come up with anything more definite.

Deathbed Experiences

Since thinking about *near* death experience has helped to firm up the evidence we got from ayahuasca, it would make sense to take a look at *actual* death experience. But of course there's a problem — dead people don't tell tales (unless you go along with the beliefs of the mediums described in chapter 1). However, witnesses and others do tell tales of the dead and dying. Some of these stories have been retold by Peter Fenwick,[13] a neuropsychiatrist who specialized in EEG studies before his retirement, and his wife Elizabeth. They collected accounts from the literature (and described their surprise at finding that the relevant medical literature is particularly sparse compared to other sources), from anecdotes that people sent to them and from structured interviews with forty nurses and other carers for the dying. They described it all in a recent book (Fenwick and Fenwick, 2008).

Since, on average, nearly one hundred people die every *hour* in the UK alone, it's perhaps not surprising that strange coincidences crop up in relation to death; they could be expected to occur by chance and get remembered because it's such an emotionally charged event. The Fenwicks can't directly refute sceptics who argue thus (nor do they attempt to do so), though the series of structured interviews that they obtained strongly suggested that weird events are actually quite common, not statistical rarities. Moreover, some of the events they described were of a type that could not easily be attributed to statistical vagaries or coincidence of any sort; also, many of them were *meaningful*, which strongly suggests that they had *something* to do with mentality and consciousness, despite the difficulty of knowing what that 'something' might be.

One allegedly frequent occurrence is that the dying either report seeing, or behave as if they are seeing, apparitions. This usually happens shortly before their deaths. The 'visitors' are often interpreted as beneficent entities come to take

---

[13] He was the specialist who measured Ruth's visual and auditory evoked potentials for Morton Schatzman.

the dying person away, by both carers and the dying themselves (when they are able to offer any views on the matter). In Western societies such apparitions are generally of deceased relatives and friends, but apparently in India a mythical figure, such as a 'messenger from the god of death', is a more likely visitor. 'But surely', you may point out, 'dying people are often confused or delirious and only too likely to have hallucinations. So what's the big deal?'

This would be fair comment were it not for the fact that the 'visitors' can appear to people who are not at all gaga before their deaths. If, on the other hand, they are confused or even apparently comatose, the visitations tend to coincide with a period of lucidity—of the dying person being temporarily, and often surprisingly as far as onlookers are concerned, 'back to their old selves'. And the visitations can give remarkably accurate predictions of time of death, which hallucinations of delirium certainly can't. For example, here are a couple of reports from nurses:

> I was attending a patient with a fellow nurse ... [he] asked us to stand one on each side of him because he wanted to thank us for looking after him. He then looked over my shoulder towards the window and said 'Hang on, I will be with you in a moment, I just want to thank these nurses...'. He repeated himself a couple of times, then died (Fenwick and Fenwick, 2008 p. 30).

> One lady was fading at the age of 97, just slipping away ... {We heard her talking] and she said it was [to] her sister Alice who had died six months previously. She said Alice would come for her the next day at 2.30 pm... Just before 2.30 p.m. [the next day] , she opened her eyes briefly, whispered 'Alice' and passed away peacefully (*Ibid.*, p. 42).

As Ruth's example showed, seeing realistic apparitions is not by itself an indication of anything spooky occurring — nor does it necessarily imply that a person has some brain abnormality or psychiatric illness. However, when old people, who have probably had absolutely no previous experience of anything similar, see realistic apparitions in their final hours that give accurate advance information about their time of death, clearly something hard to understand is going on. And the puzzles don't stop there. Real, live visitors have also occasionally reported seeing apparitions associated with a dying person, perhaps in much the same way as Ruth's husband was said to have seen the apparition that she had created of herself. The most convincing accounts of this type were from children, who were not surprised by other 'visitors' they saw by a sickbed ... until they discovered that their parents had seen no such persons.

Other phenomena that have been described by relatives of the dying include experience of lights and feelings of overwhelming compassion and the like, almost as if they had somehow been sharing in an NDE. One of the most commonly reported types of experience is a feeling of having been visited by a dying or dead friend or relative who was 'on their way out'. It most often occurs when someone is half awake, having been asleep, but can happen in clear consciousness. Such visits are usually experienced as comforting and take all sorts of forms — seeing a figure, hearing a voice, receiving a characteristic caress, or just 'knowing' that the person is there. No doubt many of these experiences can be put down to worry or coincidence. But some are more puzzling, especially those involving people who knew nothing of their relative's illness or death before the 'visit'.

Could relatives' experiences be down to the sort of 'group mentality' discussed in chapter 4? Maybe there is something about the fraught emotional atmosphere surrounding a death that makes it easier for people to merge, so to speak, with the mind of someone who is dying and share in their hallucinations and other mental states. The problem with any such explanation is that, for group mentality to occur, people have to come to share a large number of state space dimensions for some reason. They all have to be attending a football match, for example, and get swept up into the scenes going on out there on the field as well as into the emotion of the moment. But visitors of the dying simply aren't in that sort of situation. The relatives' perspectives on the world are totally different from those of someone on their deathbed, and their emotions are no doubt usually very different, too. There's probably no chance whatsoever that their state spaces could merge into a 'group mind' based on a shared state space.

So we're left with (at least) two huge puzzles. The dying commonly see apparitions that can be regarded as harbingers of death; apparitions that sometimes give extremely accurate information about its timing. Relatives report a range of strange experiences, some at least of which appear to transcend ordinary time, space and causation. These experiences, according to the Fenwicks, usually carry meaning and can often be regarded as driven by the needs and wishes of the dead or dying person, not by those of the people 'visited'.

If the Fenwicks are correct in thinking that meaning is both central to many of these occurrences and is conveyed from the dead or dying to the visitee, then we can at once rule out any idea that 'quantum entanglement' might be directly responsible for them. People trying to account for this sort of phenomenon often do point to such entanglement as offering the only possible 'scientific' basis for it. However, as pointed out in chapter 4, entanglement can convey 'information' only if that is strictly defined so as to exclude all meaning. Thus, it could enable communication from the dying to their friend or relative only if the recipient were somehow able to add their own meaning to whatever information they received. And, in some at least of the reported cases, there is no plausible 'normal' channel to allow such addition. Entanglement might contribute to an adequate explanation, but is not sufficient on its own to fully account for such phenomena.

Equally, state spaces and attractor landscapes, however 'real' they are taken to be, aren't sufficient on their own to explain the phenomena. There is simply no conceivable way in which they could by themselves provide a basis for transfer of meaning from one mind to another. The most they can do is provide a basis for meaning shared in a 'group mind', but this is possible only when the individual minds are all involved in a common dynamic, which is not the case in relation to 'visitations' and similar happenings.

However, a consciousness field envisaged as a *carrier* of attractors might just do the trick. A modulated 'qualion' field, for example, *is* a translation of a brain's objective, spatio-temporal, neural attractor instantiations into a subjective tempero-spatial format. It therefore does incorporate representations of attractors and could be said to 'carry' them. However, in order to affect the brains of visitees, any such fields originating in the brains of the dying would require non-locality in relativistic space-time, plus an ability to affect physical systems. Are such properties too fantastic to be worth considering?

We're back to hints again. The fact that the dying can be conscious of apparitions conveying accurate information about their impending departure certainly suggests that something about their awareness is not entirely bound to relativistic time — though one can't put it more strongly than that. Similarly, the apparent fact that they can convey unexpected but meaningful information to loved ones far away has to be an indication that there is something about consciousness that is, or can be, independent of relativistic space-time. Of course one can always deny the claims that such things ever happen, but I can see no adequate grounds for doing so, other than in statistical arguments about coincidence and the like which don't appear to hold water in quite a wide range of cases.

Perhaps the major sticking-point for many of us, when it comes to endorsing any such notion, has to do with the implication that this ethereal 'consciousness field' must be thought capable of affecting physical systems like brains if it is to transfer meaningful information. And it has to do so without being a physical field of any known type. All the same, there is evidence that *something* can have meaningful effects on physical systems, the best of which pertains to clocks stopping or otherwise misbehaving at the precise time of death. 'Coincidence!' you may say. Well, maybe — but how about the following anecdote told by someone who had called on his uncle to convey news of his father's death earlier that morning (at 3.15 am). The uncle already knew of it because:

> ... he said no-one had telephoned him, but told me to look at the clock on the mantelpiece—it was stopped at 3.15 am, as was indeed his own wristwatch, his bedside clock and all other clocks in the house. There was even an LED display, I think on a radio, flashing at 3.15 (Fenwick and Fenwick, 2008, p. 135).

The probability of that happening by chance is clearly vanishingly tiny. Equally, no ordinary physical field or event is going to selectively interfere with a variety of different types of clock, while apparently having no other noticeable effects. So one is left with choices about how to view the anecdote; maybe the nephew was lying about the whole episode; maybe the uncle had already heard of the death and had run around stopping all his clocks for unknown reasons; or maybe some non-local aspect of mentality can indeed affect physical systems to convey meaning. Take your pick! People do lie at times about what they have experienced or done, though less often than sceptics and conspiracy theorists like to claim. On the other hand, anomalous but meaningful events associated with the dying are said to occur rather frequently. Those with lots of experience of terminal care think of some types of event, particularly holding conversations with apparitions just before death, as being almost routine. Until we have a better understanding of them, it would seem premature to decide that some anomalies may provide useful hints about what could be going on, while others should be dismissed as 'impossible'.

This chapter is all about looking for phenomena that might allow us to 'see' what underlies experience, in the sort of way that iron filings on a sheet of paper allowed Michael Faraday to picture the magnetic field. My own feeling is that NDEs provide a clear indication of the apparently independent role of attractors in determining the content of conscious experience. One can almost see the 'lines of force', extending from a highly organized 'dance' of attractors, which constrain traumatized brains into harbouring and remembering these wonderful experiences. The picture in relation to deathbed-associated experiences, on the other hand, is not nearly so clear. They do offer hints that consciousness may have field-like properties that are independent of relativistic space-time, but which nevertheless can have meaningful consequences for us in our ordinary spatio-temporal reality. However, there are certainly no visible 'lines of force' that one can identify. All appears to be shrouded in mystery. Is there any chance that a look at mystical experience, where consciousness is typically felt to be 'outside time', might help to firm up those hints? Let's see.

Mystical Experience

> The *Cloud*[14] author [writing in the mid-fourteenth century] ... felt that he had to persuade his contemporaries that mysticism is a living fact, not a phenomenon that ended centuries before (Fanning, 2001, p. 124).

> The brightness and light that appear before the [inward] gaze are so different from those of earth that the sun's rays seem quite dim by comparison ... It is as if we were to look at a very clear stream, running over a crystal bed, in which the sun was reflected, and then to turn [on opening our earthly eyes] to a very muddy brook, with an earthy bottom, running beneath a cloudy sky (St Teresa, 1957, p. 198).

Mystical experience is still felt by many to be something of concern only to people who lived long ago and/or religious zealots prone to hysteria. But we have less excuse nowadays for any such belief, for surveys (e.g. those conducted under the auspices of the Religious Experiences Research Centre, now based at the University of Wales, Lampeter) generally show that up to half the population claim to have had one or more experiences in the course of their lives that they have felt to be very extraordinary and deeply numinous in some way.

People often report the quality of clarity and 'light' that St Teresa describes in her analogy above, as indeed do many NDEers too. But, although mystical experience may overlap NDE, the two don't appear to be identical. For example, the phenomenology of mysticism is more variable than that of

---

[14] i.e. *The Cloud of Unknowing*, an English medieval mystical text by an unknown author, based on translations of much earlier writings.

NDE, often including feelings of union with the natural world or perceptions of its extreme beauty (see e.g. Marshall, 2005), whereas NDE is all about leaving everyday nature behind; and some types of mystical experience are allegedly more common in childhood whereas, nowadays at least, the reverse is true of NDEs.

I wrote '*allegedly* more common in childhood' as the surveys of frequency have all been conducted on adults, so far as I know. People are often reluctant to talk about their experience, partly for fear of being thought mad, partly because the experience itself is often felt to be sacred and not something to be lightly divulged to others. Most of us don't feel so responsible for our childhood selves, however, and we may therefore be more willing to admit to having had 'crazy' experiences then. Some self-acknowledged mystics (e.g. William Blake) did get their experiences from quite early childhood on; others (e.g. St Teresa herself) had to wait till they were adult.

The problem with religious mystics, as far as gathering evidence relevant to consciousness studies is concerned, is that their reports of experience, and probably the experiences themselves, are so heavily contaminated by their theological and other preconceptions. Christian mystics tend to see Christ everywhere; Buddhist mystical experiences tend to conform to their own philosophical views. Although there is a fashion at present to view the Christians as wrong and the Buddhists as more on the right path, it isn't clear, at least to me, that either group has a better claim to rightness.[15] Maybe the Buddhists are better at letting their experiences inform their philosophy, whereas Christians are more likely to let their theology distort their (reports of) experience, but the belief that this imbalance occurs surely has to be regarded as 'not proven' at present. There's a nice story about a Zen master who was asked by a student about

[15] Personally, if I were to have the temerity to award stars for probable 'rightness' to any particular religious group, I'd give most to the Sufis (followers of a mystical branch of Islam). The problem with extracting evidence from what they say is that they tend to wrap up their reports in such flowery, sometimes deliberately paradoxical, language that it's often hard to understand their meaning.

what happens after death. 'Why ask me?' said the master. 'Because you're a master' replied the student. 'Yes, but not a dead one' the master pointed out.

We'll take the hint and turn to the experience of those who have had it without prior expectations about what it 'should' be like. There are plenty of such reports available these days from people without strong religious or philosophical preconceptions. That doesn't mean that they are free from 'cultural' biases of one sort or another of course, but the effect of these is likely to be relatively muted. Commonly reported features include:

- Experiences of 'light', as in the St. Teresa example, which can take all sorts of forms.
- Alterations in the sense of self; people often describe feeling that they are somehow 'one' with the world out there, or even with the entire universe, or with God.
- Feelings of the profound meaningfulness of everything, sometimes expressed as an intense awareness of universal love and compassion.
- Alterations in the sense of time.
- Awarenesses of 'presences' or 'numinous entities'.

These experiences are usually remembered at least as clearly as NDEs, and their effect seems generally beneficial. People are often relieved by them of any existential angst that they may have been suffering, and are sometimes motivated to become more charitable in their dealings with others. But they are not without their dangers. It's very probable that they provided the driving force behind many, perhaps all, of the millenarian prophets who have created so much murder and mayhem down the centuries — and are still doing so. Society, one feels, is entirely right to treat such experiences, and the people who lay claim to them, with scepticism and caution. The feeling that mystical experience should not be talked about, often reported by experiencers themselves, is surely laudable; but unfortunately not everyone is so reticent. The combination of mystic experience, an over-inflated ego and a modicum of charisma can and has resulted in centuries of misery.

Be that as it may, the alterations in the sense of time, along with a greatly enhanced sense of the meaning of everything, are probably the two most relevant features as far as our enquiry is concerned. Paul Marshall (2005, p. 72) described the time alterations as follows:

> Although momentary, some experiences seem to endure for a long time, or have 'timeless' or 'eternal' character. Sometimes transformation and motion cease completely, or, expressed more abstractly, 'time stops'. Alternatively transformation persists but alters in quality; things change in a coordinated manner, integrated in the harmoniously transforming whole ... the world is experienced not only as an integrated, interconnected whole, but as a whole that develops in an integrated way ... The transforming world is a cosmic dance.

Clearly the coincidence of a greatly altered experience of temporality with a new, or hugely enhanced, sense of universal meaning and harmony suggests that the two are linked in some way. Although there are likely to be a great many ways in which the two *could* be linked, it is at least consistent, in a broad-brush-outline sort of way, with the possibility that a time-related consciousness field acts as a carrier for attractor-associated meaning. 'But why even consider such an airy-fairy notion?', one might ask. After all, the descriptions of altered time and meaning are very similar to those given by some ayahuasceros and acid-trippers. Why not put the whole thing down to a glitch in the brain-works resulting in overproduction of DMT, or whatever?[16]

The problem for anyone trying to answer down-to-earth questions like those above comes with the next question, which is: 'why *should* a brain glitch produce these experiences?' There are only two possible strategies that can be

---

[16] Michael Persinger, writing mainly in the 1980s, became well-known for his claims that mystical experience is due to micro-seizures in the temporal lobes. And there is indeed evidence that some features of (some) mystical experiences are related to temporal lobe activity or disturbances. However, as far as the ensuing discussion is concerned, it doesn't matter what type of neural 'glitch' is envisaged. Moreover Persinger himself now pursues 'neuroquantological' ideas about the basis for consciousness; ideas far removed from any straightforward, reductive neurology (see e.g. Persinger *et al.*, 2008).

adopted here. The first is to say that the supposed glitch is merely a trigger that sets off some complex series of events, many of which, since we're talking about consciousness, are likely to involve quite esoteric concepts of one sort or another. In effect, this strategy boils down to claiming that some drug experiences *are* mystical experiences, but ones that happen to have had an identifiable precipitant. The other strategy is to say that consciousness is epiphenomenal or illusory, so you might just as well ask why the smoke billowing out of a steam engine sometimes forms rings or sometimes looks a bit like a row of houses. It's a waste of time thinking about questions of that sort when you could be looking at the workings of the engine itself!

The second strategy was hugely popular throughout much of the last century. The Behaviourists, who dominated academic psychology from the 1920s to the 1950s, simply ignored consciousness as unreal, irrelevant or 'unscientific'. When that strategy failed and 'cognitive psychology' came into vogue, innumerable books, perhaps the best known being Daniel Dennett's *Consciousness Explained*, expounded the fall-back position (i.e. that it's some sort of epiphenomenon or illusion) with varying degrees of sophistication. In many of these works (but not Dennett's) the fall-back position was adopted as a basic assumption, albeit usually implicitly rather than explicitly. The trouble with it is that it doesn't work; it's simply untrue because consciousness clearly does have effects and thus is indeed real, at least according to the definition of 'real' adopted in this book (chapter 1). The mere fact that only the existence of consciousness could result in so many books being written about it is sufficient to prove its reality.

'Aha!' a defender of the *ancien regime* might say at this point, its apparent reality is only like that of your *idea* of a unicorn, whereas consciousness itself is like an 'actual' unicorn—i.e. non-existent. Good try, but I'm afraid that doesn't work either as a defence of the strategy. A moment's thought shows that we don't know about *anything*—whether ourselves, or ideas of unicorns, or that tree outside the window—if we're not conscious of them.[17] So 'consciousness itself' is inevitably analogous to the 'idea-of-unicorn', not to the non-existent 'actual' unicorn, and thus has to be regarded as 'real'.

Why did so many thoughtful people follow what is obviously, with the benefit of hindsight, such a flawed strategy? One can point to many possible reasons. For example, the pervasive, crude, 'clockwork universe' materialism that prevailed (and still does prevail) in some circles; or the very understandable fascination with all the dazzling neuro-scientific discoveries about how brains work, combined with not wanting to be distracted by awkward questions; or the enthusiasm (now fading) for computer analogies for mind. But I suspect that the principal reason is more subtle. As we are constantly being told, we are now in the 'information age'—and very wonderful it is, too. Consciousness, however, is primarily about meaning; information is to consciousness rather as food is to our bodies—it provides the raw material, but can hardly be recognized in many aspects of the finished structure. Artists have always known this, but mainstream 'scientific' culture has preferred to ignore it. Focussing as they did (and often still do) on 'information', scientifically minded people were bound to lose sight of consciousness along with meaning.

In the current climate, it's therefore hard for many of us to 'see' consciousness itself, despite the fact[18] that it *constitutes* our 'seeing'. We are in much the same position, perhaps, as those Tierra del Fuegan natives paddling about on logs of wood who allegedly, according to accounts of early visitors,

---

[17] This applies only to the conscious 'we', of course. Our brains 'know' lots of things that 'we' don't—i.e. unconscious thoughts, perceptions and feelings. However, this doesn't help any defender of the second strategy because, if some unconscious aspect of my brain activity were to cause me to get an idea of consciousness and write about it, how could it do so without giving me the *experience* of consciousness? And the experience, of course, is 'real' as shown by the effect it has of making so many of us write about it.

[18] It's partly *because of* this fact, too, for the same reason it's hard to see a window when you are looking through it. All the same, my own feeling is that we often don't see it mainly because we don't have the right concepts to aid our vision.

didn't and probably couldn't take any notice of the galleons anchored off their shores. If we want to adequately perceive and ultimately to understand our 'galleon of the mind', we'll need to develop all sorts of new concepts about how it is built, how its anchors hold to the sea bed and its sails work with the wind. It's no good simply dismissing complex phenomena triggered by, or associated with, neural (and other) events as irrelevant or epiphenomenal; they surely need to be taken at least as seriously as the neurology, if we are ever to understand consciousness.

The main relevance of mystical experience to consciousness studies, for the time being at least, seems to me to lie in its very mysteriousness and thus the emphasis it places on the *un*understability of experiences that are related to it. Clearly it does share commonalities with drug experiences, NDEs and aspects of deathbed experience. But it occurs, usually quite unpredictably, in large numbers of perfectly sane, healthy and ordinary people. You don't have to be high on acid or at death's door in order to experience these states. In fact mystical experience seems, if anything, to be associated with normality and mental fitness. So it has to be telling us something about *normal* consciousness, or at least about the potentialities inherent in normal consciousness. By implication, therefore, the same can be said of the phenomena with which it overlaps — NDEs and the like. They shouldn't be dismissed as freaks or meaningless outcomes of neural dysfunction, but should be regarded as windows able to throw light on the fundamental nature of consciousness. Although a common 20th century strategy was to claim that experiences of this type are 'nothing more than' bizarre consequences of brain malfunction, it is arguable that adoption of this view involves turning ones back on some of the best available pointers to the true nature of all conscious experience.

Conclusions

This chapter was all about a search for experiential equivalents of the iron filings that helped Michael Faraday to understand magnetic fields. How successful has it been? We certainly haven't found any elegant, single phenomenon to match Faraday's, but maybe we haven't done too badly. The search started off with an attempt to define the ground rules for deciding what might count as a candidate for a significant phenomenon. 'The Story of Ruth' showed that an apparently normal person in good health can create realistic (as far as they themselves are concerned) 'apparitions' at will and, as is well known from other sources, can produce amazingly accurate recreations of their past dynamic states.[19] Although such abilities are very remarkable, we thought they could be viewed as 'party tricks' played by consciousness and unlikely to tell us anything of deep significance. They showed us that apparitions and hallucinations turning up in other settings, however apparently realistic they may be, are unlikely to be useful sources of evidence.

Moving on to ayahuasca experiences and NDEs, we found really quite strong evidence, especially from NDEs, that attractor dynamics appears to have a major role in shaping conscious experience; the content of the experiences, and sometimes the contexts in which they occur, make it seem very unlikely indeed that bottom-up neural causation could be solely responsible. This may sound a bit confusing; what I mean is that *something* must be responsible for extremely clear and detailed 'life review' for instance, and it's almost inconceivable that it could all be down to neurons in an apparently comatose brain in an intensive care unit or wherever. The *something* argued for in this book is a 'dance' of attractors viewed as having an apparently independent 'reality' analogous to that of natural laws. We also noted that puzzling descriptions of altered perceptions of time seem often (always?) to be associated with these 'attractor-dominated' experiences.

Then the deathbed experiences strongly suggest that temporal anomalies aren't confined to subjective feelings about

---

[19] Ruth was apparently able to reproduce the dynamic states of other people, too, such as her father and her friend Becky, but it's not known how accurate these were.

their occurrence. The dying can acquire reliable knowledge about their immediate futures, it appears. Relatives, too, occasionally appear to gain non-spatio-temporally mediated knowledge. A variety of other phenomena occur that could be taken to suggest that consciousness may be 'field-like', though not any form of physical field constrained by the time of relativity theory. However, there were hints only in these connections; nothing clear-cut.

Mystical experience, on the other hand, also involves the (subjective) temporal anomalies noted above and emphasizes their linkage with enhanced experience of meaning—often experienced as universal love. As meaning is memory, attractor and natural law related (see chapter 4), the linkage can be taken to suggest that these factors are involved somehow in whatever goes on during such experience. The fact that mystic experience is so widespread, and so obviously related to the other anomalous experiences described, gives confidence about taking then all 'seriously' and not dismissing them as 'nothing but' glitches. They appear to be potentialities implicit in all human consciousness, offering useful pointers to its nature.

But what, exactly, do they indicate? There's no answering this question yet. One can only offer rather vague ideas, for instance that consciousness can perhaps be viewed as a 'carrier wave' for attractor landscapes; that it is a kind of reflection in time of objective happenings in the brain. As we saw earlier (chapter 6), such landscapes may be mapped onto brain structures, so there's probably no 'in principle' problem about a mapping onto any 'consciousness field'—however big the 'in practice' problems to do with envisaging details may be! The biggest 'in principle' problem of all, it seems to me, concerns how one can picture the 'existence' of attractor landscapes. As we've seen, there does appear to be quite good evidence for their independent 'reality'. Do they exist in Platonic heaven, along with other mathematical objects, or are they always 'embodied'? We've seen how they may be embodied (mapped) in brains. Does the constraining influence that they appear to have on brains depend on a Platonic world or on their secondary 'embodiment' in consciousness fields? Is there indeed any valid distinction between consciousness fields and the 'Platonic heaven'?

Everyone will have their own ideas, many of them much better than mine, about possible answers to questions of this sort. And it's likely to be quite a while before we'll be able to do more than *ask* questions. Answers won't be turning up tomorrow. All the same, maybe we've now got some sort of basis now for dealing with the question posed in chapter 1 — who was Mrs Willett? Let's turn to that next.

Chapter 9

Making Sense of 'Mrs Willett'

What Does 'Who' Mean?

To make any sense of the Mrs Willett story told in chapter 1, we need to try to say something sensible about who she was and who were the various personalities that 'visited' her. So we must first take a look at what a 'who' of any sort might be. Until we're fairly clear about what the word refers to in general, there's not much point in asking how it applies to Mrs Willett and her entourage in particular. Presumably 'whos' are something to do with selfhood and, if this book has done nothing else, I hope it will have convinced all readers that selves are shrouded in mystery. Indeed a good many thinkers, from David Hume in the 18th century on, have doubted whether anything that one can properly call a 'self' actually exists. Freudians, Existentialists, Post-modernists, Deconstructionists and some psychologists, especially those with Buddhist leanings, have all added to the uncertainty.

Defining 'who' certainly looks easy enough at first sight — you just have to point at someone and say 'that's what you can ask "who" questions about.' But, as we've seen, the 'who' that you point at has quite fuzzy, leaky boundaries. Although his or her physical shape and outline stay reasonably constant in the short to medium term, almost all of the material contributing to that shape is recycled every few months. And things are even worse from the mental point of view. The mental 'self' at any given moment includes quite a lot of both the material and the social environment of whomever you point at—and that's from an objective, 'third person' point of view. From a subjective point of view, 'I' can be displaced into a robot (chapter 2), or split with some of 'me' manifesting in an apparition of myself ('Ruth'), or 'leave' my body altogether (OBE), or be temporarily non-existent (unconsciousness). Yet, unless I am completely unconscious, I still recognize myself in all these circumstances as a 'me' that could in principle be a 'who' to someone else. Even David Hume, who was an affable and warm-hearted man, almost certainly *felt* that he knew what he was talking about when he used the pronoun 'I'—whatever his intellectual doubts.

I guess the essential thing to remember is that, although we can point to someone's body easily enough, and say 'that's a person and a potential referent of a "who" enquiry', the subjective 'self' in question may feel they are somewhere else altogether.[1] And a reciprocal difficulty often occurs. I may have no problem feeling that I am the same 'self' now as the one represented by a school photograph of myself, but a friend looking at the photograph might not recognize it as having anything to do with me. This rarely causes problems from a practical point of view, since we are normally anchored to our bodies and we make allowances for the ravages of time, but it does imply that we don't actually know what we're talking about some of the time, when we use the word 'who' of other people. Because of this potential for ignorance and/or getting it wrong, pointing at someone isn't adequate as a *definition* of 'who' despite its practical usefulness most of the time. 'Who?' should in fact be regarded, I suggest, as a third-person enquiry about an 'I'. In other words, someone else's *subjective* sense of self is what users of the word 'who' should think of themselves as referring to. They shouldn't think of themselves as referring primarily to anything objectively observable, even though the subjective 'I' to which they refer often will coincide with a whole range of material, measurable factors.

---

[1] My wife often notices this and rightly complains about it! I guess most husbands have the same problem at times.

How does this suggestion cover existentialist 'who am I?' ruminations, it might be asked. Surely it risks getting into Russell's paradox[2] territory, with all its attendant difficulties. My own feeling is that there's actually no problem here. The ruminating 'I' still has a sense of selfhood, and is merely playing at seeing itself from a third person perspective — something that people commonly do in all sorts of contexts.

Although being anchored in a body generally provides a lot of our sense of self, indeed is responsible for our sense of self according to some theorists, we've seen from NDEs and the like that awareness of our own familiar, physical body doesn't seem to be needed for a *continuing* sense of self. The theorists may well be correct that a body is needed in order to *develop* such a sense, but the evidence strongly suggests that, once it has developed, it can continue apparently more or less independently of normal somatic inputs. When the self loses its anchor, its perceived boundaries do sometimes (but not always) hugely expand — as in some mystical experiences for instance — but even then something remains which I guess might be best described as a 'conscious point of view'. Perhaps that is lost, too, in the Buddhist experience of 'Nirvana'. However, so far as I know, we have never received any reports from anyone who has dissolved into Nirvana. We only have descriptions of theoretical claims about what dissolution is *thought* to be like (strictly speaking *not* to be like, since it is supposed to be a state of all-encompassing nothingness!).

On the other hand, we do have reports of other profound mystical states. All such reports of actual experience appear to describe a conscious awareness by an observing entity of something, though the 'something' in question can allegedly include the whole of space-time according to some reports, or may be nothing more than an awareness of being aware according to others. Moreover, the 'observing entity',

---

[2] 'Who shaves the barber who shaves everyone that does not shave themselves?', was one of Russell's versions. The most familiar of all versions is the one about whether to believe the Cretan who says that all Cretans are liars.

too, may feel itself to be godlike or otherwise greatly changed from ordinary human selfhood. Perhaps the appearance that all these otherwise varied experiences share a 'view-from-somewhere' property is no more than a consequence of the language necessarily involved in their description, and is not inherent in the experiences themselves. Maybe so. But at least, pending dissolution, 'whos' do report themselves as having a consciously perceived point of view, however strange it or they may be. Presumably an entity or ex-entity could no longer be regarded as a 'who' if ever that final attribute of selfhood were lost.

Taking all this into account, it seems that we need to generalize a bit from the definition of 'who' as an enquiry about a subjective 'I'. Most of the time that's adequate but, in the context of some very unusual subjective states, it may be better to think of 'who' as referring to what can be termed a (consciously perceived) 'centre of narrative gravity'. Ordinarily that's a straightforward 'I' and a lot of the 'narrative' is about a particular body and its interactions with its physical and social environments. The fact that the body occupies particular locations and has a limited range of environmental interactions is no doubt what initially, in infancy, provides virtually the whole 'centre of gravity' for its 'narratives'. As memories of all types proliferate, incorporating an ever-growing range of narrative records, the 'centre of gravity' tends to shift from the body as such to the more long-lasting 'narratives' that it harbours. Compared to all other animals, this shift is enormously enhanced in us humans by language and all that goes with it. In mystical states the 'narrative' moves on to transcendental themes, but there's still a 'centre of gravity' experienced as a 'point of view'.

As far as the picture of mentality developed in this book is concerned, a 'centre of narrative gravity' has to be regarded as another name for enduring or recurring features of an 'attractor landscape'. In infancy, genetic dynamics make the biggest dimensional contribution to state spaces harbouring the relevant landscapes; as time passes environmental, particularly social, dynamics come to predominate. Each of us builds a unique 'self', on the basis of our genetic inheritance, from all the memories, habits and skills that life affords. It's a self that manifests in our neural dynamics, but can be envisaged to 'exist' in the form of enduring state space dimensions favouring the emergence of particular attractors. Such spaces probably should not be dismissed as purely notional, the evidence suggested, for the attractors that they harbour seem to possess a 'reality' of their own; a type of reality which seems closely analogous to that of natural laws.

I don't mean to imply here that attractors can be considered to exist in a wholly separate *spatio-temporal* continuum from that of brains. Like natural laws, they are part of the everyday order; indeed constitutive of the everyday order as far as the brain is concerned. To think otherwise would be merely to re-introduce the idea of a Cartesian *res cogitans* by the back door. Attractor landscapes have to maintain what one might term a 'co-presence' with brains and the rest of the material world. If they were off in some wholly separate realm, all the difficulties over envisaging how *res cogitans* could interact with the *res extensa* of our bodies would return in full force. It was because of a particular example of one of these difficulties—that of conceiving how a 'soul' that had been Hoovered up through a tunnel into the suburbs of paradise could implant such vivid memories into the brain it had left behind—that we rejected soul-based explanations of NDEs in the last chapter.

However, it is just about conceivable, I also argued, that consciousness may be able to 'map' landscapes into a Platonic or quasi-Platonic realm. The idea was that, rather as brains and attractor landscapes reciprocally create, inform and map one another (the specific suggestion made in chapter 6 was that calcium wave/EEG dynamics provide the necessary interface for this to happen), so consciousness viewed as a gauge-like field (see chapter 7) might possibly translate or copy landscapes into a form outside the remit of relativistic space-time. As I can specify only three properties of this proposed field—that it is conscious, that it is likely to involve temporal anomalies of some sort and that it may be a sort of reflection of energetic processes in the brain—I can certainly sympathize with anyone who wants to dismiss it. About the only thing to be said in its favour is that consciousness-related temporal anomalies do occur. There's no denying the subjective ones, and the evidence for occasional objective ones (e.g. some of the deathbed experiences described in the last chapter) seems pretty good, though not rock solid. Pending any better explanation for these, I should therefore like to keep this particular field proposal in mind, on a sort of 'outside chance' basis.

The 'self' to which 'who' refers thus turns out to be a very elusive entity, according to the ideas offered in this book. But, *pace* David Hume and others, it is possible to identify something that can validly be referred to as a 'self'. It is a consciously perceived centre of narrative gravity founded in dimensions (the long-lasting ones) of state spaces, from which attractor landscapes emerge. Although originating in biology and bodies, it can certainly appear to possess a degree of independence from these. And there seems to be an outside chance that more than 'appearance' of independence is involved; maybe it can achieve actual independence via the mediation of consciousness. Let's return to Mrs Willett at this stage and see if she can help us to sharpen up our questions. We won't expect to find answers to most of them, for so much turns on the nature of time, which is a mystery within a mystery. Nevertheless, finding better questions, if we can, is never a waste of time!

Mrs. Willett

As described in chapter 1, 'Mrs Willett' was the pseudonym used by Mrs. Winifred Coombe-Tennant to conceal her mediumistic activities from the knowledge of all but a few associates. One of the few people who did know her in both guises was Jean Balfour, a perceptive woman and Gerald Balfour's daughter-in-law. Jean was perhaps a somewhat hostile witness as she was very fond of her mother-in-law Betty, Gerald's wife. Both of them knew about Mrs Willett's affair with Gerald (the one that was supposed to produce a

Messiah). Betty was hurt by it and Jean tended to take her side. Nevertheless, Jean kept in touch with Mrs Willett for years—right on into the latter's somewhat querulous old age. Here's what she was like in her prime, according to Jean:

> She was handsome, on a large scale, and moved with energy and decision ... She was essentially a primitive person but this is not to say that she did not have a very good brain without being at all 'intellectual'—she was practical rather, and had ... considerable executive ability without much psychological insight... She regarded everything in relation to herself and those she cared for (Roy, 2008, p. 232).

She was a fairly classic example, it appears, of a forceful, down-to-earth, I-know-best, English county lady; not at all the sort of person whom you might expect would spend thirty years in part-time communion with the spirits.[3] Can this be taken to imply the existence of some sort of dual personality here; might Mrs Willett have been a rather different 'who' from Mrs. Coombe-Tennant? Jean Balfour doesn't seem to have thought so. 'Mrs Willett' was there solely for the pragmatic reason that it 'wouldn't do' socially for news of Mrs. Coombe-Tennant's mediumistic talents to get out. The pseudonym didn't reflect any real change of personality and was purely a convenience, a *nom-de-plume-automatique*.

The 'narrative' behind Mrs Willett's activities wasn't foreign to Winifred Coombe-Tennant, even though she might seem at first sight to be an unlikely vehicle for it. It has to be remembered that mediumistic activities were actually quite popular in middle and upper-class circles in that period—as witness the galaxy of intellectual and social stars attracted to the SPR (Society for Psychical Research) at its foundation. Moreover Winifred's sister-in-law was married to one of the moving spirits behind that organisation, namely the gifted and charismatic Frederic Myers. She had family reasons for taking an interest in the field, and family

---

[3] People like this do sometimes have a weakness for spirits in the form of a gin bottle of course—but rarely for disembodied spirits.

was important to her. Moreover, she very probably would have taken it for granted that 'family' was unlikely to be wrong or mistaken about anything; she would have been predisposed, in other words, to accept the validity of Myers' activities without question. Then came the death of her daughter, Daphne. With her get-up-and-go approach to life, it's hardly surprising that she tried automatic writing herself to see if she could get in touch with Daphne and also that she appealed for help to Myers' old circle, with some of whom she had kept in touch after his death seven year earlier.

It seems safe to assume, therefore, that Willett and Coombe-Tennant were the same 'who', possessing a common attractor landscape. During séances, when the 'spirits' were present, additional 'whos' did apparently manifest but, if in fact they were separate entities of some sort, they can be regarded as separate from a *single* Coombe-Tennant/Willett. So I'll drop the rather cumbersome use of separate names and refer to her henceforth as 'Winifred' — it would have taken a brave stranger to call her that while she was still alive as she would have thought it grossly impertinent, but perhaps she has mellowed since and may forgive me!

Winifred not only displayed a talent for automatic writing, but later on developed a '... distinctive style of mediumship in which she could "see" and "hear" the communicators while still being able to talk to the investigator sitting with her' (Roy, 2008, p. 207). Sitters present with her could hold what some of the less sceptical among them took to be more or less direct conversations with the dead, with Winifred functioning as a sort of relay station. Moreover, she could often allow this to happen while retaining what seems to have been a normal and clear consciousness of herself, her surroundings and what the 'spirits' were saying to her. Indeed 'they' stated outright that they preferred her not to go off into a trance in the manner of so many mediums because her type of fully aware mediumship somehow facilitated 'their' communications, so they claimed, adding that they had 'trained' her to achieve this state.

Clearly major splits of some sort existed in whatever landscapes and narratives were relevant; Winifred was reporting ideas, feelings, alleged 'memories', and even displaying emotional characteristics, that were to all appearances entirely distinct from any conscious 'narrative' of her own. Independent 'whos' certainly *seem* to have encroached on Winifred. Who or what were they?

Who Were Winifred's 'Spirits'?

As noted by Jean Balfour, Winifred herself was neither particularly introspective nor psychologically perceptive. She seems to have had no conscious doubt at all that Gurney, Myers, Sidgwick and the rest were precisely who they claimed to be—discarnate spirits communicating from an afterlife. Curiously, though, she once confided to Jean that she was afraid of death. Perhaps she did harbour doubts of some sort in some secret corner of her mind, despite the sales-pitch for the wonders of the afterlife that she had been broadcasting for thirty years. Others of her circle, however, were less confident that they knew what was going on; especially Eleanor Sidgwick, widow of one the alleged 'communicators' and very active in the SPR for many years. Jean Balfour reported:

> In those days we were not aware, as we are nowadays, of the leakage of ideas that can go on beneath the threshold of consciousness: and I think she [Eleanor Sidgwick] already suspected it. Although she never entirely said so, her caution in expressing an opinion of her own upon the meaning of the [communications], suggests to my mind that she was aware of the fluidity of the Unconscious (Roy, 2008, pp. 163-64).

When discussing the occasional failures of the American medium, Mrs Piper, Eleanor Sidgwick also came up with the idea that sitters were not just objective observers of a medium's performance but also, at some level, active participants in whatever went on. She envisaged a sort of two-stage 'telepathy', in which the sitter acted as an unconscious aerial receiving messages from the 'spirits', while the medium connected to the sitter to amplify and give voice to any message.

Eileen Garrett (1893–1970) was a younger contemporary of Winifred's whom we've not met previously as she wasn't much involved with the SPR.[4] She was active as a medium for almost her entire adult life, following a childhood during which she described having had two unusually vivid and persistent imaginary playmates. Unlike Winifred, she wrote about her experiences and had an interest in the psychology behind them. Towards the end of her life, she wrote:

> I prefer to think of the controls [i.e. the 'spirits' who guided her mediumistic communications] as principles of the subconscious. I had, unconsciously, adopted them by name during the years of early training. I respect them, but cannot explain them (Garrett, 1968, quoted by Fontana, 2005).

Thus the people involved in these activities appear to have had a range of views about the nature of the 'spirits' involved. Some thought they were exactly who they claimed to be, namely discarnate entities speaking from an afterlife; others wondered whether some sort of telepathy might be involved, but were uncertain as to what sort; questions about whether the possible role(s) of participants other than the 'spirit' and the medium had surfaced, as had questions about whether it was all down to the unconscious or subconscious mind — presumably that of the medium.

There does seem often to be a clear 'narrative' discontinuity between medium and 'spirits', which is particularly obvious in the case of Winifred and her visitors. Given the definition of what 'who' should be taken to refer to, arrived at earlier in this chapter, I think we do need, tentatively at least, to regard the visitors as being separate 'whos' from Winifred herself. Why not, in that case, simply accept that

---

[4] She was, however, involved with the Rhines — the Duke University parapsychologists who were particularly active in the 1950s and 60s. Indeed, I believe she was the only medium to have been thoroughly investigated by them and she retained a high opinion of 'scientific methodology' subsequently. She's particularly famous for having provided details, two days after the event, of reasons for the airship R101's crash, allegedly obtained from one of the officers killed in it.

they were who they claimed to be? It would probably make sense to do so if all such 'spirits' were as convincing as Winifred's gang. But they're not; many 'spirit guides' are entities with weird names, claiming to be American Indians, Ancient Egyptians and the like, who are only too liable to 'communicate' banal rubbish. A particularly famous 'spirit', one of Mrs Piper's controls who claimed to be a deceased French doctor named 'Phinuit', turned out to have no knowledge of the French language.[5] Entities that could plausibly be taken at face value, like Winfred's, were and are rarities. Most are quite unbelievable for a whole range of reasons other than their incompatibility with current mainstream ideas about the nature of the world.

Moreover 'Ruth' (see chapter 8) showed that realistic 'apparitions', able to hold sensible conversations and sometimes to provide information not known to the conscious mind of their perceiver, can be produced without the involvement of any alleged 'spirits'. Her 'apparitions' evidently had a lot in common with the 'spirits' that Winifred 'saw' and with whom she could converse. The clincher, of course, showing that Ruth's 'apparitions' were (certainly often and probably always) products of her own mind lay in the fact that she could produce at will ones of herself and of Morton Schatzman while he was present with her. So it would seem no more than sensible to conclude that Winifred's were of the same nature—unusual products of the sub-conscious mind, just as Eileen Garrett eventually concluded about her own 'spirit guides'.

Winifred's case, on this view, can be regarded as a variant of dissociative identity disorder, with Myers, Gurney and the rest being secondary personalities. There's a large and

---

[5] However 'Phinuit' was logical in some matters. He claimed that he 'swapped places' with Mrs Piper herself when he was communicating through her body and that she went off to the spirit world for the duration. When asked why she couldn't remember having done so on return, 'he' stated that she had no access to her brain while out of her body, so couldn't store memories of what had happened. I have to agree with him that it's a plausible explanation for her alleged amnesia, but unfortunately he didn't explain how NDEers *do* remember!

controversial literature on the question of exactly how separate are the apparently separate personalities in this disorder. Are they actually distinct personalities, or should they be regarded as aspects of a single personality? Opinion seems to have been fairly evenly divided over the years; some saying the various personalities that manifest *can* often be regarded as separate 'whos' on definitions similar to the one offered at the beginning of this chapter; others saying they are not as distinct as that. When controversies go on for so long without any clear resolution, it's more often than not a sign that the wrong question is being asked. So I'll take the hint, drop the 'who or what were the "spirits" and were they really distinct from Winifred?' questions for the time being and ask instead where the narratives that were foreign to Winifred came from.

Where Did the 'Spirit Narratives' Come From?

Given the picture of mentality developed in the first four chapters of this book, the question above looks an easy one to answer. Winifred was very closely involved with a group of people who were passionately interested in 'spiritualism' and its validity or otherwise, many of them also having close emotional ties to the alleged 'spirits' that manifested. The group dynamics would have contributed lots of dimensions to Winifred's own dynamic states. It's hardly surprising, therefore, that she should have incorporated the group 'narratives' into her own mind. Not so easy to say why their 'narratives' emerged into her consciousness in the way they did, but there seems to be no 'in principle' difficulty about affirming that this is what must have happened. After all, the story of 'Ruth' was a neat demonstration of the capacity of intrinsic mental content to manifest as apparently realistic 'apparitions'.

Surely it's an open and shut case therefore, I might claim, and one that helps to show the usefulness and generality of my model of mentality since it can be used to explain events as bizarre as the Winifred story. Well, as it happens, no! As is so often the case, the devil is in the details. One important detail is that several mediums, two of them in different countries and not all that closely connected with 'the group', produced 'communications' that slotted in with Winifred's. Another is that obscure *factual* information turned up in some of these communications — information that certainly would not have been anywhere in Winifred's mind, though it's now impossible to say whether other group members, many of whom were better educated than her, might have harboured it.

'Ordinary' state space dynamics could not account for either of these circumstances, so far as I can see. They could account alright for rather general notions, attitudes and actions being shared between core members of a group, and perhaps spreading to a few outsiders too. But they couldn't account for transfer of specific, allegedly unfamiliar facts. Winifred couldn't, from her own resources, describe a specific fact not known to her even if it was known to other group members. She would have had to learn the fact before any group dynamics could 'resonate' with her own neural dynamic and elicit it Only two possibilities seem to remain therefore — either fraud on a rather large scale, or the existence of sources of information, and possibly of meaning, additional to those intrinsic to the group itself.

Many people nowadays would probably go for the fraud option, perhaps tempering its severity with remarks about 'unconscious self-deception'. I find it very hard to believe that deliberate fraud could be the explanation, especially as so many of the group, whatever their personal hopes for 'immortality', strove so hard over very long periods of time for both intellectual and methodological rigour. Most of them come across as being primarily motivated to uncover truth, not to con others into accepting some sort of quasi-religious belief system. Nor were they in need of money; they all had independent incomes and/or employment, while their researches were a financial drain. 'Unconscious self-deception' doesn't work either, for many people would have had to somehow mis-record or fabricate 'communications' for this to suffice as an explanation, and there's no way that could have happened on a sufficiently large scale in the absence of any conscious awareness of what was going on.

I suppose, if Winifred's 'communications' had been unique, one could dismiss them as some sort of strange, ultimately insignificant, anomaly. But in fact there've been many generically similar events. For example, the alleged 'Winifred's' post-mortem 'communications' with Geraldine Cummins, which raise very similar questions about how on earth Cummins could have obtained some of the specific information that she reported. Conscious fraud seems very unlikely and it's hard to see how unconscious self-deception could have sufficed, since she would have had to go out of her way to collect little-known details about Winifred. Cummins did once visit the Balfours (about 20 years before she first channelled 'Winifred'), but she would have had to have dug very hard to get information about Winifred, who was fierce in defence of her anonymity. Cummins could hardly have done any digging without being aware of it, nor would she appear to have had any reason to do so at the time.

My own feeling, therefore, is that there are good grounds for supposing that Winifred did have access to some extra-group source of information. The group probably played a part in helping her to focus on and channel the information, and very likely contributed a lot to its perceived meaning. Much the most striking thing about this 'source of information' is that, unless due to fraud, it had sometimes to be independent of any normal temporal and causal constraints. There would seem to be only three possibilities for envisaging a source able to supply the erudite information involved — and perhaps some of that relating to emotional matters that had allegedly never been disclosed during the lifetimes of those involved — provided one does reject the fraud hypothesis:

- An atemporal linkage between Winifred's conscious or unconscious mind and (aspects of) the minds of Myers and the gang while they were still alive.
- A 'record' of information in the minds of Myers and the gang held in some sort of universal memory field (viz.

Laszlo's 'akashic field', mentioned in chapter 8), that Winifred could access somehow.
- Myers and the gang did indeed 'exist' in some empyrean realm but were able, with difficulty, to communicate with Winifred.

Although these possibilities *look* different, it's not clear that they actually *are* different in any meaningful way. If minds can 'link' with those of their successors, they must still in a sense exist, at least from the point of view of any successor with whom a 'link' is formed. Would whatever underpins any such 'link' be meaningfully different from a 'memory field'? Would a 'record' in a memory field be any different from an 'existence' in some atemporal realm?

The whole idea of mental atemporal linkages of any sort must appear so implausible to many that they are bound to prefer explanations based on conscious or unconscious fraud. However, we arrived previously at the 'outside chance' idea that consciousness might possibly be a field with origins in memory-related broken temporal symmetry. And we've seen that a whole range of different sorts of consciously experienced temporal anomaly have been reported. Maybe, then, it's not totally absurd to suppose that linkages might occur between 'consciousness fields' originating from different people, regardless of any differences in the temporal co-ordinates occupied by their brains. So little is understood about the nature of time that one can't say anything more definite than 'maybe it's not totally absurd' to suppose this.

If the idea's not completely absurd, are there any grounds for preferring one or other of the three options outlined above, supposing that they do harbour meaningful differences? It does look as though the first two possibilities, being apparently wholly 'memory' based, would preclude any change in the source of information. However, Myers and the gang did apparently change post-mortem, or at least the meanings associated with information conveyed appeared to change from Winifred's temporal perspective. Moreover, there are reports from mystics that 'change' can occur in what is felt to be an 'atemporal' realm, which sounds paradoxical but I suspect may have something to do with what we called a 'view from somewhere' on the 'atemporal' realm allowing a sequence-like experience of it.

Perhaps, therefore, Myers and the gang were/are more than fixed and unalterable memories held in or transmitted through some extensive or universal field. Or perhaps not—maybe the information originated from a 'memory field', while the apparent growth and change of meaning associated with that information was all down to Winifred herself and her living associates. Questions about the view one should take of Myers' apparent post-mortem mutability are almost certainly unprofitable at present since it is very unlikely that progress can be made with them until we have a better understanding of time.

We've already seen (chapter 7) that current scientific pictures of time are inadequate. To be precise, the Newtonian picture, which works well enough for many practical purposes, is known to be wrong, while the relativistic picture is known to be incomplete. Both are almost totally out of synch with our subjective experience of time. In the final chapter, I'd like to look at other notions of time that may be waiting in the wings and see whether they could prove compatible with the ideas outlined in this book about the structure of mind and of consciousness.

Chapter 10

The End of Time?

I filched the title of this chapter (but added a question mark) from that of a book by physicist Julian Barbour (1999). He wants to get rid of time, hoping to 'end' it by dethronement from the place it currently occupies in science, and indeed in most peoples' everyday thinking, as an essential part of the foundations of existence. That's surely of interest from our point of view. Maybe we should also remember the alternative meaning— 'end' in the sense of a possible aim or purpose. Although our own culture generally regards time as purely linear, others have thought of it as circular or spiral; a whole range of 'shapes' for time, more complex than a straight line, are conceivable. Many of them would incorporate an appearance of goal-seeking as far as creatures like us, bound to their surfaces, are concerned. But there's not much that one can usefully say about the topology of time, other than that it might be less straightforward than is commonly supposed, so I won't pursue the second meaning and will confine myself to taking a look at 'end' the sense of abolishing or demoting time.

Getting Rid of Time

Barbour tells us that he has spent much of his adult life trying to re-think the foundations of physics in order to get rid of current weaknesses and inconsistencies. Notions of time and space are especially problematic, he avers, but any improvement to the overall picture has to incorporate all the weirdness of quantum theory. Using a Machian[1] approach, he argues that the fundamental entities are the different 'relative configurations' that could be adopted by the matter in the entire universe — an almost inconceivably huge number from a 'classical' point of view and infinite if quantum considerations are added to the picture. These configurations can be pictured as 'existing' in an enormously vast configuration space (see for comparison the RNA configuration space described in chapter 3).

> The Wheeler-De Witt equation [which, Barbour says, may be 'the fundamental equation of the universe'] is telling us ... that the universe in its entirety is like some huge molecule ... and that the different configurations of this 'monster molecule' are *the instants of time*... Time does not exist. There is just the furniture of the world that we call instants of time ... (Barbour, 1999, p. 247).

So there is no time dimension whatsoever in Barbour's theory, nor any independent spatial dimensions for these latter dimensions are secondary consequences of the relative positions of the matter contributing to whatever the overall configuration may be. The appearance of change and motion derives from paths through the configuration space. The path leading from any particular configuration to another is defined by a measure of minimum 'distance' (which is not 3-D spatial distance), while the actual paths that we ourselves are likely to experience are down to the probability of our being part of particular configurations. Some types of configuration are hugely more numerous than others, says Barbour, so we are especially likely to find ourselves in a set of those.[2] Moreover these much more numerous configurations will also usually include what

---

[1] Ernst Mach (1838-1916), an Austrian physicist and philosopher best known for his eponymous studies of the speed of sound ('Mach 1'). What's relevant to Barbour's argument is that he thought the whole universe has to be taken into consideration in many contexts. Inertia, for example, is a property that makes sense only if an object's motion is considered in relation to that of *all* other matter.

[2] Barbour's argument here is by analogy with entropy. Lower entropy states are so enormously more improbable than higher entropy ones that closed systems must almost always follow the 2nd law of thermodynamics.

look to be *records* of other, related configurations — hence the appearance of being able to remember a 'past', for instance.

It's a baroque scheme, though probably no more extravagant than the 'many worlds' interpretation of quantum theory, which is quite popular at present. It shares some of the universalist spirit of 'many worlds' in that all possible configurations are envisaged as existing in a configuration space, which Barbour dubs 'Platonia', though not all will be 'realised' (in contrast, most versions of 'many worlds' take *all* the possible 'histories' to be equally 'real'). One might suppose, too, that it has something in common with the 'block universe' view of time (see chapter 7). It's certainly a 'block universe' of a sort, but the essential point about it is that time plays no part whatsoever in its structure. So-called 'time', for Barbour, is not an independent dimension but a sort of illusion consequent on the existence of defined paths between differing, instantaneous 'relative configurations'. The chapter 7 'block universe', on the other hand, takes a temporal dimension, in the form of the temporal component of Minkowski's 'space-time', to be foundational.

And Barbour is far from being alone in his thinking. Many physicists would like to derive time and space from something more fundamental, if only they knew how. Lee Smolin for instance, who is unlike Barbour in that he would prefer to keep some sort of notion of the reality of time, remarked:

> We now know that time has no absolute meaning. There is no time apart from change. There is no such thing as a clock outside the network of changing relationships (Smolin, 2000, p. 24).

The obvious next question to ask of Smolin is 'changing relationships of what?' For Barbour the individual, universal patterns of relationship *are* what exist. They don't change, there are simply huge numbers of co-existent ones. For other physicists the 'whats' are complex mathematical objects, whether the branes and strings of string theory, or the entities of Smolin's 'loop quantum gravity', or spin networks (or maybe all three!). However, there have been suggestions on grounds other than Barbour's 'nothing changes' that the question of 'what changes?' may be wrong in the sense of being meaningless. These involve speculations that the fundamental level of reality may be described by a 'non-commutative geometry' (Connes, 2008). If it is, space and time can be nothing more than secondary properties of reality, but the same applies to individuality of any sort! There are no separate entities in situations described by this geometry. The main appeal of this idea, I suppose, lies in the fact that entangled particles appear to lack individuality, and maybe they retain or somehow reflect a situation that exists at the foundations of reality.

The most appropriate lesson to draw from all this is that there seems to be widespread agreement among fundamental physicists that time is not what we ordinarily suppose it to be, and is likely to prove to be either an illusion of some sort or an emergent property of something more fundamental. However, there's no agreement yet over how we *should* think of it that is any advance on the concept of time in relativity theory. There's not much point, therefore, in following the speculative physics any further, but I'd like to take a look at ideas from a totally different source—poetry. After all, we've argued that consciousness has a special relationship with time, whatever the truth about that mysterious concept. Maybe poets, with their finely tuned conscious perceptions, have useful intuitions to offer about its nature.

Poetic Time

Many poets appear to take a rather dim, not to say gloomy, view of time. For example:

> We are not sure of sorrow;
> And joy was never sure;
> Today will die tomorrow;
> Time stoops to no man's lure;
> And love grown faint and fretful.
> With lips but half regretful
> Sighs, and with eyes forgetful
> Weeps that no love endures.
>
> (Algernon Swinburne)

The End of Time?   221

> From low to high doth dissolution climb,
> And sink from high to low, along a scale
> Of awful notes, whose concord shall not fail,
> A musical, but melancholy chime ...
>
> The longest date do melt like frosty rime,
> That in the morning whitened hill and plain
> And is no more; drop like the tower sublime
> Of yesterday, which royally did wear
> His crown of weeds, but could not even sustain
> Some casual shout that broke the silent air
> Or the unimaginable touch of Time.
> (William Wordsworth)

I guess the two poems above express pretty much what most of us feel; time's an inexorable process, laying waste to whatever we hold dear. But here's something that neatly pinpoints the relativity of our perceptions:

> Good creatures, do you love your lives
> And have you ears for sense?
> Here is a knife like other knives,
> That cost me eighteen pence.
>
> I need but stick it in my heart
> And down will come the sky,
> And earth's foundations will depart
> And all you folk will die.
> (A.E. Housman)

Then there are magical or mystical expressions:

> Once out of nature I shall never take
> My bodily form from any natural thing,
> But such a form as Grecian goldsmiths make
> Of hammered gold and gold enamelling
> To keep a drowsy Emperor awake;
> Or set upon a golden bough to sing
> To lords and ladies of Byzantium
> Of what is past, or passing, or to come.
> (W.B. Yeats)

And here's one averring that time *doesn't* win when it comes to love, albeit a rather fierce form of love:

> but if a living dance upon dead minds
> why, it is love; but at the earliest spear
> of sun perfectly should disappear
> moon's utmost magic, or stones speak or one
> name control more incredible splendour than

> our merely universe, love's also there:
> and being here imprisoned, tortured here
> love everywhere exploding maims and blinds
> (but surely does not forget, perish sleep
> cannot be photographed, measured; disdains
> the trivial labelling of punctual brains .
>   Who wields a poem huger than the grave?
> from only Whom shall time no refuge keep
> though all the weird worlds must be opened?)
> Love
(e.e. cummings)

The great poet of time was of course T.S. Eliot. And the quotation from his work most frequently offered is:

> Time present and time past are both perhaps present in time future and time future contained in time past. If all time is eternally present all time is irredeemable.

The first sentence of the quotation betrays the influence of relativity theory and Eliot's academic friends, while the conclusion about irredeemability in the second sentence is illegitimate.[3] But he did have other and more heuristic things to say, especially in *The Four Quartets,* which are echoed by themes that have cropped up in this book. For instance, the difficulty of conceiving of any continuity in time of 'selves'; the special status of consciousness in relation to time in that the conscious moment appears to be 'out of time', but can be remembered only within a temporal context; and the possibility of 'change' in an essentially timeless zone—Eliot uses the image of a 'dance' occurring within a timeless moment.

Apart from Swinburne and Wordsworth, who seem to have endorsed a strictly Newtonian picture, it seems that there is poetic support for the views of physicists who suppose there's more (or maybe 'less' would be more apt in Barbour's case!) to time than we currently understand, but

---

[3] Eliot is basically describing a 'block universe' view of time here. But the co-presence of everything can't be taken to imply that the 'everything' could not be different. If one of the co-present events was absent, for instance, perhaps unfortunate events would have been co-present that 'in fact' were/are/will be non-existent. In that case the event incompatible with the actuality of the unfortunate ones can be regarded as redemptive.

they mostly don't add anything new to physical thinking. However there is a rather traditional thought, emphasized in the e.e. cummings quote, which is quite outside the professional ken of physicists; namely that, whatever the fate of everything else, love at least is eternal—love *does* in some sense 'escape time'. Sounds ridiculously sentimental, doesn't it? What is 'love' anyway? Is there any meaningful sense in which there could be a *fundamental physics* of love, as opposed to, say, a *physiology* of some of the correlates of love and lust? 'Unlikely' is probably the politest comment that one could expect to hear made about any such proposal nowadays! On the other hand, the link between love and meaning so often reported by mystics and others, may offer a hint about where one could start to look for any such physics. I do sometimes wonder, therefore, whether the prejudices of Mrs Willett and her associates may not have been nearer to the truth about the nature of love than those of contemporary reductionists.

John Donne, I think, described exactly the attitude needed if ever we are to understand time and consciousness:

> Goe, and catch a falling starre,
> Get with child a mandrake roote,
> Tell me, where all the past yeares are,
> Or who cleft the Divel's foot.
> Teach me to heare Mermaide's singing,
> Or to keep off envies stinging,
>   And finde
>   What winde
> Serves to advance an honest minde.

We need to go on asking silly, even childish, questions and making poetic demands, until eventually we stumble on questions and concepts that turn out not to be so silly after all. Maybe some of these will involve Eliot's idea (also in *The Four Quartets*) of a return to where we started from —and recognizing it for the first time; then, maybe, we shall begin properly to understand our own minds and the structure of the universe.

Conclusions

The quest in this book, to discern the shape of mentality and to understand Mrs Willett, has been surprisingly fruitful in some respects and frustratingly elusive in others. The 'attractor landscape' picture turns out to fit, in what I think is a neat sort of way, with all sorts of apparently unconnected fields, from the purposes of sleep through a fractal/holographic view of the neural basis of consciousness and memory, to connections with meaning and natural law. And the associated 'state spaces' provide a basis for understanding both many puzzling features of perception and the occasional appearance of 'group minds'. It's a way of looking at mentality that may turn out to be wrong, of course, once we have the tools to test it properly (i.e. tools for studying goings-on in conscious brains that have both the spatial resolution of fMRI and the temporal resolution of EEG). Many of the details I suggested for illustrative purposes, especially those in chapter 6, almost certainly *will* turn out to be partly or wholly wrong. Nevertheless, the 'landscape' model surely has heuristic value at the very least.

But the search for what puts fire into the neurology and the landscapes in order to produce consciousness itself has led us, via memory, to questions about the possible nature and structure of time. And these questions, not surprisingly given the present state of our knowledge, have turned out to be unanswerable. Nevertheless, the mere fact of being led to ask them may prove useful. There appear to be quite good grounds for supposing that they should be central to any search for the basis of conscious experience; and they imply that, from a neuropsychological point of view, it's research on memory, especially the initial stages of the memory process, that offers the most hope of getting to grips with what is going on. The direction taken by our quest also implies that we are not going properly to understand our everyday conscious experience, or the true nature of our selves for that matter, until the physicists have achieved a deeper understanding of time. I have the impression that many of them have long thought that this may be the case, although it's an idea that is relatively unfamiliar to most psychologists and neuroscientists.

A final implication worth emphasizing is that a focus on temporal anomalies — both subjective and, if any confirmed examples of such can be found, objective too — should prove specially useful in relation to both consciousness research and developing a deeper understanding of time's nature. There's still a certain reluctance in some circles to take the phenomenology of conscious experience all that seriously when it comes to theory and research. So-called 'objective' measures still tend to be given more weight and credence. But any such attitude seems illogical, for conscious experience, in all its many forms, is all we ever have. Without it there is no knowledge of theory, experimental outcomes, or anything else for that matter. At one time, to give an example of mistaken attitudes that can prevail, reports by people of their experience of synaesthesia[4] were generally pooh-poohed in academic circles. Now it's a flourishing field of study, providing useful insights into the neural basis of perception. It is time, I suggest, that we began to treat people's reports of anomalous temporal experience as a possibly *essential* source of information about ourselves.

As it happens, we're not necessarily limited to dealing with subjective evidence only. Probably the best 'objective' evidence of temporal anomaly has to do with findings that various physiological and other changes can appear *before* some stimulus is shown that might be considered responsible for the changes. For example, GSR responses of the type used in lie detection tests have been observed prior to the showing of emotionally upsetting pictures. The time interval between GSR change and subsequent stimulus can be more than one second, and thus too long for the change to be attributed to any association with Libet's 'backward referral' (discussed in chapter 5). This finding has sometimes

---

[4] Synaesthesia is the experience of sensations in one modality also being associated with sensations in another. The commonest type is to see particular letters or numbers as having a particular colour. Others include experiencing colours as having tastes, or sounds as having particular shapes.

been referred to as the 'pre-sponse' (see e.g. Batthyany *et al.*, 2009, for an account of some of the relevant literature and a description of an experiment of this sort).

As this book was at the 'final proof' stage, a report appeared of ingenious work by a Cornell University psychology professor, Daryl Bem.[5] He had taken nine fairly standard experimental protocols, commonly used by psychologists, and had simply delayed the 'stimulus' part of the experiment until *after* the 'result' part had been recorded. In eight out of the nine experiments, he saw the same sorts of 'result' that he would have seen if the 'stimulus' had been given in the normal way (i.e. *before* the 'result' was recorded). Naturally, the 'responses' he saw were much more muted than would be expected if the experiments had been done in the usual order, but they were nevertheless highly significant statistically. Bem's work appears to be a striking and meticulous demonstration of the reality of 'pre-sponse' effects. But what does it imply?

Assuming that probability theory is not awry (and if it were awry, most science would need re-writing), the 'pre-sponse' must mean either that time is not as we ordinarily suppose, or that 'mind' can somehow transcend normal temporal limitations, or both. However, it remains to be discovered whether *consciousness* has a part to play in producing the 'pre-sponse', or whether consciousness is irrelevant and the finding is a consequence of a relationship between time and 'extended mind' in general (i.e. 'mind' of the sort discussed in chapters 2 & 3). Like all good research, Bem's raises a host of subsidiary questions. Answers to them, when available, are likely to tell us a lot about the major themes of this book.

---

[5] Daryl Bem, 'Feeling the Future: experimental evidence for anomalous retroactive influences on cognition and affect', *Journal of Personality and Social Psychology*. In press, 2010. Also available at http://www.apa.org/pubs/journals/psp/index.aspx

Bibliography

Adams, Colin C., *The Knot Book; an elementary introduction to the mathematical theory of knots*, New York: W.H. Freeman & Co., 1994.
Alberini, Cristina, 'Mechanisms of memory stabilization: are consolidation and reconsolidation similar or distinct processes?', *Trends in Neuroscience*, 28, 1, 2005, pp. 51-56.
Alev, C., Urschel, S., Sonntag, S., Zoidl, G., Fort, A.G., Hoher, T., Matsubara, M., Willecke, K., Spray, D.C., Dermietzel, R., *Proceedings of the National Academy of Sciences of the United States of America*, 105(52), 20964-9, Dec 30 2008.
Arendt, H., *The Human Condition*, University of Chicago Press, 1958.
Arndt, Markus, Juffmann, Thomas, and Vedral, Vlatko, 'Quantum physics meets biology', 2009, http://arxiv.org/PS_cache/arxiv/pdf/0911/0911.0155v1.pdf.
Audretsch, Jurgen (ed.), *Entangled World: the fascination of quantum information and computation*, WILEY-VCH, 2002.
Baars, Bernard, *In the Theatre of Consciousness; the workspace of the mind*, Oxford University Press, 1997.
Baez, John, 'Noether's theorem in a nutshell', http://math.ucr.edu/home/baez/noether.html 2002.
Bailey, Lee, and Yates, Jenny (eds.), *The Near Death Experience: a reader*, New York and London: Routledge, 1996.
Balduzzi, David, Tononi, Giulio, 'Qualia: the geometry of integrated information', *PLOS Computational Biology*, Vol 5, Issue 8, e1000462, August 2009.
Barbour, Julian, *The End of Time; the next revolution in our understanding of the universe*, London: Weidenfeld & Nicloson, 1999.
Batthyany, Alexander, Kranz, Georg, and Erber, Astrid, 'Moderating factors in precognitive habituation: the roles of situational vigilance, emotional reactivity and affect regulation', *Journal of the SPR*, Vol. 73.2, No. 895, pp. 65-82.
Bickle, John, *Philosophy and Neuroscience: a ruthlessly reductive account*, Kluwer Academic Publishers, 2003.

Buonomano, Dean, and Maass, Wolfgang, 'State dependent computations: spatio-temporal processing in cortical networks', *Nature Reviews Neuroscience*, 10, 2009, pp. 113-25.
Butterfield, Jeremy (ed.), *The Arguments of Time*, The British Academy, 1999.
Cacioppo, John and Patrick, William, *Loneliness; human nature and the need for social connection*, New York and London: WW Norton & co, 2008.
Carroll, Sean, *From Eternity to Here: the quest for the ultimate theory of time*, Dutton: Penguin books, 2010.
Chalmers, David, *The Conscious Mind*, Oxford University Press, 1996.
Claxton, Guy, 'No Business Like Osho Business!', *Resurgence*, 167, 1994, pp. 58-60.
Clayton, Philip, and Davies, Paul (eds.), *The Re-emergence of Emergence: the emergentist hypothesis from Science to Religion*, OUP, 2008.
Cole, Michael, *Cultural Psychology; a once and future discipline*, Cambridge, MA: The Belknap Press of Harvard University Press, 1996.
Colgin, Laura Lee, Denninger, Tobias, Fyhn, Marianne, Hafting, Torkel, Bonnevie, Tora, Jensen, Ole, Moser, May-Britt, & Moser, Edvard I., 'Frequency of gamma oscillations routes flow of information in the hippocampus', *Nature*, 19th Nov. 2009.
Connes, Alain, 'On the fine structure of space-time', In: *On Space and Time*, ed. Shahn Majid, Cambridege University Press, 2008.
Damasio, Antonio, *The Feeling of What Happens: body, emotion and the making of consciousness*, William Heinemann Ltd., 2000.
Dennet, Daniel, *Consiousness Explained*, The Penguin Press, 1991.
Dennett, Daniel C., *Sweet Dreams: Philosophical Obstacles to a Science of Consciousness*, Cambridge MA and London: MIT Press, 2005.
Devlin, Keith, *Logic and Information*, Cambridge University Press, 1991.
Diekelmann, Susanne and Born, Jan, 'The Memory Function of Sleep', *Nature Reviews Neuroscience*, 11, 2010, pp. 114-26.
Edelman, Gerald, and Tononi, Giulio, *Consciousness: how matter becomes imagination*, Allen Lane: The Penguin Press, 2000.
Ellis, Ralph D., *Questioning Consciousness: the interplay of imagery, cognition and emotion in the human brain*, Amsterdam and Philadelphia: John Benjamins, 1995.
Everett, Daniel, *Don't Sleep, There Are Snakes; life and language in the Amazonian jungle*, London: Profile Books, 2008.
Fanning, Steven, *Mystics of the Christian Tradition* London and New York: Routledge, 2001.
Fellin, T., Pascual, O., Gobbo, S., Pozzan, T., Haydon, P., Carmignoto, G., 'Neuronal synchrony mediated by astrocytic glutamate through activation of extrasynaptic NMDA receptors', *Neuron*, 43, 2004, pp. 729-43.
Fenwick, Peter and Elizabeth, *The Art of Dying: a journey to elsewhere*, London: Continuum, 2008.

Feynman, Richard, *QED; the strange theory of light and matter*, Penguin books, 1985.
Fields, R. Douglas, *The Other Brain; from dementia to schizophrenia, how new discoveries about the brain are revolutionizing medicine and science*, New York: Simon & Schuster, 2010.
Fodor, Jerry, *The Mind Doesn't Work That Way: the scope and limits of computational psychology*, The MIT Press, 2000.
Fontana, David, *Is There an Afterlife: a comprehensive overview of the evidence*, Botley, Hants: O Books, 2005.
Fox, Mark, *Religion, Spirituality and the Near Death Experience*, London and New York: Routledge, 2003.
Frank, Lone, *Mindfield*, Oxford: Oneworld, 2009.
Freeman, Walter J., *How Brains Make Up Their Minds*, London: Weidenfeld and Nicolson, 1999.
Freeman, Walter, *How Brains Make up their Minds*, London: Weidenfeld & Nicolson, 1999.
Frith, Chris, *Making up the Mind: how the brain creates our mental world*, Oxford: Blackwell Publishing, 2007.
Gauld, Alan, *Mediumship and Survival*, London: Paladin Books, 1983.
Giaume, Christian, Koulakoff, Annette,, Roux, Lisa, Holcman, David, & Rouach, Nathalie, 'Astroglial Networks: a step further in neuroglial and gliovascular interactions', *Nature Reviews Neuroscience*, 11, 2010, 87-99.
Goswami, Amit, *The Self-aware Universe: how consciousness creates the material world*, 1993.
Gray, Jeffrey, *Consciousness: creeping up on the hard problem* (pbk.), OUP, 2006.
Hameroff, Stuart, 'The "Conscious Pilot" — dendritic synchrony moves through the brain to mediate consciousness', *Journal of Biological Physics*. Springer (published online), April 2009.
Hamilton, Trevor, *Immortal Longings: FWH Myers and the Victorian search for life after death*, Exeter: Imprint Academic, 2009.
Harris-White, M.E., Zanotti, S.A., Frautschy, S.A. and Charles, A.C., 'Spiral intercellular calcium waves in hippocampal slice cultures', *Journal of Neurophysiology*, 79, 1998, pp. 1045-52.
Harth, Erich, *The Creative Loop: how the brain makes a* mind, Penguin books, 1995.
Haydon, P.G., 'Glia: listening and talking to the synapse', *Nature Reviews: Neuroscience*, Vol. 2, no. 3, 2001, pp. 185-93.
Hendel, Tal, 'Energy Eigenvalues as Qualions', paper submitted to *The Journal of Consciousness Studies*, Exeter: Imprint Academic, 2009.
Hering, H., and Shang, M., 'Dendritic spines: structure, dynamics and regulation', *Nature Reviews Neuroscience*, Vol. 2, no. 12, 2001, pp. 880-88.
Herrmann, Christof, Munk, Matthias, and Engel, Andreas, 'Cognitive Functions of Gamma Band Activity: memory match and utilization', *Trends in Cognitive Science*, Vol 8, no 8, 2004.

Hilgetag, Claus, and Barbas, Helen, 'Are there ten times more glia than neurons in the brain?', *Brain Structure and Function*, Springer, published online 07 Feb. 2009.

Huang, Kerson, *Fundamental Forces of Nature: the story of gauge fields*, World Scientific Publishing co., 2007.

Hughes, Gethin, 'Is Consciousness Required to Inhibit an Impending Action? Evidence from event-related brain potentials', PhD thesis, University of London (Goldsmiths College), 2008.

Humphrey, Nicholas, *Seeing Red: a study in consciousness*, Cambridge MA and London: Harvard University Press, 2006.

Hutchins, Edwin, *Cognition in the Wild*, Cambridge MA and London: The MIT Press, 1997.

Jablonka E, and Lamb M., *Evolution in Four Dimensions: genetic, epigenetic, behavioural and symbolic variation in the history of life*, Cambridge MA and London: MIT Press, 2005.

Jibu, Mari, and Yasue, Kunio, *Quantum Brain Dynamics and Connsciousness*, Philadelphia and Amsterdam: The John Benjamins Publishing Co., 1995.

Jung, P., Cornell-Bell, A., Madden, K.S., and Moss, F., 'Noise-induced spiral waves in astrocyte syncytia show evidence of self-organized criticality', *Journal of Neurophysiology*, 79, 1998, pp. 1098–2001.

Kauffman, Stuart, *At Home in the Universe: the search for the laws of complexity*, OUP, 1995.

Kelley, Edward, et al. *Irreducible Mind: towards a psychology for the 21st century*, Lanham MD: Rowman and Littlefield, 2007.

Kitzbichler, Manfred, Smith, Marie, Christensen, Soren and Bullmore, Ed, 'Broadband criticality of human brain network synchronization', *PLOS Computational Biology*, March, 2009 (available online).

Klemm, W.R., Li, T.H. and Hernandez, J.L., 'Coherent EEG Indicators of Cognitive Binding During Ambiguous Figure Tasks', *Consciousness and Cognition*, 9, 2000, pp. 66-85.

Koch, Christof, *Biophysics of Computation: information processing in single neurons*, OUP, 1999.

Larock, E., 'Why neural synchrony fails to explain the unity of visual consciousness', *Behaviour and Philosophy*, 34, 2006, pp. 39-58.

Laszlo, Ervin (ed.). *The Akashic Experience: science and the cosmic memory field*, Rochester: Vermont. Inner Trafditions, 2009.

Libet, Benjamin, 'Neural Processes in the Production of Conscious Experience', in Velmans, M. (ed.), *The Science of Consciousness*, London: Routledge, 1996.

Linden, David, Kallenbach, Ulrich, Heinecke, Armin, Singer, Wolf, and Goebel, Rainer, 'The Myth of Upright Vision: a psychophysical and functional imaging study of adaptation to inverting spectacles', *Perception*, Vol. 28, 1999, pp. 469-81.

Lisman, J., Schulman, H., and Cline, J., 'The molecular basis of CaMKII function in synaptic and behavioural memory', *Nature Reviews: Neuroscience*, Vol. 3, no. 3, 2002, pp. 175-90.

Logothetis, Nikos, 'The Ins and Outs of fMRI Signals', *Nature Neuroscience*, 10 (10), 2007, pp. 1230-32.

MacCormac, E. and Stamenov, M.I. (eds.), *Fractals of brain, fractals of mind*, Amsterdam and Philadelphia: John Benjamins Publishing Co., 1996.

Majid, Shahn (ed.), *On Space and Time*, Cambridge University Press, 2008.

Marino, Lori, 'Cetacean brain evolution: multiplication generates complexity', *International Journal of Comparative Psychology* 17, 2004, pp. 1-16.

Marshall, Paul, *Mystical Encounters with the Natural World; experiences and explanations*, OUP, 2005.

Mayhew, Christopher, in D. Ebin (ed.), *The Drug Experience*, pp. 293-300, New York: Evergreen Black Cat, 1961.

McFadden, J., 'Synchronous firing and its influence on the brain's electromagnetic field: evidence for an electromagnetic field theory of consciousness', *Journal of Consciousness Studies.* 9, no. 4, 2002, pp. 23-50.

McGann, Marek, 'Perceptual Modalities: modes of presentation or modes of interaction?', *Journal of Consciousness Studies*, 17, 1-2, pp. 72-94, Exeter: Imprint Academic, 2010.

Milburn, Gerard J., *The Feynman Processor: quantum entanglement and the computing Revolution*, Reading, MA, 1998.

Mitchell, Melanie, *Complexity: a guided tour*, OUP, 2009.

Nunn, Chris, 'A Nagelian Neurology of Consciousness?' *Science & Consciousness Review*, April, 2003, http://psych.pomona.edu/scr.

Nunn, Chris, *De la Mettrie's Ghost,* Palgrave MacMillan, 2005.

Nunn, Chris, *From Neurons to Notions; brains, mind and meaning*, Edinburgh: Floris Books, 2007.

Oberheim, Nancy, et al. 'The Uniquely Hominid Features of Adult Human Asrtocytes', *The Journal of Neuroscience*, 29(10), 2009, pp. 3276-87.

Palva, S., and Palva, J.M., 'New Vistas for Alpha Frequency Band Oscillations', *Trends in Neuroscience*, 30(4), 2007, pp. 150-58.

Penrose, Roger, *The Road to Reality: a complete guide to the laws of the universe*, London: Jonathan Cape, 2004.

Pereira Jr., Alfredo, and Furlan, Fabio, 'On the role of synchrony for neuron-astrocyte interactions and perceptual conscious processing', *Journal of Biological Physics*, Vol. 35, issue 4, 2009, pp. 465-80.

Pershin, Yuiy, and Ventra, Massimiliano di, 'Experimental demonstration of associative memory and memristive neural networks', www.arxiv.org/abs/0905.2935

Persinger, Michael, Meli, Salvatori and Koren, Stanley, 'Quantitative Discrepancy in Cerebral Hemispheric Temperature Associated with "Two Consciousnesses" is Predicted by NeuroQuantum Relations', *Neuroquantology*, Vol 6, no 4, 2008, pp. 369-78.

Peyrache, Adrian, Khamassi, Mehdi, Benchenane, Karim, Wiener, Sidney, and Battaglia, Francesco, 'Replay of rule-learning related neural patterns in the pre-frontal cortex during sleep', *Nature Neuroscience*, 12, 2009, pp. 919–26.

Pockett, Susan, *The Nature of Consciousness; a hypothesis*, i.Universe.com Inc. 2000.

Poidevin, Robin le, *Travels in Four Dimensions: the enigmas of space and time*, OUP, 2003.

Pribram, K., 'Neuropsychological investigations', *The physical nature of consciousness*, ed. Philip van Loocke, Amsterdam and Philadelphia: The John Benjamins Publishing Co., 2000.

Price, Huw, and Corry, Richard (eds.), *Causation, Physics and the Constitution of Reality: Russell's republic revisited*, Oxford University Press, 2007.

Price, Huw, *Time's Arrow and Archimedes Point*, OUP, 1996.

Ramachandran and Blakeslee, *Phantoms in the Brain: human nature and the architecture of the mind*, Fourth Estate Ltd, 1999.

Robbins, Steve 'On Time, Memory and Dynamic Form', *Consciousness and Cognition*, Vol. 13, 2004, pp. 762–88.

Roy, Archie, *The Eager Dead; a study in haunting*, Sussex: Book Guild Publishing, 2008.

Sacks, Oliver, *The Man Who Mistook His Wife for a Hat*, Picador, 1986

Sautoy, Marcus du, *Symmetry*, New York: Harper Collins, 2008.

Schatzman, Morton, *The Story of Ruth: one woman's haunting psychiatric odyssey*, New York: G.P. Putnam's Sons, 1980.

Schumm, Bruce, *Deep Down Things: the breathtaking beauty of particle physics*, Johns Hopkins University Press, 2004.

Searle, J., 'Consciousness', *Annual Review of Neuroscience*, 23, 2000, pp. 557–78.

Shanon, Benny, *The Antipodes of the Mind: charting the phenomenology of the ayahuasca experience* (pbk.), OUP, 2002.

Skrbina, D., *Panpsychism in the West*, Cambridge, MA: MIT Press, 2005.

Smolin, Lee, *Three Roads to Quantum Gravity*, London: Weidenfeld & Nicolson, 2000.

Spencer, Kevin, Nestor, Paul, Niznikiewitcz, Margaret, Salisbury, Dean, Shenton, Martha, and McCarley, Robert, 'Abnormal Neural Synchrony in Schizophrenia', *Journal of Neuroscience*, 23 (19), 2003, pp. 7407–11.

Sporns, Olaf, and Honey, Christopher, 'Small worlds inside big brains', *Proceedings of the National Academy of Sciences*, Vol. 103, no 51, 2006, pp. 19219–20.

St. Teresa, *The Life of St Teresa of Avila by Herself*, trans. J.M. Cohen, Penguin Classics, 1957.

Stegner, W., *The Gathering of Zion*, Eyre & Spottiswoode, 1966.

Strassman, Rick, *DMT the Spirit Molecule: a doctor's revolutionary research into the biology of near-death and mystical experience*, Rochester, Vermont: Park Street Press, 2001.

Strawson, Galen, *Mental Reality*, MIT Press, 1994.

Swedenborg, Emanuel *Heaven and Hell*, trans. George Dole, West Chester, PA: The Swedenborg Foundation, 2000 (1758).

Tart, Charles (ed.), *Body, Mind and Spirit*, Hampton Roads Publishing Co., 1997.

Tart, Charles, 'Mind embodied; computer-generated virtual reality as a new, dualistic-interactive model for transpersonal psychology', *Cultivating Consciousness*, ed. K.R. Rao, Westport and London. Praeger, 1993.

Taylor M., *The Fanatics: a Behavioural Approach to Political Violence*, Brassey's (UK), 1991.

Todd, J., and Marois, R., 'Capacity Limit of Visual Short-term Memory in Human Parietal Cortex', *Nature*, 428, 2004, pp. 751–4.

Toksvig, Signe (ed.), *Swan on a Black Sea: a study in automatic writing, the Cummins-Willett scripts*, London: Book Club Associates, 1971.

Trehub, Arnold, 'Space, Self and the Theater of Consciousness', *Consciousness and Cognition*, 16, 2007, pp. 310–30.

Tuszynski, Jack A., *The Emerging Physics of Consciousness*, Berlin, Heidelberg and New York: Springer, 2006.

van Hemmen and Sejnowski, Terrence (eds.), *23 Problems in Systems Neuroscience*, OUP, 2006.

Varela, Francisco, Thompson, Evan and Rosch, Eleanor, *The Embodied Mind: cognitive science and human experience* (pbk.), The MIT Press, 1993.

Velmans, Max, *Understanding Consciousness* (2nd edition), New York and London: Routledge, 2009.

Vidal G., *Messiah*, E.P. Dutton & Co, 1954.

Villiers, J. de and Garfield, J., 'Evidentiality and Narrative', *Journal of Consciousness Studies*, Vol 16, Nos 6-8 pp. 191–217, Exeter: Imprint Academic, 2009.

Vimal, Ram L.P., 'Meanings Attributed to the Term 'Consciousness', *Journal of Consciousness* Studies, 16 (5), Exeter: Imprint Academic, 2009.

Wagner, Andreas, *Robustness and Evolvability in Living Systems*, Princeton University Press, 2005.

Wegner, Daniel, *The Illusion of Conscious Will*, The MIT Press, 2002.

Wiedemann, Claudia, 'Neuron–glia interactions: With a little help from glia', *Nature Reviews Neuroscience* 11, 2010, pp. 152–3.

Wilczek, Frank, *The Lightness of Being: mass, ether and the unification of forces*, Philadelphia: Basic books, 2008.

Yuval-Greenberg, Shlomit, and Deouell, Leon, 'What You See Is Not (always) What You Hear: Induced Gamma Band Responses Reflect Cross-Modal Interaction In Familiar Object Recognition', *The Journal of Neuroscience*, 27(5), 2007, pp. 1090–6.

Index

Apparitions 162–68, 183, 211
Astroglia 119–20
Attractors 38–40, 89–90, 99–100, 115–16, 131, 137, 174–75, 183–84, 198, 205
Attractor landscapes 41–43, 99–100, 129, 199
Ayahuasca 169–74

Balfour, Arthur 7, 11
Balfour Eleanor–see Sidgwick, Eleanor
Balfour, Gerald 8, 11
Balfour Jean 206–7, 209
Barbour Julian 217–19
Behaviourism 1, 22, 23, 195
Block universe–see Time
Bomb test (Elitzur-Vaidman) 65–66
Braids–see Knots
Brain–size of 19–20
Brigham Young see Mormons

Calcium (ions and waves) 117, 118–20
CaMKII 121–24
Centre of narrative gravity–see Personhood
Chalmers, David–see dual aspect theory
Chaos 39–40
Cognition 21–22
Configuration space (neural) 93, 127
Configuration space (RNA) 47–48
Consciousness–as a biological phenomenon 84–85
Consciousness–field theories of 147–51, 159, 194, 205
Consciousness–meaning of 1 -2, 79–83,
Consciousness–neural correlates of 97–102, 115–123

Consciousness–quantum 94–97
Conscious pilot 117
Coombe-Tennant Daphne 9, 12
Coombe-Tennant, Henry 11
Coombe-Tennant, Winifred 5, 9–12, 206–209
Copycat (computer programme) 70
Cross correspondences 10, 13
Culture 22–26, 37
Cummins, Geraldine 12–13, 214

Deathbed experience 185–91
Decoherence 74–75, 95–96
Disciples 60–62
Dissociative identity disorder (multiple personality) 15, 211–212
DMT (dimethyltryptamine) 169–70, 177
Dual aspect theory 66–68
Dualism (substance) 156, 179
Dynamics–brain 33–36
Dynamics–entanglement 73–77
Dynamics–genetic 34–35
Dynamics–social 36–38

EEG (electroencephalography) 97–102, 116–18, 166
EEG coherence–see synchrony
Elective democracy 46
Electromagnetism 141
Eliminative materialists 1
Everett, Daniel 24–26
Experience–size of 28 -31

Feynman path integrals 64
fMRI (functional magnetic resonance imaging) 97–98
Fraud 213
Fractals 116, 120, 129
Freeman Walter 99–100

Index

Free will 106-8

Garrett Eileen 210
Global workspace theory 88-90, 115, 159
Gray, Jeffrey 143
Group mentality 58-62, 187, 212-13
Gurney, Edward 6, 11

Hamiltonian 151-52, 155
Heisenberg uncertainty-see Temporal field, quantization of
Holland (Mrs) 9
Holography 123-25

Idealism 62-63
Information-Bateson's definition of 17, 69, 76
Information -relationship to meaning 69
Information-relationship to 'reality' 17
Introspection 80-82
Inverting spectacles 52-53
IQ testing 23-24

James, William 7

Knots 125-29
Knowledge (in physics) 64-66

Lagrangian 155
Libet, Benjamin 103-4
Lodge, Sir Oliver 8
LTP (long term potentiation) see Memory

Matter 134, 138-42
Meaning 69-71
Memory 109-12, 121, 163, 176, 179
Memory –false 180
Mentality-see Mind
Mind-boundaries of 51-58, 76
Mind-definition of 2
Mind-dynamics of 33-34
Mind-embodied 26-28
Mind-group see group mentality
Merleau-Ponty, Maurice 27
Messiahs 59-61
Mormons 58-59
Moving dot illusion 143
Multidimensionality 46-50, 115
Myers, Frederic 6-8
Mystical experience 191-97, 203-4

Natural laws 71-2, 134-38
Navigators 21-22
Near death experience 175-84
Neutrinos 16
Noether, Emmy 134
Noether's theorem 134, 155

OrchOR 95

Panpsychism 63-66
Perception 52-54
Personhood 201-5
Phenomenology 158-9, 226
Piper (Mrs) Leonora 9, 10, 211
Piraha 24-26
Present moment (specious present) 85, 159
Pre-sponse 226
Property dualism 66-69
Psychedelic drugs 169-70

Qualia space 93
Quantum counterfactuals 65-66
Quantum theory 136

Real–definition of 15-17
Reality (of attractors) 131, 157-8, 174, 183, 199, 205
Re-entrance 91-94, 117
Reflexive monism 29-30, 55-58, 180
Reportability (of consciousness)-see introspection
Rubber hand illusion 52
Ruth 162-68, 211

Schatzman, Morton-see Ruth
Seifert surfaces-see Knots
Self-see 'personhood'
Self-consciousness 87-88
Sex (evolution of) 43-44
Sidgwick, Eleanor 6, 209
Sidgwick Henry 6
Sleep (functions of) 45-46
SPR (Society for Psychical Research) 6-7, 207
Spirits 8, 209-12
Spiritualism 7
State space (dynamic) 2, 38-43, 54-55, 213
Stroop test 166
Swedenborg 7-8
Symmetry 135, 140-41, 146, 154 -55
Synchrony 100-2, 116-17

Temporal field–quantization of 151–52
Time 133, 142–47, 215, 217–20, 224–26
Timing of experience 103–5, 142–43, 172, 193, 216
Time–poetic views of 220–24

Varela, Francesco 27–28

Velmans Max–see 'reflexive monism'

Willett (Mrs)–see Coombe-Tennant, Winifred.
Wundt, Wilhelm 23

Yang-Mills equation 141